MID-TWENTIETH CENTURY AMERICAN PHILOSOPHY:

Personal Statements

MID-TWENTIETH CENTURY
AMERICAN
PHILOSOPHY:

Personal Statements

edited by

Peter A. Bertocci

Borden Parker Bowne Professor of Philosophy
BOSTON UNIVERSITY

NEW YORK
HUMANITIES PRESS
1974

Library of Congress Cataloging in Publication Data

Bertocci, Peter Anthony.
  Mid-twentieth century American philosophy.

  Includes bibliographical references.
  1. Philosophy, American—20th century—Addresses,
essays, lectures. I. Title.
B935.B47   191   73-18467
ISBN 0-391-00340-2

Printed in the United States of America

Contents

MID-TWENTIETH CENTURY AMERICAN PHILOSOPHY:
PERSONAL STATEMENTS

Preface: Peter A. Bertocci   vii

Biographical Notes   ix

1. Kenneth D. Benne
   ON LEARNING TO BELIEVE IN PERSONS   1

2. Brand Blanshard
   RATIONALISM IN ETHICS AND RELIGION   20

3. George Boas
   IN DEFENSE OF SCEPTICISM   47

4. Theodore Brameld
   CULTUROLOGY AS THE SEARCH FOR CONVERGENCE   62

5. Harry S. Broudy
   UNFINISHABLE BUSINESS   84

6. Edwin A. Burtt
   TOWARD A PHILOSOPHY OF PHILOSOPHY   104

7. Herbert Feigl
   NO POT OF MESSAGE   120

8. Charles Hartshorne
   PHILOSOPHY AFTER FIFTY YEARS   140

9. Glenn R. Morrow
   REASON AND COMMITMENT   155

10. Stephen C. Pepper
    IDEALS IN RETROSPECT   168

11. Roy Wood Sellars
    FORTY YEARS AFTER: A CLARIFICATION OF OUTLOOK   179

12. Herbert Spiegelberg
    ETHICS FOR FELLOWS IN THE FATE OF EXISTENCE   193

13. Robert Ulich
    CONFESSIONS OF FAITH   211

14. W. H. Werkmeister
    THE WORLD I LIVE IN   227

15. Paul Weiss
    THE PHILOSOPHIC QUEST   240

Index   246

Preface

The fifty years from 1920 to 1970 in American philosophy are marked by ferment. One would expect no less in a country that has been increasingly responsive to the "unfinished business" of civilization within its own shores and in the world. Whatever else may be true about philosophers in America, they have been far from impervious to philosophical perspectives expressing the ferment in other lands—and in part because thinkers from other lands have found a new home in the American academic world. Why not, then, try to record, even in a small way, some sense of the meaning of the philosophic quest during this period by asking some of the Socratic gadflies in the middle decades to reflect on "the things that matter most" as they re-view their own philosophical pilgrimages?

The philosophers who speak for themselves in this volume have done most of their teaching and writing in the last thirty or forty years. They were invited to write in the vein of *confessio fidei*—to speak, if they saw fit, beyond the limits of their systematic writings, to share the motifs in their work and to present concerns about their world.

It is always tempting to suppose that specific philosophic trends express the philosophic atmosphere of a country. The reader of this volume cannot miss the healthy variety of experience and concern that inspires these philosophers. Very much aware that philosophy cannot be indifferent to the upheavals of war, to economic, political, and social change, to new discoveries affecting every area of life, they would be the last to say that they speak for their times. Yet their essays suggest their commitment to the persistent problems of philosophy.

It is worth noting that four of our scholars have dedicated their talents to the construction of a philosophy of education. They remind us of the task that significant thinkers from Plato to Dewey have considered integral to the philosophic venture.

Both circumstances and necessity always limit the scope of a volume of this sort. While no premium was put on representation of influential perspectives, had some other philosophical statesmen found it possible to contribute, as anticipated, the volume would have been the richer. The editor restricted himself to philosophers beyond the age of sixty-three. Had he chosen to include philosophers younger than sixty-three, the scope would have had to be limited even more arbitrarily. As one reads these testaments of wisdom, he cannot but be grateful that such visions form part of his past and part of the heritage of the future.

It is with special pleasure that I acknowledge the professional advice of my colleague, Robert S. Cohen. The aid of Judith Bleiwas Wilkis, of Ned S. Garvin, the Edgar S. Brightman Fellow in Philosophy, and the constant encouragement of my wife, have made the privilege of editing this book an even more meaningful experience.

February, 1973   *Peter A. Bertocci*
Arlington, Massachusetts

Biographical Notes

KENNETH DEAN BENNE was born in Morrowville, Kansas on May 11, 1908. He earned the B.S. at Kansas State University in 1930; the A.M. from the University of Michigan in 1936, and the Ph.D. from Columbia, 1941. In 1969 Lesley College and in 1970 Morris Brown College honored him with the D.H.L. He began his teaching career in a rural school in Kansas. He served as a teacher of physical and biological sciences in Concordia, Kansas (1930-35) and became an associate in the social and philosophical foundations of education, Columbia University, Teachers College (1938-41). He continued his career as philosopher, educator, and specialist in human relations at Horace Mann Lincoln Institute, Columbia University (1946-1948), at the University of Illinois (1941-46 and 1948-53), and as Berenson Professor of Human Relations at Boston University (1953-1973). Professor Benne was a recipient of the Kilpatrick award for Distinguished Contribution to American Philosophy of Education, 1945. He served as Centennial Professor, University of Kentucky, 1965; and was a founder of the National Training Laboratories and Institute of Applied Behavioral Sciences (1949). He is a member of the Adult Education Association of the U.S.A. and a past president (1966-67). He has been president of the Philosophy of Education Society (1950-51) and of the American Education Fellowship (1949-52). He was a founder of the International Association of Applied Social Scientists and Chairman of its Board (1971-   ). His bibliography includes more than 150 items, some of which follow: *Education in the Quest of*

Identity and Community, 1961; *The Planning of Change,* 1st Ed. 1963, 2nd Ed., 1969 (joint editor and author); *T-Group Theory and Laboratory Method,* 1964 (joint editor and author);*Education for Tragedy,* 1967;*A Conception of Authority,* 1943, 1971.

BRAND BLANSHARD was born in Fredericksburg, Ohio, on August 27, 1892. He received his A.B. from the University of Michigan in 1914, his A.M. from Columbia in 1918, a B.Sc. from Oxford in 1920, and the Ph.D. degree from Harvard in 1921. Blanshard is the recipient of many honorary degrees, including Litt. D., Swarthmore, 1947, Concord, 1962, Albion, 1966; L.H.D., Bucknell, 1954, Colby, 1956, Trinity, 1957, Roosevelt University, 1959, Simpson, 1961, Kenyon, 1961; and LL.D. from Oberlin in 1956 and the University of St. Andrews in 1959. Blanshard was a Rhodes scholar from 1913 to 1915. He began his teaching career at the University of Michigan in 1921. Subsequently he taught at Swarthmore College and at Columbia University. In 1945 he became Professor of Philosophy at Yale where in 1956 he was appointed Sterling Professor, and served as Chairman of the Department of Philosophy from 1959-61. In 1929-30 he was a Guggenheim Fellow, and in 1961-62 he was a Fellow at the Center for Advanced Studies at Wesleyan University. He has held many distinguished lectureships, including the Carus (1959) and the Gifford (1952-53). He has been President of the American Philosophical Association, Eastern Division (1942-44), and of the American Theological Society (1955-56). In addition to editing philosophical works and contributing to numerous scholarly publications, Blanshard has written: *The Nature of Thought,* 2 vols. (1940), *Reason and Goodness* (1960), and *Reason and Analysis* (1962).

GEORGE BOAS attended the public schools of Providence, Rhode Island, where he was born on August 28, 1891. He received a bachelor's and a master's degree from Brown University in 1913 in English and from there went to Harvard, Columbia, and the University of California (Berkeley) where he received his doctorate in 1917. Boas spent two years in the Army, with eighteen months foreign service from 1917-1919, and two in the Navy, 1953-55. His books have been mainly divided among three fields, aesthetics, the history of ideas, and the philosophy of science and epistemology. Among his works are: *The Heaven of Invention* (1962); with A. O. Lovejoy, *Primitivism and Related Ideas in Antiquity* (1935); *Dominant Themes of Modern Philosophy* (1957); *Rationalism in Greek Philosophy* (1961);*A Critical Analysis of the Philosophy of Emile Meyer-*

son (1930); *The Inquiring Mind* (1958); *The Limits of Reason* (1960); *The Cult of Childhood* (1966); *The History of Ideas: An Introduction* (1969).

THEODORE BRAMELD was born in Neillsville, Wisconsin, on January 20, 1904. He received his B.A. from Ripon College in 1926, his Ph.D. in philosophy at the University of Chicago in 1931, and was honored with an Ed.D. by Rhode Island College in 1959. A Fellow in Philosophy at Chicago, 1929-31, he began his career as instructor of philosophy at Long Island University, 1931-35, continued at Adelphi College, 1935-39, became Associate Professor of Educational Philosophy, University of Minnesota, 1939-45 (Professor 1945-57), before moving to New York University for the years 1947-58, and then to Boston University as Professor of Educational Philosophy, 1958-69. He has been a Visiting Professor and Lecturer at Teachers College, Columbia; School for Workers, Wisconsin; University of Puerto Rico; New School for Social Research; William Alanson White Institute of Psychiatry; Dartmouth College; Springfield College; and the University of Hawaii; and is at present Visiting Distinguished Professor in Urban Education, City University of New York (1973-74). In 1964-65 he was a Fulbright Research Scholar in Japan; and in 1971-72, Senior Fellow, East-West Center, Hawaii. In 1944-45 he was President of the Philosophy of Education Society, and, among varied professional responsibilities, is Vice-Chairman of the Council for the Study of Mankind, 1969- . Among his many scholarly contributions are: *Philosophies of Education in Cultural Perspective* (1955); *Toward a Reconstructed Philosophy of Education* (1956); *Cultural Foundations of Education* (1957); *The Remaking of a Culture—Life and Education in Puerto Rico* (1959); *Education for the Emerging Age* (1961); *Education as Power* (1965); *The Use of Explosive Ideas in Education* (1965); *Japan: Culture, Education, and Change in Two Communities* (1968); *Patterns of Educational Philosophy* (1971).

HARRY S. BROUDY assumed his present position as Professor of Philosophy of Education at the University of Illinois in 1957, after serving as Professor of Philosophy and Psychology of Education at the North Adams and Framingham State Colleges in Massachusetts for 20 years. He has also been a visiting lecturer at Boston University and New York University, and at the Universities of Southern California, California at Berkeley, and the Florida State University. Broudy received the A.B. degree from Boston University, and did his graduate work at Harvard University, receiving his Ph.D. degree in Philosophy in 1935. He was awarded the honorary degree of Doctor of Humanities by Oakland University in 1969. His major publications include: *Building a Philosophy of Education* (1954), revised 1961 and translated into Korean and Spanish; *Paradox and Promise* (1961); with John S. Palmer, *Exemplars of Teaching Method* (1965); with M. J. Parsons, I. S. Snook, and R. D. Szoke, *Philosophy of Education: An Organization of Topics and Selected Sources* (1968); *Enlightened Cherishing: An Essay on Aesthetic Education* (1972); and *The Real World of the Public Schools* (1972). He served as senior editor, with R. H. Ennis and R. H. Krimmerman, of *Readings in the Philosophy of Educational Research* in 1973, and has served as general editor for the University of Illinois Press of a series of readings in the philosophy of education. He has contributed chapters to a number of yearbooks and symposia volumes, and many of his periodical articles have been reprinted in books of readings and anthologies. He delivered the Boyd H. Bode Memorial Lecture in 1963, the first Cornell University School of Education Lecture in 1962, and one of the Jennings Scholar Lectures in 1965-66. In 1967-68 he was a Fellow at the Center for Advanced Study in the Behavioral Sciences. He has been editor of *The Educational Forum* since 1964. He is past President of the Philosophy of Education Society and of the Association for Realistic Philosophy.

EDWIN A. BURTT was born in Groton, Massachusetts in 1892. He was educated at Yale and Columbia Universities, receiving his Ph.D. from the latter in 1925. He taught philosophy at the University of Chicago (1923-1931), and at Cornell University (1932-1960), where in 1941, he became Susan Linn Sage Professor of Philosophy. He has held visiting professorships at Harvard, Stanford, and the University of Hawaii. He has served as President of the American Theological Society and of the Eastern Division of the American Philosophical Association. He was honored by the degree of L.H.D. from the University of Chicago. Among his varied philosophical publications are included the books: *The Metaphysical Foundations of Modern Physical Science, Right Thinking, Types of Religious Philosophy, The English Philosophers from Bacon to Mill, The Teachings of the Compassionate Buddha, Man Seeks the Divine,* and *In Search of Philosophic Understanding.* During 1946-47 he travelled extensively in the Far East, as a representative of the American Philosophical Association, to promote a closer contact between Western and Eastern philosophers. In 1953-54 he spent several months in India and Ceylon studying Hinduism and Buddhism, and lecturing on Western philosophy and religion. In November 1956 he was invited by the

Government of India to participate in the Buddha Jayanti celebration under its sponsorship. A series of lectures delivered at the University of Calcutta in 1967-68 will probably eventuate in a book whose title will be *Toward and Beyond the Community of Man.*

HERBERT FEIGL was born in Reichenberg, Austria-Hungary in 1902. He earned his Ph.D. at Vienna, having studied also in Munich. He taught at the University of Iowa from 1931-1939, and has been a Regent's Professor of Philosophy at the University of Minnesota since 1941, and director of the Minnesota Center of Philosophy of Science (1953-1971). He has been honored by distinguished lectureships and fellowships in America and abroad, and has been President of the Western Division of the American Philosophical Association (1962-63) and of the International Institute for the Unity of Science (1967-71). He is co-editor of *Minnesota Studies in the Philosophy of Science,* and of *Philosophical Studies.* Especially notable among his publications is *The 'Mental' and the 'Physical': the Essay and a Postscript* (1967) and his contribution to the *Fifty-Fourth Yearbook of the National Society for the Study of Education* (1955); *Moral Problems in Contemporary Society* (P. Kurtz, ed.) (1969); his memoir in *The Intellectual Migration: Europe and America 1930-1960* (eds., D. Fleming and B. Bailyn (1969)).

CHARLES HARTSHORNE was born in Kittanning, Pennsylvania, on June 5, 1897. He received his A.B. (1921), M.A. (1922), and Ph.D. (1923) all from Harvard. After two years of post-doctoral study abroad he returned to Harvard to begin teaching as an assistant to A. N. Whitehead. In 1928 he joined the Faculty at the University of Chicago, and became Professor of Philosophy in 1949. From 1955 until 1962, he was Professor of Philosophy at Emory University in Georgia, and since 1962 he has been Professor of Philosophy at the University of Texas. Professor Hartshorne was Terry Lecturer at Yale University in 1947 and Fulbright Lecturer at the Universities of Melbourne and Kyoto. He was Visiting Professor at Goethe University in Frankfurt, and at Banaras Hindu University, Varanasi, India. In 1948 he served as President of the Western Division of the American Philosophical Association. In addition to numerous articles, including original contributions to ornithology, Hartshorne has written: *The Philosophy and Psychology of Sensation* (1934); *Beyond Humanism* (1937); *Man's Vision of God* (1941); *The Divine Relativity* (1948); *Reality as Social Process* (1953); *Philosophers Speak of God* (with William Reese) (1953); *The Logic of Perfection*

(1962); *Anselm's Discovery* (1965); *A Natural Theology for Our Time* (1967); *Creative Synthesis and Philosophic Method* (1970); *Whitehead's Philosophy: Selected Essays, 1930-1970* (1972); *Born To Sing: An Interpretation and World Survey of Bird Song* (1973).

GLENN R. MORROW was born in 1895. At the time of his death, 1973, he was Adam Seybert Professor Emeritus of Moral and Intellectual Philosophy, University of Pennsylvania. Professor Morrow received his A.B. from Westminster College in 1914 and his Ph.D. from Cornell University, 1921. He taught at Westminster College (1914-16), Cornell University (1922-23), University of Missouri (1923-29), University of Illinois (1929-39), University of Pennsylvania (1939-65). Between the years of 1944 and 1952, Professor Morrow was Dean of the College, University of Pennsylvania. He was American Field Service Fellow in France, 1921-22, Guggenheim Fellow in Greece, 1952-53, and Fulbright Research Scholar in Oxford, 1957-58. Morrow has served as President of the American Philosophical Association, Western Division (1940); and of the Eastern Division (1953). He was American Editor of *Archiv für Geschichte der Philosophie,* 1960-65. Among his publications are: *The Ethical and Economic Theories of Adam Smith,* 1923; *Studies in the Platonic Epistles,* 1935; *Plato's Law of Slavery in its Relation to Greek Law,* 1939; *Plato's Cretan City,* 1960; *Plato's Epistles,* 1962; *Proclus' Commentary on the First Book of Euclid's Elements,* translated with Introduction and Notes, 1970; numerous articles and reviews in philosophical and philological journals.

STEPHEN C. PEPPER was born in Newark, New Jersey in 1891. He earned the A.B., A.M., and Ph.D. from Harvard University in 1913, 1914, and 1916 respectively. After teaching at Wellesley College in 1916-17, he went in 1919 to the University of California and became professor of philosophy in 1930 and chairman of the department of philosophy from 1953 to his retirement. Colby College honored him with the degree, Doctor of Humane Letters, in 1950. Among his varied writings are: *Aesthetic Quality* (1938); *World Hypotheses* (1942); *The Basis of Criticism in the Arts* (1945); *Principles of Art Appreciation* (1950); *The Work of Art* (1956); *The Sources of Value* (1958); *Ethics* (1960). Professor Pepper died in 1972.

ROY WOOD SELLARS was born in Ontario, Canada in 1880. His A.B. and Ph.D. were earned at the University of Michigan in 1903 and 1908 respectively. He began his teaching at the University of Michigan in 1905 and was Professor from 1923 to 1956 and is now Emeritus. He was President of the Western Division of the American Philosophical Association, and is listed in the *International Dictionary of Biography*. Among his many essays and thirteen books are: *Critical Naturalism* (1921); *Religion Coming of Age* (1928); and *The Philosophy of Physical Realism* (1932), *The Principles, Perspectives, and Problems of Philosophy* (1969).

HERBERT SPIEGELBERG was born in Strasbourg, France, on May 18, 1904. He was a student at the University of Heidelberg, Germany (1922-24), the University of Freiburg, Germany (1924-25), and received his Ph.D. from the University of Munich (Germany) in 1928. In 1938, Spiegelberg came to the United States. He was an instructor and research assistant at Swarthmore College, 1938-41, and became a member of the faculty of Lawrence College (Wisconsin) 1941-1963. He has been Professor of Philosophy at Washington University since 1963 and is now Emeritus Professor. Spiegelberg held the position of Fulbright lecturer at the University of Munich in 1961-62 and gave the Alfred Schutz Memorial Lecture in 1972 at Boston University. He is a member of the American Philosophical Association and of the Metaphysical Society of America. His writings include: *Antirelativismus* (1935); *Gesetz und Sittengesetz* (1935); *The Phenomenological Movement* (1960; second edition, 1965); *Phenomenology in Psychology and Psychiatry* (1972).

ROBERT ULICH was born in Bavaria, Germany in 1890. After attending the Humanist Classical Gymnasium in Saxony, he continued his education at the Universities of Freiburg, Neuchatel, Munich, Berlin, and earned his Ph.D. (1915) at the University of Leipzig, where he was research fellow in 1915-16, and librarian from 1917-1921. From 1921-23 he was assistant counsellor in the Saxon Ministry of Education, and he served as counsellor in charge of Saxon Universities from 1923-1933. In 1934 he joined the faculty of the Harvard University School of Education. His many writings include: *Fundamentals of Democratic Education* (1940); *History of Educational Thought* (1945); *Conditions of Civilized Living* (1946); *Three Thousand Years of Educational Wisdom* (1947); *Man and Reality* (1948); *Crisis and Hope in American Education* (1951); *Education and the Idea of Mankind,* editor (1964, 1968).

W. H. WERKMEISTER was born August 10, 1901, in Germany. He came to the United States in 1924, after studies at Münster and Frankfurt, and received his Ph.D. from the University of Nebraska in 1927. He was a xvi / MID-TWENTIETH CENTURY AMERICAN PHILOSOPHY

member of the faculty at Nebraska from 1926-1953. The years 1953-60 were spent as Director of the School of Philosophy, University of Southern California. Since 1966 he has been Professor of Philosophy at Florida State University. He has been Director, *pro tem,* of the Institute for American Culture, University of Berlin, and visiting lecturer at Harvard. In 1964-65 he was President of the Pacific Division of the American Philosophical Association. Among his publications are: *A Philosophy of Science* (1940, 1965); *The Basis and Structure of Knowledge* (1948, 1968); *Introduction to Critical Thinking* (1948); *A History of Philosophical Ideas in America* (1949); *Theories of Ethics* (1961); *Man and His Values* (1967); *A Historical Spectrum of Value Theories* (Vol. I, 1970, Vol. II, 1973). He has written eighty or more articles in professional journals, and chapters in various books.

PAUL WEISS was born in New York City on May 19, 1901. He received a B.S.S. degree from the College of the City of New York in 1927 and an A.M. and Ph.D. degree from Harvard, 1928, 1929. He has honorary degrees from Grinnell, Pace, and Bellarmine Colleges. Weiss began teaching at Harvard and Radcliffe in 1930. He taught at Bryn Mawr College from 1931 until he went to Yale in 1946, where in 1962 he was appointed Sterling Professor of Philosophy. He is currently Heffer Professor of Philosophy of the Catholic University of America. He is the founder of the Philosophy of Education Society, Inc., The Metaphysical Society of America, the Philosophical Society for the Study of Sport, and he is a past President of the American Philosophical Association, the Metaphysical Society of America, and the Philosophical Society for the Study of Sport. In addition to editing, with Charles Hartshorne, *The Collected Papers of Charles S. Peirce* (6 vols.), he is the author of many books, some of which are: *Reality* (1938); *Nature and Man* (1947); *Man's Freedom* (1950); *Modes of Being* (1958); *Our Public Life* (1959); *The World of Art* (1961); *Nine Basic Arts* (1961); *History: Written and Lived* (1962); *The God We Seek* (1965); *Sport: A Philosophic Study* (1969); *Philosophy in Process,* vols. 1-6 (1955-1971); *Beyond All Appearances* (1974), *Cinematics* (1974).

On Learning to Believe In Persons

Kenneth D. Benne

Learning to believe in persons begins with believing in myself. Belief in persons does not stand by itself. It is interrelated with other knowledges and beliefs about man in society, in history, in nature, in the world. But it begins with the originating center of all my knowing and believing, whatever and whoever the objects of my knowledge and belief—myself.

I aspire to believe in myself as a human person. I often, perhaps always, fall short of my aspiration. When I fall far short, I recognize familiar processes of self-obfuscation, self-division, self-diminution occurring within me. My thinking becomes confused and divided. I listen to the evidence, pleas, demands of some voices in me and ignore or reject the evidence, pleas, demands of other voices. My choices become partisan as among various parts of myself. My energy flows into defense and justification of partial and partisan positions taken against the criticisms of repressed or rejected interests and evidences within myself. I project minority positions within myself hatefully upon others around me. In diabolizing these others, I diabolize part of me and in the process further weaken and divide myself. I grow rigid in defending thoughts, orientations and courses of action which were formed in the past, which were, perhaps, liberating, unifying and strengthening at some past time but which now deflect me from investment in creative and integrative processes which might liberate, unify and strengthen me in present and future thought, choice and action.

When, recognizing processes of self-obfuscation, self-division, self-diminution within myself and naming and accepting these for what they are, I re-enact my belief in myself, the voices within me are joined again

1

in fruitful, dialogic conflict. I become open to the invention and incorporation of new, liberating, unifying and strengthening patternings of impulse, aspiration and response in and to my world. I become open to the resources of others outside me in pursuing my creative quest. I learn and grow. I am reconfirmed in my belief in myself as a human person.

Persons in History, Submergent and Emergent

It is difficult for me, as it is for other men, to maintain faith in the capacity of human persons to learn and to grow as the main resource and hope of man in our historical period. We are painfully aware of deep schisms in the body social. Familiar ways of dealing with such schisms, familiar rites, have lost their power to suppress, repress or reconcile. And schisms in the body social, not surprisingly, have engendered schisms in the human soul. We live in a period of time in which historical movements and events are experienced by most men as "meteorological" or "geological" cataclysms. On this view, no individual body, mind or spirit can stop, divert or direct them. Individual men who once emerged from history to choose for themselves have lost the support of beliefs and institutions which once gave credibility to their assertion of effective freedom and to their belief in their creative power to shape events through their own thoughts and actions. Men feel lost, alone, in the midst of historical eruptions and counter-eruptions. Their personal lives seem to count for little or nothing in the massive reequilibrations of institutions, societies and cultures in which their personal lives are fatefully involved. Can a man sanely maintain faith in himself in such a period of history? And, even if it could be demonstrated that he can, since faith in himself requires that personal choice not be dissolved in the machinations of historical necessity, should he do so? I believe that I can and should maintain faith in myself, in my capacity to learn, to grow and create. And I feel justified in recommending the same faith to others as a saving faith. I have found justification as I have come to trust the power within myself to say no to the environing powers which threaten to engulf and destroy me.

The rhetoric of power is a potent rhetoric in a time such as ours. It is largely out of a feeling of impotence to resist the commands and cajolements of collective power in the presence of cataclysmic events that persons are now alienated from faith in themselves. It is in negation of this rhetoric of power that faith in one's self is both manifested and generated. A poem which, when I wrote it, I called "A Dream", seems to me now to depict a reality for men if they choose to see and believe it.

A Dream

The light—so dim it drew the horizon near—
Showed giant figures, almost human, hemming me round,
Faceless or with averted faces. I stood alone and I could hear
Their almost human voices—impressive sound
Well-amplified, most high fidelity—commanding "Kneel!"
I did not kneel. And from me came a bleat—
Most poorly modulated, low fidelity—"I do not feel
Your right to make me kneel." Came their repeat
"Kneel!"—computer-programmed, nuclear-driven now—"We
    have the power.
We are the nations, churches, races, collectivities.
You are a piece of us—without us, nothing. In this dark hour
Of dire emergency, to stand upright is treason, sacrilege—
    down on your knees!"
Darkness had further dimmed the scene and it was cold.
Wavering, my voice came to my ears, perhaps into their almost
    human ears, whispering "No!"
From near around me, like a significant secret told
By friend to friend in private, came fellow-sounds—at first low
Then amplified by human power—a chorus free
Praising man and singing "NO!" Above me dawned a dim but
    brightening star.
I saw faces of men—a company of little men standing tall and
    welcoming me.

Collectivity and Community

Men depend on their institutions for facilitating and regularizing the satisfaction of many of their needs. In turn, institutions depend upon the internalization and acceptance by persons of patterns of conduct, belief and relationship, of subordination and command, for their viability and perpetuity. In an historical view, institutions are artifacts invented and affirmed by men at some past time, recent or remote. But they must continually be reinvented and reaffirmed by the men who live in and through the patterns of conduct and rationalization which their operability requires, if they are to survive in actuality.

When men bow down to institutions—familial, economic, political, or religious—granting to them some rightful power to create and to destroy the persons who depend upon them, they are engaging in idolatry, worshiping that which they themselves have created and re-created, alienating themselves from their own inherent power to create and to destroy. When men say no to the demands of any institution for their unquestioning allegiance and obedience, they are reducing their alienation from their original power to legitimize any and all social arrangements—a power which lives only within and between themselves.

To assert the originating power of persons to destroy and to create institutions is not to deny the social nature of man. It is rather to assert the validity of Martin Buber's distinction between collectivity and community. Collectivity lives in the regularization of predictable I-It relationships among people. Relationships between persons are functionally rationalized into role relationships in the service of externalized objectives and goals. In a just collectivity, there is reciprocity in role relationships and equity in the distribution of the products of joint efforts. But in a community, persons meet as persons in I-Thou relationships. Relationships in a community do not depend on the curtailment or arrest of personal existence in the interest of efficient service of external goals, as in a collectivity. The intention and result of communal relationships is the enhancement and augmentation of personal existence. There is, as Aristotle once said, no need for justice among friends. I-Thou relationships are characterized by spontaneity, creativity, surprise. Collective relationships are characterized by predictability, routinization, minimal surprise. Men in a livable society must maintain an intricate and precarious balance between collective and communal relationships.

The Idolatrizing of Artifacts

It has been a temptation of contemporary scientific students and managers of social life to conceive sociality and to coach the practice of sociality in the image of collectivity to the virtual exclusion of community. And most have yielded to the temptation. I have already mentioned man's tendency to idolatrize his artifacts in commenting on his worship of institutions which live only through his continual re-creation and re-affirmation of them. This has been apparent also in man's use of his latest and most powerful technological creations analogically to shed light on his own nature as a man. In the heyday of machines, scientific students of man sought to interpret man as a machine. No doubt this mechanical metaphor shed much light on mechanical aspects of human functioning, both in body and in mind. And no doubt also, it led many men to strenuous efforts to organize human effort after a mechanical model. But it also trapped men into forgetting that the creator of the machine was not exhaustively explained after the model of one of his own creations.

It is not surprising that with the human creation and development of computer technology, men are widely interpreting man's mental functioning after the model of computer functioning. Nor is it surprising that human efforts are being widely coached and organized to conform to the demands and to the image of the computer. Cybernetic man is an idol just as mechanical man was and is an idol to many men. The difficulty lies not in the invention and use by men of mechanical or computer models and technologies in facilitating human projects. The difficulty lies in the tendency of man the creator to deify his own creations, to ascribe to them a reality prior to the reality of himself, and to put himself abjectly into the service of his own artifacts. In this process he comes to feel powerless before the powers which he has released and loses faith in the creative power that lies within himself to use his artifacts in the service of personal and communal ends or to refuse to use them at all.

The accelerated march of bureaucracy in the organization of human life in the modern world combines two of the depersonalizing tendencies already noted. It reflects man's tendency to conceive and to practice sociality in the image of collectivity to the attempted exclusion of community in the organization of human relationships. Another way of saying this is to say that modern men have attempted to cultivate and foster I-It relationships throughout the range of organized life to the exclusion of I-Thou relationships. It reflects also modern man's tendency to place his faith in technologies as a way of solving human problems, even to the extent of modeling his view of himself in the image of this most recent and most powerful technology. He has tended to forget that only he himself can heal the schisms in his soul. That these tendencies of modern men have proved abortive is evidenced: by the widespread despair, quiet or clamorous, of men, affluent or poor, who live their lives enmeshed in bureaucratic structures; by widespread withdrawal of personal investment in the fate and fortune of bureaucratized institutions, whether this withdrawal takes the form of psychological or physical dropping out; by growing attempts, especially among the young, to destroy and discredit bureaucratized forms of life and relationship, and by the weakness of bureaucratic leadership to learn from these various forms of protest and withdrawal and to generate the spontaneous allegiance of persons which the renewal and perpetuity of established institutions require.

The Affirmation of Person and Community
through the Negation of Idols

It is in the widespread and growing negation by persons of dehumanizing and depersonalizing demands placed upon them by many of our customs and institutions that I find reason to believe that faith by persons in themselves today is not a forlorn faith. For in the negation there is also an affirmation. Actually, there is a double affirmation in every negation of dehumanized and depersonalized ways of life and of the idols which men have made of these. When I negate demands upon me which contravene my humanity and my personhood, I am affirming the irreducible and ineradicable reality of the human and the personal in me and in others. But I am also, as I negate a dehumanizing and depersonalizing social order, affirming an alternative social order which is dedicated to the enhancement rather than the attenuation of the human and the personal in me and in others. In my negation, there is thus an affirmation both of person and of community.

Why is it hard for many men to hear the affirmations in the voices of contemporary protest? The difficulty comes in part because, in the dominant vocabulary in terms of which man and society are discussed today, it is hard for protesters to name or to declare clearly or unequivocally the affirmation of themselves out of which their protests arise. In the conventional view, protest arises out of weakness and deprivation, not out of strength, and is addressed to those who are assumedly strong and undeprived. And both protesters and those against whom protest is directed tend to share this conventional view. On this view, the "haves" possess goods which the "have nots" do not possess. The protest is motivated by a desire to deprive the "haves" of their valuable possessions and to endow the "have nots" with valuable possessions of the same sort. No doubt current social and political protest does in part conform to this model both in the national and the international scene. But there are good reasons to believe that this model fails to illuminate significant aspects of current protest against established institutions. For protest arises from the ranks of those now in possession of the conventional goods of our society—the affluent young, socially conscious intellectuals and artists, voluntary adult drop-outs from established institutions, the mentally ill. They are saying that they do not want that which the "haves" in established society now possess and tend to call good. They are rejecting the criteria of success, the value orientations, the conventional over-valuation of credentials and statuses which permeate much of established society. They are groping toward more life-affirming and person-affirming, more "humanized" values, and toward social forms and relationships which incorporate and support the pursuit and actualization of these values. I do not believe that it is beyond those in charge of institutions to join the protesters in their human quest if they can come to believe that they themselves are more important than the positions they occupy or the privileges they possess.

And the case is not unlike that among many of the "have nots" as well—American Blacks who reject the values of the dominant society and seek to build their own society based on more life-affirming and self-affirming value orientations; "third world" groups who reject the dominant values both of Soviet Communism and American Capitalism and who seek to image and achieve some non-imperialistic alternative in society and in culture; "liberation" front groups among women, homosexuals and others.

The human struggles which many contemporary protest movements precipitate and embody are thus not fully illuminated by conventional models of political struggle, even though proponents and opponents frequently speak a political language and are often enamored of and bewitched by political modes of action as the only way out of confusion and conflict. The struggles are easier to comprehend fully if they are seen as struggles toward a more human way of life than men are now living and enjoying, toward communal arrangements which support souls in their varied quests toward a meaningful life, toward a more person-centered existence. They are struggles toward a more humanized world culture. They are religious struggles in which men seek ways of finding or building a home in the universe in which they have come to feel homeless. This view does not deny the political dimension of the struggle. It does tend to put this dimension in its place. Thus widespread attempts to conceive and practice the contemporary human struggle in exclusively political terms becloud the affirmations of person and community that are implicit in contemporary protests against established institutions and ideologies.

The Fragmentation and Repersonalization of Men

The implicit affirmations are further obscured by factionalized support of various fragmented views of man, his nature and his destiny. This fragmentation of views of man characterizes academic life, the life of social practice and the life of contemporary action. Departmentalization in the study of man reflects the rampant specialization of language, assumptions and activities in the conduct and organization of contemporary research. But it also supports a segregation of research efforts with only limited communication between psychologists, sociologists, anthropologists, economists, linguists, critics of the arts, historians, political scientists and theologians—all presumably seeking to contribute to human understanding and comprehension of the nature and destiny of man. Specialization and segregation characterize research efforts *within* each of these fields of study as well. Efforts to build communication between persons in various segregated disciplines or to synthesize, to confront and inter-criticize findings, concepts and assumptions from different disciplines receive little support and are often opposed vigorously by proponents of the disciplines and by those who finance their efforts. Philosophers of man have widely abandoned these tasks. It is hard to say how much light specialized knowledges of man might shed upon our dark and confused human situation, since efforts to focus such light are infrequent and unsustained.

But it is easy to see that people seeking to understand and deal with their human puzzlements and pains get either little or highly abstract and misleading intellectual help from academic sources of knowledge about man. This is illustrated well by students who, seeking to understand themselves and their human condition, increasingly find little help in studies organized along specialized disciplinary lines. It is dangerous to themselves and to others when they conclude that "objective" studies of man, which the scientific disciplines of man profess, are worthless in the pursuit of their purposes and when they are confirmed in a one-sided subjectivity in their view of what "knowledge" of man is apt to their purposes. It is dangerous but it is also understandable that many students and other actionists identify *themselves* with an uncritical and undiluted subjectivity in their choices and decisions.

Fragmentation has also come to characterize professionals in their learning and use of technologies of social practice—in and among the health professions, in social work, in administration and management, in schooling and education, in organized religion. Each operates with varying assumptions about human behavior, human potentiality, the ends of human life. And, since professional practice has tended to shape its patterns of service to the forms and requirements of established institutions, protesters against established institutions tend to discount the validity of professional, knowledge-based expertise, and to discount also the values of objectivity and rationality, with which professional experts over-identify themselves, in seeking to coach and influence human practice and action.

The departmental and bureaucratic organization of knowledge-building and of knowledge-application has tended to limit interpersonal exchange between researchers and practitioners and between both and the "ultimate" consumers and clients of research and of professional practice. When they do meet they tend to meet in formalized and stereotypic role-to-role relationships. Their differences are emphasized in such meetings. They rarely meet as selves and as persons, possessed of a common humanity but differing in needs and resources, with hope for the possible joining of needs and resources in processes of mutual and common benefit. The need for cultivating such community among scholars, among scholars and practitioners, among scholars, practitioners and "consumers" of knowledge and professional practice is now widely recognized in health, in education, in welfare, in religion and in industry and business. Roles and statuses as now defined and enacted thwart the development of such community. Only persons and selves can meet in community. Specialization becomes fragmentation when specialists fail to affirm themselves as selves and persons first and as specialists second. Creative and humane mergers of specialized knowledge, of specialized technologies, of specific human needs take place only as persons with specialized knowledge, persons with specialized technologies and persons with specific needs meet as persons in community. And such meeting occurs only as people come to believe in and affirm themselves as human persons. Without such meetings our specializations will destroy our common humanity as they are now tending to do.

Only Selves Can Reconcile the Subjective and the Objective in Man

A more basic factionalized fragmentation of man has shown itself, as we have explored the effects on man's vision of himself of departmentalization of effort in the study of man and in the development and utilization of technologies of social practice. This has to do with man as "subjective" and man as "objective". Some assert the priority of the subjective existence of man over any or all characterizations or conceptualizations of man as an object among other objects and see dependence by persons upon these as escapes from freedom. Others assert that only objective knowledge of man furnishes a valid basis for understanding, treating, teaching or managing him and relegate subjective visions of man to an irreal world of fantasy, wish or dream—perhaps to be totally discarded as evidence of his nature, perhaps as evidence to be explained or explained away in terms of "real", objective, publicly manipulable variables and their relationships.

The effects of this fragmentation of man are most apparent morally in differing views of how man validly grounds his choices and decisions about what to do with himself and how to deal with others. On a highly subjectivist view of decision, men make their choices alone, unjustified and without excuse, on the basis of inner spontaneous promptings and impulsions. Only in such decisions is man freed. The objectivist view asserts that man is freed only through objective knowledge of himself and his situation. The free man makes up his mind to act one way or another on the basis of knowledge of the motivations and consequences of alternative actions, keeping his subjective wishes and fantasies out of the "rational" calculus utilized in the decision.

It seems to me that both subjectivist and objectivist partisans have split human capacities that are conjoined in the selfhood of man. Whatever else selfhood includes, it involves the distinctively reflexive power of human beings. I affirm myself. I understand myself. I respond to, take responsibility for myself. In each of these statements, "I" somehow appears as both subject and object. In self-processes I and my situation appear as object to be understood, analyzed and diagnosed whether historically, in terms of my present involvements, or in relation to some future perspective or project. But it is I, as subject, with various and often conflicting wishes, fantasies, impulses, aspirations, preferences, who is objectifying myself and my situation in the hope of fuller, less deluded, more harmonious expression, investment and fulfillment of my complex and conflicted-subjective-objective person in present action and future consequence. "Selfing" is a process which conjoins subjective and objective modes of human actuality, hopefully to the mutual and beneficial service of both. It is this "selfing" process in which I believe and seek to believe more fully and responsibly.

This is not to say that all my choices and actions are at any one time involved in self-processing. I am sometimes moved by an inner impulse which impels me to actions that involve no recognition of the claims and welfare of other regions of myself or of other persons within the ambit of my action. My self must pay a price for such inconsiderateness. The price may not be too great to pay if the impulse which moved me was a repressed part of my person which now I am aware of and which I can include, perhaps for the first time, within the councils of myself. But the price must be paid and I would hope to develop a self, through such experiences as these, which in the future is less repressive of, more attentive to minority voices in and around myself.

At other times I am moved to action by the weight of external demands and evidences which leads me to ignore or repress the demands of "subjective" voices and doubts within my person. Such action is debilitating to myself. For I am dishonoring and supressing parts of my subjective person in such decisions, perhaps through idolatrizing some externalized projection of myself at the expense of the invention of new modes of response which might do greater justice both to external demands and to internal demands—modes of response which can become part of my learning-growing person. Such "objectively" grounded actions are, from the viewpoint of this potentiality, unfaithful slayings of myself.

Both internal and external censorships and curtailments of whole, integrated and free responses in and to my world are possibilities and probabilities which continually threaten me. To abet internal censorship by invoking the sacred name of "subjective" freedom or to elevate external censorship in the name of "objective" reality is to perpetuate divisions within persons and to block the building of community out of the conflicts among men.

Decisions and choices present themselves to persons as ambiguities, confusions and conflicts. There is a strong tendency in human as in other organisms to make a quick end to ambiguity, confusion and conflict within the organism by externalizing the conflict, by rushing to some inner equilibrium, whether impulsive or rationally engineered, which is a wilful falsification of both outer and inner reality. Belief in the self supports the human person in staying with the conflict, in joining the dialogue between inner voices and between outer voices, and in seeking and affirming the creative resolution of conflict which is likely to issue from the conflict as it is taken into the persons of the contestants and worked through to a humane conclusion. For one who affirms the potency and benignity of the self, easy resolutions which would foreclose conflicts by excluding them from the self are seen as temptations to irresponsibility or, as I have expressed the idea poetically, as burdens of false peace.

The Burden of False Peace

I seek no peace which gives the lie to life—
No peace which speaks extinction to the mind
Or chills the hot projection of the will.
Oh take from me the burden of false peace.

Life is the aching pressure of the will,
The flickering, posturing pageant of the mind.
What dulls my mind and saps my will steals life.
Oh take from me the burden of false peace.

I would begin (not end) my quest for life at
     Bethlehem.
I would find strength to will and fail, and learn
     to will anew,
To know that loss and pain in love can strengthen
     me.
Oh take from me the burden of false peace.

Only Persons Can Reconcile the Rational
and the Non-Rational in Man

The factional struggles between proponents of "subjective" and "objective" man often polarize a related disjunction between "irrational" and "rational" man. When *rationality* is used to name processes of resolving issues by cool manipulation and logical processing of facts, with an exclusion of human feelings and aspirations evoked by the issue from the arena of judgment as "non-facts", it is not surprising that feelingful and aspiring persons thus excluded from influence on the resolution should find in rationality an enemy. Nor is it surprising that they should seek to elevate "sub-rational" urgencies of feeling and impulse, *Blut und Boden,* or "super-rational" revelations and absolutes, whether of nation, race or God, above rational processes as legitimate arbiters of human choice and action. The effect of the polarization is to blind both the opponents and proponents of a depersonalized and dehumanized version of rationality to their own incoherences. "Objective rationalists" are blinded to the part which their own unacknowledged feelings, aspirations and preferences play in the judgments they make. "Subjective irrationalists", as they seek to justify to themselves and others some favored urgency or revelation as worthy of acceptance as a ground for choice and action, fail to see that they are enlisting processes of rationality in the service and propagation of their own "irrational" devotions. Both are deluding themselves.

The problem is to invent and enact a more adequate conception of rationality. The purpose of rationality in human affairs is not to suppress human impulses and their satisfaction. It is, rather, to seek to facilitate the fuller and more harmonious satisfaction of human impulses and interests where various impulses and interests present contrary and conflicting demands upon finite human energies and resources. In a situation demanding harmonization, rationality creates an ideal which has pertinence and authority to persons seeking to actualize goods which are seen as irreconcilable without the mediation of such an ideal. An ideal is perforce a creative blending of things actual and things desired.

My belief in myself and in the selves of others leads me to accept Santayana's criteria for evaluating the work of rationality in human affairs.

> A rational will is not a will that has reason for its basis or that possesses any other proof that its realization would be possible or good than the oracle which a living will inspires and pronounces. The rationality possible to the will lies not in its source but in its method. An ideal cannot wait for its realization to prove its validity. To deserve loyalty it needs only to be adequate as an ideal, that is, to express completely what the soul at present demands, and to do justice to all extant interests.[1]

A self, when it behaves rationally in the presence of an issue, must seek reliable information concerning relevant matters of fact. And human aspirations, aversions and preferences are important facts to be blended and reconciled with other more technical and external considerations in forming decisions and attainable ideals. Knowledge of what now is or has been never determines completely the direction or form of future action. Reason in a self that operates in self-respect is an inventive, imaginative and reconstructive reason alive to new possibilities and desirabilities in improving human arrangements and correcting human derangements. A hopeful self learns to use failures in action to envision new desirabilities and to generate new and more attainable aspirations.

1. George Santayana, *The Life of Reason*, Vol. I., (N.Y.: Scribners, 1929), pp. 254-55.

Another distinction with respect to rationality in human affairs helps to explain in part men's current penchant for polarizing "irrational" and "rational" man. This is Karl Mannheim's distinction between substantial and functional rationality in contemporary society.[2] Mannheim used "functional rationality" to refer to the objective analysis of functions required for various collective tasks and the organization of task production through an ordered lay-out of interrelated functions into which "personnel" are fitted through deliberate processes of selection and training. Functional rationality in human organization was exemplified in Germany in the movement to rationalize industrial organization, and in America, in the scientific management movement. With refined and augmented power, functional rationality flourishes today in the disciplines of operations research and systems analysis. The rationalization of human organization has moved out of industry into government, education and the provision of health and welfare services and has touched men and women in every aspect of their lives.

Mannheim used "substantial rationality" to refer to the "reason" I described earlier, operating at the personal and group levels of human organization to achieve a flexible, harmonious and viable patterning among various and conflicting impulses and interests. But substantial rationality operates integratively, voluntaristically, with full communication and interaction between cognitive, affective and conative aspects of living when it operates well or fully.

Mannheim remarked that an increase in functional rationality often led to an increase in substantial irrationality on the part of people expected to accede to its demands upon them. He did not, as I recall it, explore the opposite hypothesis. But perhaps that opposite hypothesis is what protesters against functionally rationalized organizations—student leftists, Black Power advocates and Hippies among others—are exploring today. Does a committed effort by a group to articulate and assert its substantial rationality lead to an increase in functional irrationality within a highly rationalized social system or organization? I think that we have evidence that it does. But the task of practical reason as it operates through selves and communities does not end there. It must move on to the normative questions—Need the requirements of functional rationality and those of substantial rationality be opposed, segregated and polarized in the organization of human life and action? Should we invent and bring into being

2. Karl Mannheim, *Man and Society in an Age of Reconstruction*, (N.Y.: Harcourt, Brace, 1951), pp. 51-60.

forms of human organization in which the claims of substantial rationality and of functional rationality are reconciled and harmonized?

Early "human relations" protests against the sweep of functional rationality within industry were often couched in terms of its neglect and frustration of the affective and conative needs of men who work but often fail to live in industry. The newer "human relations" protestants must speak also of the frustration by rampant functional rationality in the management of human life of the powers of substantial human rationality which operate in and through human persons as well. And the protests must be addressed not least to the organization of our life of learning and education.

Persons in Community and Community in Persons

In commenting earlier on the premature and facile pseudo-resolutions of issues which thwart growth and learning in human persons, I did not emphasize my need, the need of all persons, for the help of other persons in shedding the burdens of false peace. I must continually validate myself against others in maintaining and deepening my reality orientation. Sensory deprivation experiments with human subjects have shown how persons, deprived of encounter with and feedback from others, lose the power to discriminate between fantasy and veridical perception, lose the boundaries which, however fluidly, identify them as persons. Consensual validation is not an option, it is rather a necessity in the maintenance of a viable self. Consensual validation by persons possessed of a common false consciousness confirms them in this false consciousness, whether of self-image or of ideology.

A self committed to growth in reality orientation must deliberately seek consensual validation against others who differ in value orientation, in life style and commitment. A growing self must seek encounter with others who can and will challenge, if necessary, the very foundations of his beliefs and life commitments. And he must reciprocate the challenge to others in mutual exchange. Each in a growthful encounter must speak truth to the other in a spirit of love and mutual respect. This, as I understand it, and try when at my best to practice it, is what Martin Buber described as a life of and in dialogue. Faith in myself places upon me the responsibility of seeking to develop an adequate validating community around me. Only through experience of such relationships can I internalize an adequate validating community within myself. As I encounter fresh conflicts between myself and others, I must renew and refresh my internal community through new encounters and dialogue with those who challenge me. Social arrangements which thwart, discourage, and punish dialogue between those who differ are poisoning the wells of personal and social renewal.

Self in Nature

So far I have spoken of self and person largely in the contexts of human exchange and sociality. But faith in self requires also supporting beliefs concerning the relations between myself and non-human nature in which persons and societies are born, seek to flourish and die. I have explored some of these relationships in a prose poem.

Meditations on the Self in Winter Time

And is this I? The sun around which planet roles revolve?
Despair sloughs off some non-essential trappings of the
    self—the me's that batten on bright public praise,
    that preen before the public smile.
The I enduring is a lonely I, yet can not spurn
    its debt to other men—its piety toward Man,
    generic and collective.
How can I find my tortuous way to Man beneath, beyond
    a maze of statuses—statuses filled and yet denied
    by me as inessential to myself?

There is a cruelty unfathomable in willful, will-less
    crowding of a man into the shape of ruin.
The will-less cruelty—lacking light of self-awareness—
    is the more unfathomable.
And yet the pain induced in victim shows a weakness there—
    a lack of calm acceptance that the cosmos is in me, in
    my tormentors too; that Man looks through my eyes when
    they see clearly, lovingly.

A thousand you's may judge a single me, may call me
    devil, thing, may name my name which canting
    lips can only hint or whisper, or for my acts
    unnamed intone dark censure.
But Man to which essential I responds may yet elude
    the judgment. So where is Man and where am I?
    The questions are the same.

My floods of fantasy break into froth and foam,
    whirling and churning, propelled by deep dis-ease
    within myself.
Creation moves within my floods of fantasy, joining my
    self to others, to Man, to world at levels which my
    ego can not see by light refracted through distorting
    screens of conscience and self image.
How can I feel, follow creation through torments of
    prideful pain? How can I find among all pains
    the pain, which, conquered, yields a new articulation
    of myself, which shapes me, node of the cosmos,
    into a form that shows forth truth?

And all these words are lame things, brittle defense-
    offense toward human cruelty and sightlessness within
    myself and others, cruelty and sightlessness which would
    deny myself and other selves unquestioned human
    membership.
Yet heartfelt words may light a heliograph, which
    others on some lonely hill beleagured see,
    interpret, may fashion bonds of new community.
Or if no heliograph gets built, if no one reads
    a message in the flickering images evoked, the
    words may kindle new light in myself, may
    quicken hope that others will be found who feel
    all mankind kin;
who do not draw harsh circles round the love they
    give, doling it out to those "deserving" it,
    which means no gift, no overflowing of a
    tribute, unmandated, undeserved;
who look through customs, credentials, relativities to
    see a core humanity, forged in despair, living by hope,
    which knows of truth because it is the source of truth.

One connection with non-human nature with which I am intimately involved from birth to death is my body. I am not always on good terms with my body. I sometimes resent its illnesses, its lack of grace, its resistance to my efforts to make it into something which it cannot be. I am most whole when I admit the voices of my body, the voices which speak of strength and limitation, of health and death, of lust and satiation into the councils of myself. For man, the animal species, with its ancient memories of a long and continuing evolution of life out of non-life, of

simple life forms into intricate and differentiated life forms, of complicated energy exchanges between organism and environment, speaks to me
through my body when I learn to hear its messages. To accept my body
as part of myself is for me to see and feel myself as nature becomes
conscious of itself in one unique center of feeling, thinking, evaluation
and choice. To feel myself as continuous with nature is to see myself as
responsible for continuing the process of evolution of life through deliberate variation and selection, not through the dumb and silent processes
of inter-adjustment which lie behind me and others like and yet different
from me. I gain strength in negating the idolatries which would arrest and
delay the continuing processes of creative evolution of which I as a
person am an indispensable part.

I believe that I am a "node of the cosmos". I have not been able to
understand those who look for evidence of the nature of nature only
outside themselves and fail to find evidence of the nature of nature also
in the self that looks beyond itself and tries to make sense of what it sees
and finds there. In myself, as I function fully and adequately, I am nature
seeking to understand itself, to direct itself consciously, to reshape itself
planfully. To recognize, as I must, if I am to become a self at all, that
otherness is as real as I does not negate myself. It means rather to me that
nature is variegated and individualized, that I, if I do not fail myself, am
in some way unique.

When I find conflict within me and around me, I am not appalled. For
I know from my own experience as a self that conflict, if I can face it and
help to work it through, can yield a wider consciousness, a creation and
realization of new good in which old good is not wholly lost. That
conflict can also destroy good puts a responsibility upon me to find ways
of augmenting the creative, rather than the destructive, uses of conflict. I
must recognize variety, differences and conflict within nature as I must
recognize it within and around myself. I must also recognize the reality of
community which supports me both in actualizing my individuality and
in the enhancement of common experience. My own power, with the
help of others, to see possibilities beyond my present powers of empirical
verification also endows me and others with the power to delude myself
and others. Truth is not possible without the concomitant possibility of
error. Without faith in myself as a node of an evolving cosmos become
conscious, critical and responsible, I lose my zest for the continuing
struggle to distinguish truth from error, to communicate truth, and to try
to live by it.

My realization that I will die quickens my sense of the importance of my life. I will not wholly die if I have allowed myself to become a memorable part of others even as I have welcomed others in becoming memorable parts of myself.

Immortality

I have found death in friends' forgetfulness
And immortality in loving memory.
Hell lives in tortured memories sharp with pain.
If hell should be the fate that I have earned,
Forget me, friends. Grant me quick death and cool oblivion.
But if love glows among the ash of time
Where we kept watch together on time's flame,
Save me from death, grant immortality.
Remember me, my friends, remember me.

And so—I aspire to believe in myself as a human being.

Rationalism In Ethics and Religion*

Brand Blanshard

Perhaps I should confess at once that I have never been much tempted by any philosophy except the one, such as it is, that appears in my books. I do not know whether this fact is to my credit or greatly to my discredit. But it can hardly be due to a lack of exposure to other ways of thinking, for in that respect I have been exceptionally fortunate. I worked at Columbia with Dewey, Woodbridge, and Montague, at Harvard with Perry and Lewis, and in England with Prichard, Ross, and Moore. The debt I owe these great men is beyond calculation, but I did not feel regarding any one of them that I could take as my own the general pattern of his thought. It was probably Bradley more than any other who helped me to find my vein. When I went to England in 1913 as an undergraduate, the whole of philosophical Britain was living in his shadow in a way that it is hard for students of today to understand; and it fell to my lot to live in the little college, Merton, in which he was still a fellow in residence, to see something of him personally, and to study his *Logic* under Harold Joachim, an admiring exponent of his thought. Though I cannot claim to have mastered his system, I was greatly impressed and influenced by it.

The Philosophic Enterprise

The main thing I owe to Bradley was his conception of what philosophy was seeking to do. This borrowed stone became the head and corner

*Some parts of this essay will re-appear in the forthcoming Library of Living Philosophers, ed. Paul Schilpp, on Professor Blanshard's Philosophy. (Ed.)

of my philosophy. When I came to write a book on *The Nature of Thought,* and tried to make clear to myself what reflective thinking was attempting to do, the only answer that seemed plausible was that it was seeking understanding, that understanding was explanation to oneself, and that explanation lay in placing something in a context of relations that rendered it intelligible. Since this is probably the cardinal idea of my philosophy, perhaps I should dwell on it a moment.

According to this idea, philosophy is an activity pursued by everyone, and common sense, science, and philosophy are stages in a continuous enterprise. The boy who picks up a smooth stone on the beach and wonders how it got its shape has taken the first step in that enterprise; he has begun to think things out for himself in the interest of understanding them. If he grows up and becomes a geologist, he will be doing the same thing still, though with more knowledge, skill, and precision. The boy asks why the stone is smooth, and conjectures that it is because it has been constantly rubbed by the stones around it as the tides rise and fall. The geologist says that too, but presses the inquiry further; he asks why the tides rise and fall, and explains them through a precise law that connects them with the approaches and recessions of the moon. The philosopher is not deserting the path of this inquiry; he is still pressing the question why, still seeking clarity and fullness of understanding. This gravitational law that governs the tides—why is it to be accepted? Is it intelligible in the sense of logically necessary? If so, why can we not discover it by sitting down and thinking? If not, how are we to know that it holds without exception? And what exactly does it mean to say that the moon 'pulls' the tides, or that anything 'causes' anything else? These are questions that spring straight out of any sustained endeavor to understand one's world.

As the endeavor goes on, it is bound to raise questions of great technicality and difficulty. And there are persons who think of the philosopher as a specialist in such questions, a dealer chiefly in esoteric puzzles. He is not really that. Indeed he is so little of a specialist that he often finds himself embarrassed in describing what he does; in trying to think things out, he seems merely to be doing whatever everyone else on occasion does. He is not a specialist as the biologist is who confines himself to arachnids or hymenoptera, or the historian who concentrates on the Long Parliament. These specialists till their particular plots of ground because they happen to be interested in them, not because they have seen that certain questions must be raised and answered if they are to understand the world. But it is precisely this that makes the philosopher raise some questions rather than others. If he marches through certain thickets, it is because, if he is to reach his ulterior goal, he must. But there is nothing whimsical or esoteric about this goal or his motive in seeking it; what drives him on is theoretic interest, the need to get clear about the world he lives in, the desire to see why things are as they are and behave as they do. Because plain men also feel this, they have commonly turned to their philosophers with some expectation of light and leading, as men who were doing with determination and skill what they had themselves tried to do more gropingly; the philosophers were walking the same path but were further along, and had news of what lay ahead. Unfortunately that feeling of community between the plain man and the philosopher seems to be disappearing; the philosopher now appears to be not so much a wise and reflective human being as an expert in analyzing the meanings of words and in solving logical puzzles.

Is there anything new in the idea of philosophy as a peculiarly determined effort to press the question Why? Probably not. But in the form in which I have developed it there are three components that have seemed to me of importance.

The Theoretic Impulse

The first is the notion of thought as springing from a distinct drive in human nature. A drive is an urge or impulse directed to a distinctive end. Thinking has been identified with many processes—by the pragmatists with the seeking of a practical end, by many psychologists with a sequence of associations, by behaviorists with certain bodily responses. It is not primarily any of these things. It is the search for a peculiar kind of satisfaction, namely intellectual or theoretic satisfaction. This end is only implicitly present when thought begins in the perceptual interpretation of the given, but it steadily rises in the explicitness and firmness of its control as thought approaches its maturity in systematic reflection. Thinking can be responsibly studied only from the inside, for it is a conscious and purposive process, distinguished from all other processes by the uniqueness of its end.

Granting, however, that the end lies in theoretic satisfaction, what is it that thus satisfies? In what sort of content or arrangement does thought come to rest? Only in understanding, we have suggested, only when something that has frustrated and puzzled it is explained. But what does it mean to explain something? It means, we have said, to place it in a context that renders it intelligible. "What is that man doing up in a tree?"

"He is cutting a branch that interferes with the telephone line." "Why do porcupines have quills?" "Because such quills afford protection to their owners and thus enable them to survive." "Why do triangles have internal angles that equal exactly two right angles?" "Well, take this triangle as typical, draw a line through the apex parallel to the base, and extend the two sides that meet at the apex. Then these two angles at the base equal these two beyond the parallel line, and the one that is left equals the remaining one on that line. The three together are therefore equal to a straight line, and a straight line is equal to two right angles. Do you follow?" In all these cases explanation is the same in general pattern; it places what is not understood in a context that makes it intelligible. Not that the contexts are all of the same kind; the context in the first case is one of means—end; in the second, of causation; in the third, of logical necessity. But in all, what explains is the relations within a little system, formed by the thing to be explained and its context.

In most men the theoretic impulse is no very powerful drive; "the love of truth," says Housman, "is the faintest of human passions." Few men sit down like Rodin's *Thinker* and think for its own fascinating sake; they wait till thinking is needed for some practical purpose—getting the car started, getting rid of this troublesome cold—and drop it when the purpose is attained. But they could always go on with their theorizing if they cared to. No theoretical satisfaction is ever more than temporary and partial; the question Why? can be asked again and again, without apparent limit. One sees why the angles of a triangle must equal two right angles, but the little set of insights one uses to show it do not make an island of their own; they are so connected with others in Euclid's system that their denial would carry the whole system down with them. They are warranted by that system as a whole. And what warrants the system? Again, its place in a larger system which, sooner or later, can only mean the universe. All this puts me gratefully in a special tradition of philosophy, one that runs back through Whitehead, Bosanquet, and Hegel, to Spinoza, Sankara, and Plato.

The first two points, then, are that thought is an activity with an end of its own, and that this end consists in seeing things in relations that explain them. The third point consists in an answer to a question that inevitably rises here. What guarantees that the system which satisfies thought should also answer to the nature of things? Might not a philosopher raise the question Why? about some fact that puzzled him, and place it in a system of relations that perfectly satisfied his theoretic sense, while still being really defeated? For how does he know that the system which satisfies his intellect is also the system, if any, that holds in nature? It would seem that the very rigor of his logic might carry him farther from nature at every step, since between the logic that he finds satisfactory and the actual structure of things there might be an impassable gap.

The Postulate of Rationality

There is no way of *proving* this gap away. Any proof that the laws of logic are valid of the world would have to use those laws in the process, that is, assume their validity for that world, and this validity is the point at issue. But we may at least ask the skeptic what he means by saying that logic may not hold of the world. Does he mean this, for example, that though a certain spot on this stamp is pink, it may also and at the same time *not* be pink? That would be the case if the law of contradiction did not apply. One can say such things easily enough, but can one think them? Press the skeptic as to what a state of things would be like in which a spot was both pink and not pink, and he is not helpful. He may reply that this only confirms his case; we are so hamstrung by logic that we cannot even think what freedom from it would be like; but that only shows our slavery anew; we are so sunk in it that we cannot frame the idea of an escape. There is not much force in this reply. Freedom to think irrationally and act impossibly offers no genuine alternative to our present state, and it is called freedom only by a confused analogy. Freedom from coercion means something definite and desirable; freedom from logic means nothing conceivable nor, therefore, desirable.

So far, then, as the end of thought is the explanation of things by seeing them in a coherent system, we can only suppose that this system reflects the world as it is. But we have intimated that in the ideal thought sets before itself, more is involved than coherence. In our ordinary logic, two beliefs may be consistent without being related otherwise; "it is raining" is consistent with "Miltiades commanded at Marathon," but they seem utterly unconnected. According to the logic of *Principia Mathematica,* they do, to be sure, "imply" each other, but that is because implication is there so defined that any two propositions imply each other if both are true. But no rationalist could be content with such mere juxtaposition among the items of his knowledge, since that would mean that his inquiry was shelved at the outset; the question, 'why, in a world in which this is true, should this also be true?' would have no answer. Facts, perhaps systems of them, would stand side by side for no reason at all. Now much of the world may consist of this sort of heap or litter of facts; at least I find myself distrustful of a priori proofs that it cannot. That the world is an intelligible system rather than a congeries of accidents seems to me rather a postulate of speculative inquiry than a conclusion decisively made out. One may say, if one wishes, that it is a matter of faith. But that suggests that the postulate is dispensable or arbitrary, and it is clearly not. Thought is an unavoidable human enterprise; if it is to succeed, the question Why? which it continually raises must be answerable; to assume that it is answerable is to assume only what is necessary unless the enterprise is expected in advance to be a failure. There is no self-deception in a "faith" of this kind. One is not running gullibly beyond the evidence; one is assuming at each step of the journey that there is solid ground ahead and that this will hold for each subsequent step. In this one may be mistaken. But there is no very wild credulity in assuming, when one presses the question Why?, that there is an answer to the question.

My conception of philosophy, then, involves three theses: (1) that the theoretical impulse at the root of philosophy is a distinct drive in human nature, (2) that the end of this drive is to order things in an intelligible system of relations, and (3) that as our understanding advances, there is a closer approximation of the system within to the system without.

But the question we are asked in this volume is not merely what we believe on matters of ultimate concern, but in what sort of conclusions our philosophies issue when we turn to the life around us. This gives anyone with an outlook like mine an opportunity not to be missed. For I am a rationalist, and one of the salient features of our time is its distrust of reason. Clearly, I should say something about this distrust and my attitude toward it. I should like then to go on and point out how my rationalism has affected my views in two fields where that distrust is most apparent, ethics and religion.

The Revolt Against Reason

That reason has fallen from its former estate is plain enough. Even in philosophy it has been brusquely demoted. Wittgenstein, whose influence has been enormous, held that no fact in the world has any logical connection with any other. The imposing tradition in metaphysics extending from Plato to Whitehead, in which the thinker undertook by patient reflection to trace the outlines of the world order, has been dismissed on the grounds that it was unaware of the verifiability theory of meaning and the analytic character of a priori statements. Ethics has been declared off bounds for reason, since a "judgment" of value is the expression of an attitude, and hence neither true nor false; and political thinking, being essentially applied ethics, has shared in this skepticism. Logic is considered by an influential school as a body of conventional rules without significance for the nature of things. The philosophy of religion has been declared by Karl Barth to be impossible on the ground that it is presumptuous to suppose God a respecter of human logic and ethics.

These are important developments. What makes them important is not only that if they are true, philosophy is a less significant enterprise than has been supposed; it is also that, once this traditional stronghold of reason has surrendered, the minor outposts are likely to follow suit. Indeed they have not waited for philosophic insurgency to declare their own independence of reason. Those of us who were brought up, rightly or not, to believe in standards that were objective and rationally defensible are facing a scene so chaotic as to force us to reexamine much or most that we took as self-evident. Meaninglessness in poetry; the theatre of the absurd; a God-is-dead religion; art without form and void; an anthropology in which no culture is better or worse than any other; an education in which examinations and academic distinctions are to be abolished as involving odious comparisons, and subject matter determined by social "relevance;" an exaltation of the primitive in music; the retreat of many youths from responsibility into a world of narcotic fantasy; a crime rate suggesting that for large groups of our population the line between right and wrong has been largely obliterated—these are some of the marks of the revolt against rational standards that I have in mind. In philosophy the reaction has been against rationalism; in these more populous areas, it is against rationality itself.

Some definitions are called for at this point. When talking the language of epistemology, I mean by "reason" the grasp of necessary connections, best exemplified in logic and mathematics. "Rationalism," when used in the same context, is the belief that reason, as distinct from sense experience, is an independent source of knowledge. Rationalism in metaphysics is the theory that the world is a whole whose parts are connected by necessary relations. Now it is clearly not reason or rationalism in these somewhat technical senses at which the present revolt is aimed. The reason that is under suspicion is the whole knowing side of our nature, and the protest is against making this dominant over the sides of feeling and impulse. The rationalism that is rejected is that which would set up objective and impersonal thought as the arbiter in matters of taste, morals, and religion, as well as of fact and theory. The revolt, we may say, is against intellectualism and the type of man it is believed to represent, the man who would reduce all problems, theoretical, practical, and personal, to intellectual problems that may be cleared up by taking thought. And this, it is said, is making thought into an idol. The impersonal, reflective thought that is quite rightly appealed to in the sanctuaries of science, philosophy, and courts of law is no authority for the world outside them. Poets do not want to be dictated to by such an authority, nor artists to be straitjacketed by it, nor experimenters with new drugs or nostrums to be preached at by it, nor minorities with grievances to be moderated and restrained by it, nor youths whose pulse is high and whose impulses are strong, to be forced into subjection to it.

Some Rationalist Convictions

Now the rationalism to which I subscribe is not of the merely academic kind. I must admit to the belief that just as there is an answer to the question Why?, when asked about what is, so there is an answer to it when raised about what ought to be, about rights and duties, about taste, or religion or conduct. Indeed I think the great need at present is the recognition that there are standards in all these fields and that reason can provide them. The reason here invoked varies somewhat with its subject-matter, but it involves throughout the grasp of objective relations. The problems that torment and divide us may be as difficult as one cares to make them, but they are not in principle insoluble, and if one is serious about solving them, I see no alternative to the appeal to reason. If that makes me an intellectualist, I must accept the name.

It may be replied that 'from the practical point of view, this exaltation of reason is futile; the difficulty is not that men distrust the power of reason to give an answer; it is rather that they cannot agree what that answer is. And there is not much point in urging men to be reasonable if, when they do, they come up with the same vehement differences as before. Men on both sides of an issue have often professed an intense devotion to reason, but this has not prevented them from denouncing each other's conclusions as perverse, or even on occasion from cutting each other's throats. What is the point of urging reasonableness upon them if, even when they accept it as an ideal, they differ as deeply as before over what in particular it requires?

This is not as convincing on reflection as it seems at first glance. If two men who profess allegiance to reason are confronted by the same problem and the same facts, and yet arrive at conflicting conclusions, that shows that at least one of them, in spite of his profession, is *not* being guided by reason; a reason that contradicts itself belies the name; at some point the reasoner has been pushed or pulled off the rational track. The forces exerting the pushes and pulls are innumerable; Descartes gave one oversimplified account of them, Freud another; Mill tried to classify them in the section of his *Logic* on fallacies; Professor Thouless has tracked down many of them in his useful little book on *Straight and Crooked Thinking.* They will perhaps never be exhaustively listed. Suffice it to say that to an unambiguous question there is, as a rule, only one right answer, while there are numberless ways of reaching wrong ones. And on a question of any difficulty it is far easier to go wrong than right.

When people professing allegiance to reason do go wrong, it is not because reason has failed or misled them, but because, innocently or not, they have defected from it. Their professed devotion to reason has not been strong enough to deal with distorting agents such as impatience, egotism, and prejudice. These tendencies are so ingrained in human nature that any attempt to get rid of them altogether would be utopian. But one can at least reduce their influence by becoming aware of them and remaining on guard against them. When men have identified their self-respect with thinking impartially, whole classes of them, for example judges, have succeeded in achieving it in considerable degree. Most men at present are so far from tying their self-respect to objectivity of thought that the very notion of an ethics of belief, the notion that adjusting one's belief to the evidence, is an obligation like paying a debt, would seem visionary to them. It is coming slowly to be realized that there is such an ethics of thought, and that it is a duty not only to tell the truth, but to try to see it. The world would be an astonishingly different place even if men came to feel that being unreasonable was bad taste or bad form. Wilfrid Trotter, the student of herd instincts, wrote: "If rationality were once to become really respectable; if we feared the entertaining of an unverifiable opinion with the warmth with which we now fear using the wrong implement at the dinner table; if the thought of holding a prejudice disgusted us as does a foul disease, then the danger of man's suggestibility would be turned to an advantage."

Skepticism in Ethics

Present-day skepticism about reason, however, goes far beyond these doubts as to whether reason can achieve control. It questions whether in one vast area of life, the field of values, reason has any relevance or competence. To say that an experience is good or that an act is right, it holds, is not a judgment at all, but an expression of liking or some other favoring attitude. This view was adopted by logical empiricists because it seemed to be required by their division of cognitive statements into a priori and empirical. The statement that stealing is wrong is plainly not a priori, since there are exceptions to it; and it is just as plainly not empirical, since rightness is not a characteristic that can be sensed. Hence the statement is not a cognitive statement at all, but an expression of attitude, perhaps of emotion, perhaps of entreaty or command. In any case since an attitude is not true nor false, neither is the alleged judgment. Statements about good and evil, right or wrong, beauty or ugliness, therefore fall outside the sphere of rational discourse altogether.

In my *Reason and Goodness* I have tried to examine this new subjectivism in some detail. Various forms of it have been persuasively urged by Messrs. Ayer, Toulmin, Stevenson, Hare, Urmson, Nowell-Smith, and others, and an adequate criticism would call for a separate examination of many theories that differ from each other only slightly. All of them seem to me to run aground on the same fact, namely that when we make an ethical judgment, we normally mean to say something true, and that when others differ from us about it, they normally mean to say that it is not true. This the attitude theory denies. It holds that when I say "Brutus did wrong in stabbing Caesar," I mean to say nothing about Brutus' act, but only to express my present attitude toward it.

That there is something wrong with this analysis may be seen by a simple experiment. Let us ask ourselves whether what we meant to say when we made the statement would still hold if we had not made it. The natural answer is: Of course it would. The rightness or wrongness of a remote act does not depend on whether we make a statement about it here and now. The rightness or wrongness of Brutus' act surely belonged to it when it was committed, and did not have to wait twenty centuries to come into being. Yet that is substantially what the attitude theory is saying. It holds that the only meaning expressed by "right" or "wrong" is one that is exhausted by the present inward stance of the judge, and this implies that if we had happened not to make the statement, nothing we mean by "right" or "wrong" would have belonged to Brutus' act. Indeed nothing really evil has ever occurred in history. The black death, the influenza epidemic of 1918, the two world wars of the present century, did seem evil to their contemporaries, but that is irrelevant; it is not what *we* mean when we say that they were evil. Our meaning is supplied entirely by our present attitude, and therefore in the only sense in which we are permitted to use the terms, the good and evil of past events depend entirely on present attitudes. If my mood changes and I come to admire Brutus' action, that action has changed from wrong to right in the only sense in which any action is wrong or right. If this is offered as an analysis of what we actually mean when we call actions right or wrong, it seems to me preposterous.

The moralists who preceded the Wittgenstein era, Rashdall, Moore, Ross, Carritt, Joseph, Prichard—all of them happily among my teachers—seem to me to have had a stronger grip on ethical fact and intention than their successors. They agreed that a moral judgment was really a judgment, that it meant to say something true about the character of an action, a character owned by it independently of what was thought or felt about it. Of course they had their differences—and serious ones—about what precisely was being asserted (though it would never have occurred to them to go to the *Oxford English Dictionary* to settle a philosophical question, or to appeal to the usages of street and supermarket as authoritative for ethics). Their method was essentially that of Socrates, to start with what the plain man thought he meant, then show that this meaning did not square with his other applications of the term, and, if necessary, to go on refining it till it did. The meaning that in the end emerged might well be something remote from the first crude result of self-examination, something that was not explicitly present in the user's mind at all and would have met with rejection if presented at the start. Nevertheless at the end it would be recognized as the only definition that would consistently cover the ground and one that he had been reaching for all along.

Intrinsic Goodness

It is this process I have tried to employ in my own examination of ethical terms. I follow Sidgwick, Rashdall and Moore in thinking that the rightness of an action lies in the way it works out. But I am not a utilitarian in the sense in which they were. I hold that the rightness of an action depends on the intrinsic goods and evils involved in the way of life to which that action belongs. And what makes an experience intrinsically good? Sidgwick, Rashdall, Moore and Ross held good to be indefinable because incapable of analysis. I have not felt easy with this conclusion. Is this all we can say about experiences we find good? Whether through illusion or not, I have found two characteristics which are both present in some degree in all experiences we call good. The first is the characteristic of fulfilling some urge or drive or interest of the man who experiences it. If a man has no desire to know, he will not find study a good in itself; if he lacks an ear and interest for music, if it fulfils nothing in his nature, as it presumably fulfils nothing in a dog or a horse, he will find it a bore. Here I suppose I am following Aristotle, and am certainly closer to my teachers Dewey and Perry than I once was. My debt to the self-realizationists will be obvious. But there is another character always present in intrinsically valuable experience; some flush of pleasure. Aristotle was surely right in saying that pleasure is the normal accompaniment of fulfilment; if the fulfilment of one's desire for knowledge or one's interest in music brought no trace of enjoyment, it would be ashes in the mouth. That is the lesson of Mill's famous breakdown at twenty, in which, while retaining his intellectual powers to the full, he lost all the satisfaction he had once taken in exercising them. The result was that he did not care whether he lived or died.

Truth in Moral Judgment

With this view of what rightness and goodness mean, the settlement of ethical questions becomes a rational affair. To say that an action is right is to say something true or false, something about which there is an objective truth to be found, and reflection on the evidence is the way to find it. Supporters of the attitude theory have often been embarrassed by the realization that on their theory there was no objective truth to be found about the rightness or wrongness of anything. Some of the most distinguished of them had suffered under the Nazi regime in Germany and had the best of reasons to condemn that regime as cruel and unjust. They found themselves curiously handicapped, however, when asked to defend this condemnation. "On your theory," it was pointed out to them, "there was nothing really or objectively wrong about the treatment you received; the Nazis liked it; you disliked it; that is all; by your own testimony, there is no rational ground for preferring one response to the other." This brought home a difficulty felt by others in their position; their ethical theory and their ethical convictions seemed out of line with each other. They might say, of course, "The two attitudes are not on the same footing. No one is entitled to feel approval for injustice and the infliction of needless suffering." But this, upon their theory, is only a further expression of distaste, directed now upon feeling rather than conduct; and except to those who share the distaste, it carries no authority.

Some defenders of the attitude theory have sought to escape from their predicament by saying that while a moral "judgment" is not a proposition and therefore cannot be proved or disproved, one can still give reasons for it and see that some reasons are stronger than others. Nazi persecution of the Jews was wrong because it was a persecution of innocent people, because it was brutalizing to the agents, and because it inflicted needless suffering. But if these relevant reasons are moral judgments offered as true, the theory has been deserted; and if they are mere ejaculations, they are not reasons for anything. Professor Hare has contended that attitudes themselves may have a kind of consistency, so that Christians could support an attitude by arguing that consistency with their other attitudes required it; but if asked why the Christian view as a whole is to be preferred to a rival view, for example the Nazis', Professor Hare would hold that argument breaks down; one cannot argue for a way of life as a whole; such a choice must be an ultimate non-rational commitment. But is this not an abandonment of reason at the most crucial point of all?

Reason in International Disputes

The defection from reason in ethics seems especially unfortunate when one considers its implications for international disputes. It has been assumed in the past that whatever the bitterness of the particular quarrel, there were always outlying areas of agreement that could be taken for granted. The multiplication table and the laws of logic were plainly not matters of taste but were objectively valid, and were therefore binding on both sides equally; and though disputes about fact were common, the scientific canons for establishing fact were also generally accepted. Were there any similar agreements in ethics? There were, though they were less sharply defined. In spite of notorious differences in custom, there were certain great goods, answering to man's fundamental needs, whose claims on men's recognition were nowhere denied. A life rich in these goods was regarded as self-evidently better than a life deprived of them. It was better to know than not to know, to be happy than to be unhappy, to be responsive to art and music and literature than to be a lump of dough regarding them. There was nothing arbitrary in these judgments; indeed they seemed so obviously true as to be scarcely worth formulating. Nor was there anything "relative" or parochial about them. If they were true for persons in Moscow, they must be equally true for persons in Manchester or Malawi. They provided, as it were, a set of fixed stars by which an international tribunal or a United Nations body could plot its course in dealing with the suppression of rights or a charge of inhuman treatment.

Now for the attitude theory there are no fixed stars. If South Africa decided to treat its blacks in the way the Nazis treated the Jews (I say nothing here about fact), on what ground could an international body protest? It could express a feeling of disapproval of such conduct, but if the South African whites expressed an opposite feeling, what could it say? It could not claim that its attitude was "really better" than that of the group it condemned, for if that were not a mere reiteration of its feeling, it would be a claim to the objectivity it abjured. The standards by which courts in the past have been governed, described as standards of justice, humanity, and decency, could no longer be invoked. For the court's case in giving judgment has been essentially this: "You admit that a life that is fulfilled and happy is better than a life that is stunted and meagre, and you admit, as a rational being, that if this holds of you, it holds of others. But the course you are pursuing repudiates these principles, and hence you are behaving irrationally." Such reasoning is implicit, I think, in every court decision. The judgment of a court is not an explosion of vindictiveness from the bench or the imposition on a deviant of an arbitrary social taste; nor is it merely the application of a legal rule, even if the judge so conceives it. Law is an instrument of the community employed for the communal good; its basis and sanction are ethical; and its claim on us is that the good to which it is an instrument is not an arbitrary imposition, but an end that our own intelligence would ratify if we saw things as they are. Justice is not a whim, but a rational requirement, and the common good derives its authority from a common reason.

Such authority the attitude theory abolishes. If two men or two nations differ, there is no way, according to this theory, by which the difference may be arbitrated, for there is no such thing as an objectively right course, and hence there are no standards by which the case can be adjudicated. If each side feels approval for what it has done, what it has done is right in the only admitted sense of the term. The court may plead with one side or both to change their feelings, but it can offer no rational grounds for its plea, and besides, the court's judgment is only the expression of a third feeling or attitude, no more objectively right than the others. One is thus presented with the curious spectacle of a United Nations or a World Court, brought into being to substitute reason for force, having to admit that on the most fundamental of the issues that come before it, reason is incompetent. In such a case what alternative is left but the appeal to force?

This was admitted by the most eminent exponent of the attitude theory, Bertrand Russell. He was converted to the theory in middle life, and though he disliked it, and it was clearly inconsistent with his constant appeals to reason on moral issues, he did not know how to escape from it.

> Nietzsche's here differs from a Christian saint, yet both are impersonally admired, the one by Nietzscheans, the other by Christians. How are we to decide between the two except by means of our own desires? Yet, if there is nothing further, an ethical disagreement can only be decided by emotional appeals, or by force—in the ultimate resort, by war.[1]

Of course war does settle things; it has settled the fate of western civilization a good many times over, from Marathon to Stalingrad. The objection to such a settlement is that the force at the disposal of a cause and the rightness of it are two totally different things, and that if they are both present in a given case, it is coincidental. So it is depressing to hear from the mouths of philosophers that there is now no rightness *except* that which is determined by emotion or by force.

In view of considerations like these, I think rationalism has far more of value to offer than the anti-rationalism now current. "The solidarity of mankind," Bosanquet once said, "lies in the intellectual life." There is not much hope, even if it were desirable, to get men to *feel* in the same way; it is difficult, but not quite so hopeless, to get them to *think* in the same way. They already do so, for the most part, in logic and science, and, I would add, in their thought about the principles of justice.

I have been urging the practical advantage of a rationalist ethics. There is a danger here to which I am alive. It may be urged that the analysis of a statement is one thing, and the practical advantages of adopting it quite another, and that the second cannot be used as an argument for the first. This is in general true, and I am quite ready to stake my case for the objectivity of moral judgment on analysis alone. At the same time I cannot think that the practical consequences of one analysis as compared with others is in this case wholly irrelevant. We have seen that the meaning of such terms as "good" and "right" is difficult to come by, and that the meaning finally fixed upon may be far removed from the one that comes to mind first; many suggestions have to be dismissed because they conflict with our thought as employed in wider areas. Now I

---

1. *History of Western Philosophy*, p. 116.

suppose that most reflective persons, when they think of courts, local or national, do think of them as striving after a justice that is objective and impersonal, to be ascertained only by a careful exercise of thought. If it is shown to them that a new and tempting analysis of moral judgment would entail the loss of all objective standards by which such courts could act, they might well say, "I certainly do not accept that, and if a proposed analysis of my meaning is shown to entail it, then the analysis must have gone wrong." Analysis in ethics cannot be divorced from our practical thinking in the same degree as in mathematics or metaphysics.

Reason and Race

I have stressed the advantage of ethical rationalism in dealing with international problems because they are so much to the fore today. But I think that this position offers the most hopeful approach to many other urgent issues. Of all our internal problems the most threatening and insistent is that of race. There has always been tension between black and white, but with the diffusion of blacks throughout the country and their increasing sense of their deprivations, tension is growing in every American city. The problems that result cannot be dealt with by leaving them to instinct or impulse or feeling, or even to urgent exhortations to feel differently. The verdict of feeling is negative; throughout the world of sentient beings it is a preference for one's kind, and indifference or hostility to those of other kinds. This attitude is so natural, strong, and universal that if it is permitted to have the decisive voice in race relations, we shall end up as two peoples having as little to do with each other as practicable.

It may be said that the only way to cast out this somewhat ignoble feeling is to fall back on "the expulsive power of a new affection" and to acquire the nobler feeling of Christian love. Such love has worked wonders, and its power is not to be disparaged. But traditionally it has been bound up with the Christian creed, that is, with certain intellectual convictions, and these convictions are not available on call. Furthermore, such love is not a feeling merely, for it is something that Christians are divinely commanded to have, and feelings cannot be directly willed. Christian love is less an emotion than a fixed disposition of the will, which is supposed to continue through the ups and downs of feeling. Such a disposition needs intellectual support, either that of a creed or that of the conviction that it is right and a duty.

It is no accident that the communities most consistently friendly to blacks have been communities of intellectuals, such as the colleges and universities. The case for equal rights on an intellectual level is irresistible, while on the level of sentiment it is as variable as the wind. Is it replied that this cognitive approach may be self-defeating, since it may reveal that blacks are on a lower level of intelligence and educability than whites, and therefore *should* be treated unequally? The inference does not follow. Even if statistical inquiry did show such a difference, which I understand that the experts do not admit, this would not justify discrimination in the treatment of individuals. A dozen Jews may on the average show more ability than a dozen Anglo-Saxons and a dozen Anglo-Saxons a higher average than a dozen blacks. But there is no way to find out what they can do as individuals but to give them all the same opportunities and see how far they can go. Of course equality does not mean factual equality—equality of muscle, nerve or brain; it means ethical equality, equality of right to consideration, the right to the recognition and use of such ability as one has. This principle lay behind the Supreme Court decision of 1954 which did so much to further acceptance of civil rights. It is time to recognize that the relation between reason and feeling is a two-way street. Everyone knows that political and religious beliefs may be determined by half-conscious fears and desires, and some philosophers of standing are maintaining that all speculative beliefs are similarly determined. This I deny. I wish I might turn the tables and show the enormous extent to which rational conviction can mould feeling and impulse.

Early Interests in Religion

I have been discussing how rationalism in philosophy may affect one's views in ethics. Some persons may be curious about how such rationalism affects one's views in religion. In my case its influence has been decisive, though gradual and slow. A little autobiography may here be in order.

My religious interest began early. Both my father and grandfather were ministers, my grandfather a Canadian Methodist, my father an American Congregationalist; and for many years I had a half-formed intention to follow their lead. During most of the summers of my teens, I worked in a northern Michigan summer resort, Bay View, where there was a Chautauquatype series of lectures and concerts. There I was exposed to a number of well known preachers of the time—Edwin Holt Hughes, Frank W. Gunsaulus, and Elbert Russell among others, and I recall reporting for the local newspaper William Jennings Bryan's famous address on "The Prince of Peace." I acquired an interest in preachers and preaching which I took with me to England when I went there for study in 1913. I attended many university sermons in St. Mary's, Oxford, and since they began at 8:30 in the evening and the gates of my college, Merton, closed at nine, I had regularly to pay a penny fine for attending. In the vacations I made a round of some of the better known preachers of London, Dean Inge in St. Paul's, Campbell Morgan and Maude Royden in Westminster Chapel, Fort Newton and R. J. Campbell in the City Temple. To this day I enjoy reading sermons, and have on my shelves many volumes of them by Newman, Martineau, Phillips Brooks, Charles E. Jefferson, and others. I attended numberless services in the Merton College chapel, which must be one of the most beautiful in the world, though the hour at which they were held—eight in the morning—and the arctic atmosphere of an imperceptibly heated stone church in winter somewhat cooled my enthusiasm for Anglican services.

When I began the study of philosophy, I thought of it as a formidable weapon that ought to be mastered if one were to defend religious belief. My reading tended to follow a religious line; Mark Hopkins' *Evidences of Christianity* seemed in those days very convincing; I was much impressed (and still am) by the eloquence of John Caird, described by T. H. Green as "a master of style" who could make even Hegel intelligible; and I was captivated by James Martineau, who, though too lush and tropical in rhetoric for my present taste, does combine imaginative writing with critical thinking in a remarkable way. Eager to know how much could be proved by the appeal to experience in religion, I read James's *Varieties* with fascination. While at Oxford I read a paper to some intercollegiate society on "The Subconscious Self in Religion," pored over books on mysticism, and listened with much interest to the Catholic exponent of mysticism, Baron von Hügel, when he came to Oxford to lecture. In 1914-15, I began the writing of a thesis on the influence upon each other of the idea of God and the idea of man since Augustine, working under the admirable direction of C.C.J. Webb, who was to become the first Oxford professor of the philosophy of the Christian religion. Webb was convinced that the Absolute was a person; by then, I had received a massive infusion of Bradley, and was not so sure about this. In any case, the thesis was never finished. As a result of the war, I left Oxford for four wandering years, two of them in the far east with the British Army YMCA, one at Columbia with Dewey and Montague, and one in the American army, chiefly in France. When I returned to Oxford in the fall of 1919, my interest in the thesis had so far lapsed that, to Webb's disappointment, I abandoned it and turned to logic and the theory of knowledge under H.H. Joachim.

When I signed up with the YMCA in London in the summer of 1915, I was sent first to India. A week after arrival in Bombay, I was re-shipped up the Persian Gulf to Busrah, in what was then Mesopotamia, for eight months of work with British and Australian troops along the Tigris. The work was chiefly of a secular kind, designed to support the morale of men living under hard conditions—organizing canteens, providing reading matter, distributing odds and ends in hospitals, writing letters for the wounded, and arranging shows (I used to crank an old Pathé moving picture projector, pointed at bed sheets stretched between palm trees). But I also conducted occasional religious meetings. The next year I was called back to India to serve as student secretary of the Association in Bombay, where I was in charge of a hostel in the Girgaum district, housing fifty students of Bombay University. During part of the year I had as my guest Dr. James Hope Moulton, the veteran British scholar on the Greek New Testament, who was making a study of Zoroastrianism; and I could have stayed on in India as a student of this religion, which was the faith of the large and prosperous Parsee community in Bombay. But I was not greatly attracted by any of the Indian religions, though I might have been by Buddhism if I had been able to read more deeply in it. Philosophy and religion have in the past been so intimately blended in India that it is sometimes hard to distinguish them. This seems to me to have affected Indian philosophy adversely, while doing less for religion than might have been expected; a philosophy so bound up with mystical experience loses some freedom of movement and finds it hard to be disinterested.

The two years 1919-21 I spent in rounding out degrees at Oxford and Harvard. In the summer of the latter year I gave a course in the philosophy of religion at Columbia, which must have been inadequately thought out. During the next four years, 1921-25, I was hard at work learning the ropes of the teaching profession at the University of Michigan, and my religious interests were more or less in abeyance.

The situation changed when I went to Swarthmore in 1925. Swarthmore is a Quaker college with a Meeting House in the center of the campus. I was attracted by the simplicity, good sense, and sincerity of the Society of Friends, and by its tolerant acceptance of diversities in belief. I joined the Society, and in course of time became chairman of the Committee on Ministry and Council of the Swarthmore Meeting; and one of its most frequent speakers on "First Day" mornings. What I had to say was ethical rather than religious in tone. For my ethical convictions were far clearer and stronger than any I held in religion, and I suspect that some of my hearers felt a sad lack in my "ministry." Ethics in my view has no necessary connection with religion, and religious seriousness does not carry with it any single type of morals. The nearest thing to a religious dogma entertained by the Friends is the belief in an "inner light," and even this is interpreted in various ways. My own inclination was to take it simply as the knowledge of values, more particularly moral values. Of course that falls far short of the lofty sense attached to it by George Fox, for whom it was the very voice of Deity. But I must confess that I was repelled rather than attracted by Fox and his teaching. His attitudes towards philosophy, art, music, and secular literature were as dogmatic as they were ill-informed, and have narrowed the Society's contact with the larger life of the human spirit.

Over the issues of war and peace I felt uncomfortable with the Friends, and they with me. When the Japanese invaded Manchuria in 1933, I thought that the League of Nations ought to take vigorous steps, economic and military, to halt the aggression. It seemed to me inevitable that if this overt violation of international law were allowed to succeed, it was bound to be repeated and that the world would probably sink back into the old international anarchy. Concerted action against Japan might cost thousands of lives; non-action might cost millions. And of course it did. Mussolini was soon bombing Ethiopians and Hitler storming into the Ruhr, both of them thumbing their noses at the dying and discredited League. When Hitler started his paranoiac career of conquest, I did not think the United States should stand aside as a neutral, a course that came painfully close, I thought, to neutrality between right and wrong. I recall a debate I had with a pro-Nazi in the Friends Meeting House on the question whether the responsibility for the war lay more with the Nazis or with the allies, and the best I could do in that Quaker community was to get an evenly divided vote. Of course the Friends, who are the kindliest and gentlest of people, were not pro-Nazi, but it seemed to me that their interest in peace had carried them to a belief in peace at any price, a belief I could not accept. I wrote some articles critical of pacifism in the Friends' journals, and it speaks well for Quaker tolerance that these were published.

I retain and prize my membership in the Society, though it is no longer an active one. When I came to Yale in 1945, I decided after some heart-searching not to renew at New Haven the sort of activity I had carried on at Swarthmore. That was partly because I had to assume at once the chairmanship of a large department, partly because the Battell Chapel, with its stream of eminent preachers, provided admirably for the religious needs of the students, and not least because of a growing sense of difficulty in meeting at once my hearers' standards of religiousness and my own standards of sincerity.

The Ethics of Belief

The inquiry into the idea of faith, Catholic and Protestant, that I undertook for the Gifford Lectures of 1952-53, left me with unorthodox views on the subject. I could not believe that there were two strata in the universe, nature and supernature, or that there were two storeys in man, one of faith without reason, the other of reason without faith. The world seemed to me one whole, and reason (meaning in this context our natural cognitive faculties) the only instrument we had with which to explore it. But if so, could the standards of belief that we applied in philosophy and science be dropped when we turned to religion? I did not see how they could. The western religious tradition was here against me, with its branding of doubt as sin and its blessing of those who have not seen and yet have believed. I looked into those apologists who defended the right to believe beyond the evidence, such as Pascal and James, and found their position logically and ethically questionable. There seemed to me to be an ethics of belief whose clear mandate was "Adjust your belief to the evidence," and I could not see why, if this was valid for common sense and science, it should not be valid for religion also. I thought, as Leslie Stephen did a century ago, that there was something queer in insisting, on the one hand, that we avoid gullibility and think with critical care when we do an experiment or make an investment, and on the other hand, that we profess unwavering certainty, in advance of any inquiry at all, on questions of ultimate theological difficulty. This double standard for belief has often been defended on the ground that religious belief is necessary for morals. But this is untrue. The person who has seen for himself that knowledge is better than ignorance, for example, and happiness than unhappiness, carries the best of all sanctions within him and needs no supernatural promise of reward or punishment to weight his choice.

Most defenses of exceeding the evidence in religious belief take the pragmatic line. Belief that is positive leads to so much that is desirable—confidence, serenity, hopefulness, perhaps even the assurance of another life, with its bliss and inestimable rewards—that such belief is justified by its fruits. But with a full exposure to pragmatism, I have never been convinced by it. The intellect may be used, of course, to attain practically satisfactory ends as well as to determine what is true. But it is a fundamental confusion to take the practical value of a belief as evidence of its truth, to say nothing of constituting its truth. One of the main contentions of my philosophy has been that the intellect has a goal of its own. And intellectual integrity calls for preventing all other ends, however valuable, from deflecting the intellectual compass from its pole.

A Divergence from the Idealist Tradition

Suppose the rationalist does keep fear and desire out of his thought on religious issues, where will he arrive? Rationalists ought, no doubt, to agree with each other in religious outlook, since there is only one correct way of interpreting the facts, and conflicting answers cannot both be right. But the truth is that the major rationalist thinkers have given a disconcerting variety of answers to the questions of religion. Descartes was a Catholic and Leibniz a Protestant; Spinoza, Hegel, Bradley and Royce were pantheists of varying stripe; McTaggart was an atheist, though a devoted member of the Church of England. On reflection, these divergences are not surprising, for the leap from man's minute floating platform in the universe to the ultimate power or substance is far too long to enable all who make it to land in the same place. Perhaps no two rationalists have conceived the final whole in quite the same way.

I suppose that the main difference between my way of conceiving the whole and that of the men who have most influenced me has to do with the place of values in the universe. Bradley, Bosanquet, Royce, and Hocking all thought values were objective in the sense that if the human race were blotted out tomorrow, beauty and goodness as well as truth would continue to be. These goods belonged to the Absolute, not indeed in their most familiar forms, but in forms that were at least akin to these. I wish I could accept this view, but I cannot. Intrinsic goodness is tied, for me, to the fulfilment of impulse or desire. The goods that men universally recognize as goods, those that satisfy their drives for food, drink, sex, friendship, knowledge, beauty, are all fulfilments of major human needs, and in the absence of interests derived from these needs, would cease to be goods. Let one put oneself this question: suppose there were no sentient life on earth; with no one to eat or drink, would bread and wine be good? Would a sunset be intrinsically good when the reds and yellows and the human delight in them had all (as I think they would) have disappeared? Would the multiplication table be good even when the knowledge of it, which I agree is good, had ceased to be? I can only answer No to all these questions. Intrinsic goods are relative to finite and seeking minds.

This implies that the problem of evil in its traditional form is unreal. That problem is how to reconcile the amount and distribution of evil in the world with the existence of a God who is good. When the question is put in this way, it is very difficult to avoid an opposite conclusion to the one so generally accepted and desired. A God powerful enough to create human beings need not have produced so many botched and destructive forms, so that there would be, for example, fewer mongoloid and cancer-ridden children, and fewer animals that, in order to get food, must tear other animals to pieces. The creation certainly does not look like the work of a being with our scale of values, concerned to produce a maximum of good with a minimum of evil. Able theologians like Rashdall and Brightman have proposed the idea of a finite deity, striving to mould the recalcitrant matter of the world into a more satisfactory form. But it is hard to give any account of the nature, residence or history of such a being, or explain how he could have the power to produce the goodness in the world without also having the power to avoid much of its apparently pointless evil. And if he produced this pointless evil deliberately, he cannot be good in our sense.

If one turns from a finite deity to an Absolute, the problem is scarcely less tractable. I feel very much as James did about Royce's bland attempt to prove the goodness of God from the fact that as we view evil in larger perspectives, the sharpness of its painful edges gets blurred and we are able to see it as a necessary element in a blessed whole. If one tries to work this out in a concrete case and to show how a child's dying in screaming agony from a tumor contributes to the Absolute's blessedness, the argument, to say the least, seems less real than the pain. On my own view, whatever its worth in other respects, this problem does not arise. For if good implies need and impulse, and evil implies their frustration, it is difficult to see how an absolute being could be either good or evil. To suppose the universe as we know it, with its millions of galaxies, is a being like ourselves, with needs that it is trying to fulfil, with delight in satisfying them and frustration when they are blocked, is a return to the anthropomorphism of the myth-makers rather than responsible philosophizing. There is something absurd in the notion of an Absolute's struggling after knowledge when there is nothing but itself to be known, or as loving when there are no others to love, or as seeking to realize itself when all the means and material for such realization have been in its power through infinite time. And what is one to say of the need of an absolute for sexual expression?

No doubt it makes sense to say that the universe is predominantly good or bad if this means that the total of goods would tip the scale against the total of evils, or vice versa, though our knowledge is so limited that such a calculation would be wildly speculative. But it is meaningless, I think, to speak of the universe as good or evil in the sense in which we speak of a man as morally good or evil, or in Browning's sense when he exclaimed, "How good is man's life, the mere living!" As for the imputation of moral goodness, the universe has no duties to others, for there are no others, and there is something grotesque in conceiving the whole of things as (let us say) violating its conscience by neglecting self-education for pleasure. And when Browning spoke of man's life as good, he made clear what he meant when he went on, "How fit to employ/ All the heart and the soul and the senses forever in joy!" But is there any reason to suppose that the universe has feelings, aspirations and appetites whose fulfilment gives it joy? If the ground on which the religious man is urged to worship or reverence the universe is its goodness in either of these senses, he has small reason for worshiping at all.

The True and the Good

There is thus a sharp contrast in my philosophy between knowledge and value. The object known need not be confined to our experience of it; the value of an object *is* so confined. The multiplication table and the law of gravitation are in some sense there to be found, and it would be absurd to say that we invent or create them. But when we read *The Hound of Heaven* or hear the *Ninth Symphony*, the goodness or value involved belongs to the experience itself and has no being apart from it. Astronomy would be a monstrosity unless we could believe that the stars in their courses, including our earth, had gone about their business before human beings became aware of them. On the other hand, suppose the manuscript of *The Hound of Heaven* had got lost in some editor's pigeonhole and no eye had been laid on it since; would the value we find in that poem somehow attach to the unread script? Surely not. No doubt the unseen pages would have value in the sense that if they fell under human eyes, they would arouse experiences that had value, but that is another point. The value did not exist before man's experience of it in the sense in which the stars and their courses did. Truth requires an object to which thought conforms; goodness does not.

My idea of the Absolute is thus arrived at by a different road from that of Bradley, Bosanquet, or Royce. In their thought, the various demands of our nature, moral and aesthetic as well as intellectual, are somehow already realized in the Absolute. It is a postulate of my own thought that the intellectual ideal is so realized, and a postulate of my ethics that the moral ideal is not. Indeed it is precisely because the actual world is so imperfect that an obligation lies upon us to make it better; and I have never been able to understand why, if a fully developed moral nature would find it satisfactory as it is, we should be called upon to change it. Such commands as "Be ye therefore perfect" and "do good to them that hate you" would be meaningless unless we really were imperfect and our charity were really called for toward the imperfection of others.

The assumption of our effort to know stands in sharp contrast with this. Whereas the attempt of morality is to bring into being a non-existent goodness, the attempt of thought is to discover what independently exists, what must be there already as a condition of the discovery. Unless Newton had believed that there was a law governing the motions of the planets, he would not have searched for it; unless Einstein had suspected a further law subsuming under one formula the behavior of gravitation, magnetism, and light, he would hardly have devoted his last years to the attempt to find that formula. Such inquiry finally rests, I think, only when it reaches necessity and the question Why? cannot intelligibly be asked again. The postulate of philosophy is thus that its central question is answerable and its search for understanding legitimate, in short that the world set for its dissection is intelligible. My view that the Absolute is a logically articulated but not a morally perfect whole thus accords with the natural assumptions of our activity in these two realms.

Such a view has important implications for religion. It frees us from the tension and contradiction of worshiping an omnipotent power that is both perfect and the cause of much gratuitous evil. It limits reverence, to be sure, but fixes it on objects to which reverence is due. Wonder and awe may be justly felt for the starry heavens, as Kant suggested, but one can hardly *reverence* the stars; that attitude is reserved for moral beings or the moral law. And on my theory, these two, of course, would remain. The great of the earth would still be fixed stars in the moral world; they are, or should be, always with us and their qualities need renewal in every generation. Moral law I hold to be a means to the moral end, namely the greatest good of sentient beings. To be sure, this end is not an existent object, and if the religious attitude requires an existing perfection as its complement, my position would leave it deprived and groping. But, as Dewey reminds us in *A Common Faith,* "religiousness" is not religion, and we can dissociate the valid element in traditional religion from the cluster of dogmas that have formed its intellectual center. These dogmas are largely incredible to the modern mind, and if religion insists on nailing itself to their reeling mast, it and they will founder together. They are not the valuable and permanent part of religion. What *is* valuable and permanent is the religious attitude, the humility, the moral seriousness, the largeness of concern, that have marked all deeply religious minds. It would be a tragedy for the race if these were lost. There is no reason, on my theory, why they should be. And the task of living the moral life is more than enough to engross man's faculties and energies to the utmost.

It will be evident that my attitude toward religion is ambivalent. In matters of the intellect, the Christian church seems to have been generally wrong, while in matters of the heart it has been generally right. Church history is replete with intellectual timidity and dishonesty, leading to dogmas that put a brake on human compassion. It is not surprising that rationalists should occasionally have broken out in words like Russell's: "I consider all forms of religion not only false but harmful."

Essential Religion

That is not my view. Without forgetting the witches or Torquemada or St. Bartholemew's Day, one need not take the leprous diseases that have disfigured an old institution as essential to it. St. Francis and John Woolman are nearer to the essence of Christianity than any of the inquisitors, probably than any of the Popes. Religion is too central in human nature and history to be dismissed by a wave of Russell's hand. For religion is essentially the adjustment of a man as a whole to what is ultimately true, good, and real. It is therefore an unavoidable enterprise in which all men share, each in his special degree. It is a man's window into infinity, the extension of his reach beyond his grasp, his bid for an ultimate perspective, an attempt to achieve what Emerson said prayer was, a contemplation of the facts of life from the highest point of view. It is no illusion, Freud to the contrary notwithstanding. There *is* an ultimate whole of things in which we have to live, a whole stretching infinitely beyond the small area of our immediate concern, and each of us has some notion of it, however vague. A creed is the intellectual attempt to articulate that notion at some plateau of racial advance. Furthermore each of us has some idea, again vague as a rule, of the way life should be lived in the sort of universe we accept. Religion is the fusion of the intellectual and the moral enterprise into one massive thrust.

Religion, so conceived, is not a superstition to be got rid of, but the coefficient of expansion of the human spirit. The more of it, the better. The danger is that ossification should set in on one or other side of the great enterprise. On the intellectual side, men may fail to note that all creeds are provisional only. The Apostles', the Athanasian, and the Nicene creeds were attempts at accurate formulation of the finalities by the honest minds who composed them, but the Catholic church has sought to make of them a crate for the religious intellect. But the imprisoned intelligence is bursting out through the crevices and threatening to break the venerable crate to pieces. The church, having committed itself to preserving its creeds intact, is in distress, for it cannot understand how, if the creeds go, religion can remain. It does not understand that what demands the amendment is religion itself in the larger sense here used, indeed that an intellectually static religion is something like a contradiction in terms. The same holds on the moral side. The monks with their poverty and celibacy, the Puritans with their long faces about the natural man, were perhaps taking morals more seriously than those around them, but looking at them in retrospect, we can see that human nature would have been put in irons if their notions of the ideal life had prevailed. Religion, if it is a moral and intellectual reaching for the ultimate, "the desire of the moth for the star," is not a preservative of codified conceptions and ancient practices, but a source of their rethinking and remoulding as the expression of an expanding mind.

In Defense of Scepticism

George Boas

One of the most peculiar aspects of philosophy, in view of the classical theories of knowledge, is that all people do not agree. For if, to take one outstanding example, British empiricism, all knowledge was a compound of elementary sensa, then there would be no reason why two people should ever disagree unless one of them had an abnormally narrow breadth of experience, lacking one or more sense organs.[1] But as a matter of fact, as this volume will show, the condition of philosophy is one of confusion and as the history of philosophy shows even more clearly, confusion has always been the rule. It is reasonable therefore to open a confession of faith with the question of why this should be so.

To begin with, words do not have the same meaning to everyone. Such words as *democracy, beauty, liberty, justice, Christianity,* all have both a eulogistic and a demonstrative function. Almost everybody has his own definition of such terms. And, what is more, two people may argue about whether the Soviet Union is a democracy and not be aware that they differ in their use of the word *democracy* until their discussion is well under way. It has often been the hope of philosophers that debaters should get together before arguing and clearly define their terms. But

1. Unless there are some people who are utterly passive and whose perceptual powers may be said to be standard, the perceiving individual contributes something to what he perceives. I see no reason to believe that there are any standard perceivers, though there are probably some who might be called "modal." But all I want to suggest is that the perceiving subject is not inert, the classic blank wax tablet or white paper of Locke. This idea is anticipated by Reid and in a special fashion by Kant.

there is a grave question whether all terms can be so clearly defined that they can be used without disagreement.[2] For one must first have that which is named before one with the name which one proposes to give it. How can one define *consciousness* so that everyone will know precisely what one means? Or *beauty* or *poetry?* It would be possible to frame a nominal definition of all such terms as a basis for a purely rational, or *a priori*, argument. But in genuine debate about the world of experience nominal definitions are not wanted. What is wanted is a sentence which will adequately describe an experience to which a name has already been given, a name determined if possible not by fiat but by long literary, social, and sometimes political and religious associations. We are all rooted in a culture and in modern times such a culture is likely to be pluralistic. No one description will fit all aspects of modern urban and rural culture. A man belongs to a sub-culture, whether he is aware of it or not, and he speaks the language of the sub-culture.[3] The first assumption that is required of a philosopher is either that all men are alike, which is contrary to fact, or that the differences in human nature partly determine how a man will think. Thinking, then, it will be assumed, is an individual enterprise and the clarity and precision of a definition depends on whether what is wanted is a label for a *thing* or a true description of an *experience.* This essay assumes as an article of faith that it is the latter.

A second reason why men disagree is that they use different premises in argument. If the men in question are sincere, then their premises will not be framed for sophistic ends but as a reflection of the experiences which they have had. These experiences are the outcome of the social conditions in which the men were educated. Such conditions include not only the schools which a man has attended, the books he has read, the teachers with whom he has talked, the religious leaders by whom he has been guided, but also his submission or recalcitrancy to them. Ideas will seem self-evident if he is accustomed to them and one of the effects of

2. For it to be possible, it would also have to be possible for two people to make the same primitive judgments about some experiences. This seems to happen when two people see the same color and agree that what they want to say about it is its name. But I see no reason to believe that there are some inevitable judgments associated with so-called elementary perceptual experiences. It is obvious that naming what is perceived is only one of a number of things that can be said on such occasions. It might also be pointed out that a mere color, or any other sensum, says nothing in itself, is not an assertion.

3. This becomes clear when one reflects on the assumptions, both methodological and substantial, of such philosophers as Locke and Descartes. The assumptions of the former, as is well known, emerge from physical science, of the latter from scholasticism. Are these the results of revelation?

habitually hearing the same ideas repeated is to make them appear indubitable. But this depends in part on the character of the individual concerned, some men attempting to reject the habitual, others gladly accepting it. There is probably some somatic reason for this difference in character, but to date no one has ever discovered what it is. But even if it were to be discovered, there would be little chance of eradicating it. For example take the simple word, *why?* This may mean, "What caused it?" or "What general class of beings does it essentially belong to?" or "On what level of reality is it found?" Which of these meanings is adopted will surely depend on a man's education and no one of them can claim priority over the others. The meaning used will be determined historically. The teleological *why?* was in general use well into the seventeenth century and indeed is used even today in describing animate behavior. It does not seem unreasonable to say that a bird builds a nest in order to lay her eggs in it. It certainly makes more sense to say that than to attribute the function to blind instinct, the instinct of nest-building. But to do so does not contradict any findings of a physico-chemical sort, for a bird could not build a nest unless she had a body.

Since people are bound to a culture which in turn varies from time to time, it is futile to ask them to change their premises for those of another period or culture. A modern physicist will not speak of bodies moving towards their natural positions nor will a biologist look for salamanders to find an inhabitant for the fourth element, fire. There are still men and women who deny the fact of evolution, the fact not the theory, but they are not in biological laboratories. The past is carried along in history and the old exists alongside the new. But since no man invents all of his premises, there will always be disagreement. This would not be true if there were such a thing as human nature, homogeneous both mentally and physiologically. The problem then for the philosopher is whether the individuality of people is to be taken seriously. I assume that it is.

The third important cause of disagreement is the drawing of different inferences from the same premises. Inferences do not simply appear spontaneously propelled by the sheer force of logic. They are drawn by human beings. No one to speak of sees the evils which new legislation will introduce, once it has been demonstrated that the evils which it has been framed to eliminate will indeed be eliminated. Thus the popular election of the judiciary did away with political favoritism but it also introduced the worst features of party politics into the choice of men who should be free of all political obligations. What determines that one does not see this? Again, in theology it is usually believed that God is omniscient. One of the consequences is that God must know the future as well as the past. In that event no man can be free and hence, it will be inferred, that no man is guilty of any sin. For he cannot have free choice if what he is to do is already knowable. But others will infer that all this simply implies that men should submit, like Job, to the will of God. But can one choose not to submit? If not, then whatever one does is already determined before one does it. And the well known Augustinian conclusion follows that we are all damned anyway and that God chooses those whom He will save for no reason open to man. To take a third example, it has been assumed for generations that the artist should copy nature. But there are both beautiful and ugly things in nature. One school of nineteenth century painters, following Courbet, inferred that anything natural would be beautiful when painted and another school argued that the ugly was deformed and hence unnatural. Here to be sure disagreement about the meaning of terms was also involved.

In real discourse, not discourse as it might be in a world of perfect forms, all three of these difficulties are mixed up together and it is only on paper that they can be untangled and treated separately. What inferences you will draw from a set of premises depends in part on the value that you associate with key words. "Nature" is a term which with its derivatives has sixty six meanings. "Idea" and "ideal" have about twenty seven. Some of these meanings will determine what premises a person will accept as well as the inferences he will draw from them. Thus a person who admires the natural will draw one inference from a premise in which the term appears and one who prefers art to nature will draw another. Such preferences are not self-revelatory; they appear in the use that a person makes of the terms involved. And that use will vary from man to man, depending on one's makeup, which in turn is dependent on his anatomy and physiology, his education in the broadest sense, and especially on that part of his education which occupies his youth.

My first article of faith, then, is the real existence of individuals, by which I mean not only the existence of human beings but of every thing and event that occurs in space and time.[4] This is a form of nominalism.

---

4. I state this as an assumption, though I have reasons for making it. The main reason is a rejection of the Aristotelian notion of essence and accident. From my point of view these terms name something which varies with the problem which one is trying to solve, and what is essential for instance in biology is accidental in chemistry or bio-chemistry. Other reasons are the result of observation. Whatever differentiae have been given to me in the books I have studied turned out to be applicable only to the particular thing or group of things that was under consideration. But considerations are not absolute nor determined exclusively by non-personal conditions.

II

The problem that inevitably confronts the nominalist is that of making universal statements. Universal statements are predicated on the assumption that certain groups of things and events have common properties, usually known as universals. All red things have redness in common and all material objects have mass in common. These common properties make it possible to classify things and events and to attribute to the classes qualities and properties which pervade the class.

The last thing that a philosopher would wish to do is to abandon reason. And if the existence of universals is essential to the efficacy of reason, they ought at all costs to be preserved. But reason is not exclusively occupied with Platonic ideas. The whole technique of statistical operations is rational and if one knows the technique, one will not substitute intuition, emotion, animal faith, or mystic visions for mathematical deduction. But it is true that no absolute truth will result from statistical reasoning. One will at most attain a degree of probability and will have to be satisfied with that. This does not imply that mathematics in its classical forms is itself statistical. Once the premises, including definitions, are framed, and the laws of the game obeyed, the inferences will be absolutely true. But they will be true within the framework of the rules and need not apply to the world of perceptual experience. The same for that matter applies to statistics.

But there is one important difference between a statistical and what I shall call an Aristotelian class. In the latter a common property is found in all the members. In the former the common property occurs in various degrees, the best example of which is illustrated by the Gaussian curve of distribution. It would be nonsensical to ask the frequency of triangularity in plane triangles, if one is talking geometry. But if one is talking experience, asking how really triangular a set of triangles drawn on paper is, the question is not nonsensical. The importance of this is first the gap between logic and history, or pure reason and total experience, and second the realization of how the selection of common properties is a function of the investigator, not of that which is being investigated. The investigator decides on a method of investigation, after framing his problem, and that method should not change. The method may be simply looking and seeing, in which the weakness of the visual apparatus will eliminate differences which a magnifying glass would have revealed. Anyone who has ever studied painting as it was taught in the early twentieth century knows that an area of a given color varies in hue as the light plays over it. It is impossible to place two objects in exactly the same light and even two stamps of the same denomination will be found to vary in hue as they are actually examined by a real pair of eyes. What will be selected as the distinguishing property of an object is not determined by any natural law. It is determined by the intellectual interests of the observer. And in scientific investigation it is usually used as a sign of some other more interesting property, as in tests made by litmus paper. It is obvious that if real human beings are subtracted from investigation, then what is observed will seem to be independent of them. That is a truism. We try to eliminate the observer as much as possible by equalizing laboratory conditions, canceling the personal equation, and repeating experiments under invariable conditions. But here the method again determines what the results will be and it takes the place of the investigator. The value of all this for scientific purposes need not be underestimated, but for philosophic purposes it must be integrated into all the conditions which make classes of things and events possible. What remains to be proved is the possibility of keeping the method invariant.[5]

In actual scientific investigations the uniformity of method is assured by repetition by a group of different investigators and by the variation of all the details which are suspected of being irrelevant or trivial. The scientist is always scrupulous to include the probable error, moreover, which admits that some error is probable. But what truth emerges is also probable. And, what is of more interest, one knows just how probable one's results are. Thus rational procedures are not alien to statistical investigations and nominalism is no enemy to reason.

The nominalistic approach, it is true, has to accept a duality between the human mind, whether under this name or some other, and that which it studies. The concepts which a man uses are of his making or are accepted on the authority of a colleague. They do not pave the floor of the natural world as tesserae in a mosaic. They must be thought of as tools for intellectual purposes not as objects of perception. This obviously is not an original thought of mine. It is one which I have taken over from my reading of Royce, Dewey, and Poincaré. As Royce used to put it, an idea has an internal meaning which is a purpose. But, as he would not have said, a purpose is a purpose of an individual man and need not be the purpose of any other man. I am giving to his "internal meaning" restrictions that he would have repudiated. For I doubt that disagreement

5. It actually never is absolutely invariant nor could it be in the nature of things. But one decides how much variation is tolerable and neglects it. This is of course common practice in engineering, but epistemologists have overlooked its implications.

would be so prevalent (we can limit ourselves to philosophic argument) if people in general used the same concepts for the same purposes. The individual has his own purposes which may accidentally be those of others or which may agree with those of others by fiat. But it is to be expected that individuality should be rooted in the entire personality of a man, in those impulses that are unconscious as well as those which are conscious. The junction of two minds is an aim that is difficult to realize. From the extreme agreeableness of one man to the extreme hostility of another is a long gap and agreement in the sense of two men spontaneously forming the same idea is very rare. Such unanimity requires abdication on the part of one man or something very close to it, that which is called "agreement for the sake of argument."

I am assuming that the purposes which are the internal meaning of ideas need have little if anything to do with gross action, such as is found in politics, pedagogy, the arts. Peace of mind is a value which we need not satirize. Those feelings that the existentialists have done so much to call to our attention may not be so common as they say, but nevertheless anxiety, nausea, self-contempt, hope even in vague and ill defined ways, have produced some of the most moving poetry, painting, drama, and possibly music. To alleviate these feelings men have submitted themselves to a will which they believe to be greater than their own and such submission has been a remedy for the horrors of frustration. I have no analgesic to offer for such pain. My interest in this here is to point to them as one of the origins of personal meanings in ideas.

I am not saying that there is no agreement among minds and no possibility of any. People are not so different as all that. But the way must be left open for personality to satisfy itself. In short what I am suggesting is that epistemology should be studied by psychologists. Then knowledge would be supplanted by belief and error or disagreement would be considered to be normal. Dewey's "quest for certainty" would be seen as the rule, not the exception, and it would be recognized that it is seldom successful. Belief is a product one of whose factors is social tradition. That tradition makes itself known in the history of language and comparative linguistics. The relative stability of language gives us the illusion that the things and events named have an equal stability, whereas they are all in a process of change, either slow or fast. By naming what we perceive, we fix it and conceal its dynamism. What is of peculiar interest psychologically is our desire to have a stable and uniform world to live in. If ever there was a death wish, its clearest manifestation would be here. Just as science began with the sciences of matter, which reduces all change to motion, so our philosophic life begins with an ideal of contemplation, contemplation of a world to which mutability is alien. Time was only the measure of motion to Aristotle; we might be expected to see it as the measure of life. Whereas in the history of religion it looks as if men first projected their inner life upon the cosmos, in the history of science life was the last thing to be considered. What passes for biology in the sixteenth and seventeenth centuries would now be called by the deprecitive name of natural history, simple observation of the mores of the birds and beasts. And the study of the psyche arrives on the scene even later. Scientific language was not developed to express the dynamic.

III

I obviously assume as one of my premises that time is not to be explained away.[6] I am assuming that it is one of the fundamental characteristics of the world of experience. It is possible that in the world of relativistic thermodynamics the flow of time may be reversed. But we do not live in that world nor do the problems of life that confront us come from that world. I am assuming that time is irreversible and that history is real. The acceptance of time is relatively recent and is probably attributable to the developments in biology in the nineteenth century. In fact the very concept of an event as distinguished from that of a thing is probably a biological metaphor.

If time is real, no two events of different dates can be exactly alike. It might be said that there can be sufficient similarity between them to justify generalization, but historical events are so connected laterally with other events that lopping them off from one another is always done at the risk of disfiguring them. Historians, it is true, are forced to use common nouns to name their subjects, but the differences between, for instance, the wars of the Romans and those of Louis XIV, to say nothing of our own, are such that "war" simply means two groups of people trying to kill each other. Similar remarks can be made about any of the activities which characterize human life, religious, aesthetic, political, economic.

It appears therefore to be futile for us to imagine that we can identify ourselves with our ancestors. What they held sacred, even what they held comic, just, noble, are so different from our estimations that all we can do is to point to the differences and make them seem plausible. Few of

6. As "merely subjective," a "form" of sensibility, or a feature of the phenomenal world.

our contemporaries, one hopes, can read the Old Testament without horror at the slaughter commanded by God. And yet generations of our forebears have read these same passages and found them reasonable. To interpret the ethics of the past in the language of the present is a falsification. But it is also a falsification to speak of "the past" and "the present" as if they were homogeneous. There are plenty of people alive today who do not shudder at the extermination of Jericho and who think that sinful people should be defined as the Bible defines them and that they should also be annihilated. This may seem strange, but, after all, those who call themselves Fundamentalists, if they are sincere, must take that attitude. The reason why the past seems more homogeneous than the present is that we have only the opinion of a single social stratum for the most part about what went on in it. This stratum would be called today the Upper Classes or the Intellectuals. The others did not write books. Yet we do have enough evidence to show that there was as much intellectual and moral confusion in the past as in the present. Fifth century Athens, for instance, usually thought of as all of a piece, really demonstrates a welter of ideas and standards. Even a man like Socrates, whom we think of as a saint, was ridiculed as a mountebank by Aristophanes. In fact one of the benefits of studying the history of ideas is the awareness it brings of conflict at all times.

The acceptance of time also leads one to a consciousness of the basic differences among contemporaries. No two people of the same date have exactly the same memories and the same past experiences which are the basis of those memories. Time, as we use the term, expands to cover all the events of a given date. But each event has its own time as it is lived, which, as Bergson has shown us, is quite different from time as the measure of motion. A man born at the end of the nineteenth century lived through two world wars and, if he graduated from college in 1914, was already of a different "age" from someone who was born between the two wars or after the second one. The whole concept of ages and generations needs revision, for there are always people of a given date whose lives have been passed in the previous age and others who have not yet grown to the point of having a definite cast of experience. By the time a man is twenty five or thereabouts he has chosen for himself the society in which he will live and whose values he will adopt. But he was born into a society and has carried along with him as he grows the values of that society. He may continue to live as if his "home society" were still vital or he may rebel against it and deliberately join another. The fact that according to the calendar he is a contemporary of thousands of other people is no indication that he shares with them anything more than what he reads in the newspapers or hears on the radio and even then he may skip everything except the sporting or financial pages. Thus it is very difficult to communicate with one's contemporaries unless they are of the same formation as oneself.

Social groups may well be in conflict with one another and indeed a single person may belong to several groups which are in conflict. The fact that a man is a nuclear physicist does not imply that he must like non-objective painting, twelve tone music and dislike nineteenth century romantic music. There is no consistency or inconsistency among systems of belief unless they are derivative from the same premises. But there is no common premise traversing science, religion, and aesthetics. There are the names of interests that are basically diverse and the only reason why someone should assume that relative novelties in each of the fields are based on common assumptions is that it is true that some men prefer the novel in any field regardless of consistency. It is also true that one need not like or admire a work of art for "reasons;" the appeal of art is like that of a woman. It is unfortunate that historians have used the concepts of schools of art and of thought, for to do so looks as if great groups of people all accepted the same ideas to the point of living by them. But the hard fact is that even the Catholic Church, *semper eadem,* has changed certain of its ideas in the sense of modifying only one from time to time. Witness the history of the idea of the Blessed Virgin's immaculate conception.

It is sometimes lamented that people of a given period should disagree. It is, as we have said, known by the name of intellectual and moral confusion. But as far as the records go, this has always been the case and I think that I have given reasons at the beginning of this essay why this should be expected. The moral seems to be that one should increase one's tolerance of other men's ideas, if possible, even when they eventuate in action. One should not expect more agreement than is normal. But this lofty ideal is perhaps too far beyond our reach to be realized. Tolerance itself is something that may be conditioned by factors beyond our control and for all anyone knows it may be so closely woven into the fabric of a personality that change is impossible. Just as some people are born, it would seem, submissive or recalcitrant, so some people may be born tolerant or intolerant. Liking and disliking appear to be non-rational, though approbation and disapprobation are based on reasons. Furthermore, whatever one's attitudes towards other people are, by the time one is able to express them openly, one's character is fixed. A child who has a bad temper may be reproved and possibly may learn to control it. But if he continues to express his bad temper as he grows, obviously it will become an integral part of his character. He will perhaps give all sorts of reasons to justify it and even refuse to call its effects by such names as bias or prejudice, but he alone will be taken in.

It is probable that what I say entails the belief that social reform on a large scale is impossible. This will seem lamentable according to who sponsors the reform in question and who opposes it. There are people today, for instance, who are opposed to capital punishment. There are others who believe it is the only way to prevent the commission of certain felonies. Since the truth of this depends on an experiment which in the nature of things cannot be made, one's attitude probably depends on the horror or indifference which one feels towards the taking of life. Social reform to be successful would have to be based on the feelings of a representative sample of the total population and since such a sample would be made on an oversimplified version of the problem, proposed reforms will continue to be made on a majority vote. No plan so far in recorded history has eliminated felonies or even diminished their number, though the rate of criminality varies significantly in various countries. The concept of felonious behavior has of course been modified in the last two hundred years and that may well be the answer to the whole problem of eliminating crime. The modification in question has been in the direction of greater tolerance of what used to be thought intolerable. I refer especially to the public's attitude towards chastity and homosexuality.

The acceptance of time has led to this sort of tolerance in an indirect fashion. It is assumed, an assumption with which I do not agree, that as history changes periods arise and each period has its own spirit which determines what will happen in the period. "Times have changed," is the rallying cry of men who themselves have changed, not because of any *Zeitgeist* but because of new discoveries in such fields as psychology and sociology. Since these sciences are relatively new, it is not remarkable that before they were elaborated men could not have possessed the information that they have unearthed. This information is far from being dispersed throughout the whole population and indeed even in philosophic circles there exists an ignorance of some of its most important theses and even an unwillingness to learn them. For example, if this were not so, then theories of knowledge would be called theories of belief and the unconscious influences on belief would be given the attention that they deserve. Again, the social environment of ideas would be studied with more seriousness in philosophic circles and not relegated to a special discipline whence its influence upon the formation of ideas never leaks out.

To accept time as real is also to accept the possibility of the obsolescence of ideas in all fields. This is peculiarly true of ethical and religious ideas. What we do to disguise this fact is to use old terms to name new concepts. The most interesting case of this is the preservation of the word "God" to name ultimate metaphysical entities which have nothing in common with the God of religion. The Ground of Being or the Principle of Concretion are not beings who created the world, who are loving fathers, who will judge the quick and the dead, who have been incarnated in human form, and so on. To inform a reader that these metaphysical concepts are really God is a cruel deception. One is tempted to believe that the reason why such implausible identifications are made is the desire on the part of philosophers to retain as far as possible sacred terms, as if the terms themselves had some magical power. This is similar to, but not identical with, the difference in ethics between ethical principles and morals. The latter are what men do with the approval, tacit or avowed, of the social group with which they are identified. The former are the abstract principles by which morals are to be judged. Yet the books on ethics which I have read, and they are far from all that exist, end up by justifying the ideals of the Decalogue, plus sometimes those of the Sermon on the Mount. It seems to be taken for granted by their authors when they descend to commenting on actual sins and virtues, that lying, adultery, theft, and so on must be proved to be sins on some universal principle such as Kant's categorical imperative. The logical demonstration of obligation is illusory and the ethics of a Schopenhauer or a Nietzsche, as far as deduction goes, are just as consistent and reasonable as those of Kant and Fichte. But consistency and reasonableness are not required. What is required apparently is a rationalization of what tradition has established as right and proper. Since ethics is divorced from morals, one can live on the level of time and reason on the level of ideals.

This shocking opinion needs some support. I should suggest that one give some thought to the obsolescence of such ideals as honor and courage. These are but two ideals which come to us from chivalry. As one reads the literature of the chivalric age one sees what sacrifices of life will be made to preserve one's honor and to what lengths one will go to prove one's courage, that is, bodily courage. The personal warfare which was characteristic of chivalry is now supplanted by sport. It would probably seem comic to a young man of the present day to get on a horse in heavy armor and go forth in search of adventure, attacking other men on horses upon meeting them. The *Morte d'Arthur* is hardly a book of sociology but it preserves in literary and hence moving form ideals which were already obsolescent at the very time it was being composed. It is such works which give one the illusion of the timelessness of values. As men have become more and more absorbed into the state—I do not say "into society"—they take on the morals of states and satisfy whatever primitivistic yearnings they have by savage and unethical behavior. Today some younger men are rebelling against this situation. They seem to want ethics and morals to merge. But the dualism between a system of ideals on the one hand and human conduct on the other is too great to be successfully bridged. It is understandable that this should be so, for our ideals are usually, if not always, an abstraction from a code of living that may change before the abstraction is completed and organized. One can live and live satisfactorily without much thought; habit will take care of that and custom will justify habit.

Finally, nominalism and the acceptance of time will give one grounds for believing in free will. If each person is an individual, he will by definition have characteristics that nothing else has. If one believes in universal determinism, one will have to grant that these characteristics in combination are not without influence on the course of events. Among them are our preferences, our likes and dislikes. This must be granted, above all by those who think that nothing is without some effect on the future. Just as table salt has effects which neither sodium nor chlorine has, so a man's total character, his will, his personality, his type of choices, will help in determining what he does. What a man does will be determined by a number of things and events, but among them is his peculiar personality, the enrooted habit of choice which seems to him either self-justified or justified by something analogous to natural law. A conscientious objector to war cannot be said to be living a life entirely determined by forces external to his character. Some of these determinants are external without doubt, that to which he is objecting above all. He is not objecting to everything; he is objecting to military service and the reasons he has for doing so are his reasons, not those of others. It is sheer obscurantism to deny the efficacy of character by whatever name character is called, if we are willing to believe that causal law is really universal. Why should one item in the cosmic collection be powerless to modify to some extent the curve of history? That there are causes and reasons for human decisions is undeniable. And equally undeniable is the variation in people's submission to these causes and reasons. But in any event a thing is not identical with its causes and once in existence, a thing is a new cause in itself.

IV

I have called this essay a defense of scepticism. I have done so because, to repeat, I have identified knowledge with belief and have admitted that beliefs are of various degrees of certainty. Any opinion, even of that which is perceptually before one, is relative to the context in which it appears. This has been emphasized since the time of Sextus Empiricus on. There is nothing novel here. Moreover, simple statements of identification, such as "This is a cat," are relative to what purpose the information will be put. If what one will perceive and what classifications one will make are determined by some natural law over which human beings have no influence, then what I say is stupid. I also admit that people are often very similar in their beliefs, just as they are similar in their anatomy and physiology. But beliefs are not fashioned entirely by what all men possess in common. Otherwise it would be difficult, if possible, to explain the history of science, to say nothing of philosophy.

Experience, I grant, is a determinant of belief. But experience is not simply a passive reception of impressions from the external world. To begin with experiences are selected from all the possible "impressions" and they are selected by interest. To continue, most of them have a factor of agreeableness or disagreeableness. These two considerations suffice to convince one that people are bound to differ in what they experience and to differ significantly. For every man's attention will be oriented by his past, by what he has been habituated to look for, and it requires a certain re-education to reject the past of oneself for that of someone else or for that of all who have written books. Once a man's past has become funded, as Dewey would call it, it takes on a kind of authority and will be named "the voice of experience." But one has only to read one of the great classics of philosophic prose to see how experience has several voices.

This may look like an ingrained anti-intellectualism. As a matter of fact it simply gives a new role to intelligence, the role of harmonizing one's beliefs if only for aesthetic purposes. There are, however, limits to the possibilities of harmony. Unless all things are the same, which is hard to believe, harmony stops with difference. And though we may give the conditions of difference, we cannot do more than that. Indeed in the credo which I am writing there is no more than that. Where mathematics turns into physics and physics into chemistry and chemistry into biology, wherever a new quality has to be accepted, there is a logical surd. The quality of individuality is one of these surds. There is no way of explaining why two human beings should be individuals and not simply samples of a species; that is something which we have to accept or deny. Language would induce rejection. But by all the tests of inspection, it would look as if acceptance were more reasonable, if less rational. We can easily deny individuality and nominalism and build up a metaphysics and an epistemology on the basis of logical realism. This has been frequently done, but the results have led to only more and more confusion. The reason why this has happened lies in the history of ideas. Science began with mathematics and went on through physics and chemistry to its present state. But the mathematics, physics, and chemistry which were developed seem to have had their justification in their utility to society, in measurement, commerce, and medicine. But even if this bit of historical interpretation is rejected, it is easy to see that we might have begun with biological data and finally arrived at mathematical theorems. The fundamental question is why primitive scientists were so uninterested in their fellowmen.

I have been invited to jot down a confession of faith. I have made few pretentions of giving proofs for anything. I admit that there is something paradoxical in justifying scepticism on the basis of dogma. But the dogmas are simply the premises with which all reasoning starts. The dream of assuming nothing and arriving at certainty is only a dream and even Descartes had a protophilosophy. The problem boils down to admitting that one does have premises and stating them as frankly as possible. But to refute them requires another set of premises which will in turn be dogmas. There may be some statements which are undeniable and at the same time factual. But so far no one has discovered any. It is undeniable that black is not white and round is not square, but one need not be a logician to see the logical premises and the accepted definitions and the rules of inference which lie behind such assertions. If philosophers were more given to studying the history of their subject, they would become more aware of what is entailed in it.

Culturology as the Search for Convergence

Theodore Brameld

I

If I were asked to pinpoint my outlook upon the world, I should wish to call it "an anthropological philosophy of education." In this phrase, three major disciplines converge. The pivotal one is, in crucial ways, philosophy itself, yet its significance becomes dependent upon each of the other two, anthropology and education, just as these in turn depend upon it.

Before tracing some of the steps that have led to this multiple term, let me sketch a few of its broad characteristics. One may immediately infer, of course, that philosophy, as I regard it normatively, is, or at least should be, concerned above all with the culture-building animal, man, about whom we can learn most, or at least much, from the science of anthropology. Equally, philosophy is concerned with the principal instrumentality through which man learns formally or informally to perpetuate, modify, and transform his existence when characterized as this culture-building animal—that is, the instrumentality of education. Immediately, therefore, the philosophy of culture and the philosophy of education can be viewed as co-partners. To symbolize the interrelationships of the three fields very crudely, one may think of a triad in which each angle supports both of the others. But the triad is not in the least static; it shifts with varying degrees of acceleration in both space and time.

Stated in these terms, no one could claim that any formulation of an anthropological philosophy of education is very original. Innumerable influences, direct and indirect, attest to centuries of intellectual history—

some extending at least as far back as ancient Greece in the West and to civilizations such as ancient China in the East. Yet it is probably true that the solid groundwork for such a triadic interpretation has been laid within less than two centuries. The idea that philosophy and anthropology could fuse into one unified interpretation of man and nature was scarcely taken seriously until the last half of the eighteenth century or, perhaps still more correctly, until well along into the nineteenth. To be sure, Immanuel Kant, Ludwig Feuerbach, and others were already pointing the way—indeed, "philosophical anthropology" was beginning to win respect more or less in its own right. But this subdiscipline, too, remained largely speculative until the advent of anthropology as an embryonic empirical science—the centennial of which may be marked by Edward B. Tylor's publication of *Primitive Culture* in 1871. Meanwhile, and probably with greater impact than that of any other two nineteenth-century theorists, Karl Marx and Frederich Engels (influenced by Feuerbach, Hegel, and Darwin, among others) were forging the way for rapprochement not only between philosophy and anthropology but also between philosophy and several other behavioral sciences including economics, political science, psychology, and sociology. In an implicit but meaningful sense, however, anthropology still pervaded most of their writing; it is, after all, the most inclusive of all the human sciences because, strictly, it is the only science of culture—an inclusiveness toward which their entire world view was constantly, if not always systematically, groping.

The quest for a philosophy of anthropology has been partially paralleled by the quest for a philosophy of education. While giant thinkers from Plato to Rousseau and beyond were already deeply concerned with perennial problems that the education of man generates, one would have to strain to make any respectable case for the philosophy of education as a pre-nineteenth-century discipline. In America, for example, its "origins," according to the educational historian, J. J. Chambliss, extended from 1808 to 1913. Only by the latter date, he contends, could it be recognized as a "distinct discipline."[1]

But still another step—to amalgamate *both* anthropological philosophy and educational philosophy—remains to be undertaken. Thus far, this step has rarely been ventured either seriously or effectively, and for several reasons. Even so, I consider the need for an anthropological philosophy of education as of utmost urgency—an urgency compounded

1. J. J. Chambliss, *The Origins of American Philosophy of Education* (The Hague: Martinus Nijhoff, 1968), p. 107.

by virtue of the gap that not only continues to separate the subdisciplines I have just mentioned but, even more so, in the propensity toward meticulous specialization that keeps even these two from attaining mature stature.

The point is better exemplified by the current image of educational philosophy than it is by anthropological philosophy, although the latter, too, remains more tangential than not. The regard for most educational philosophers as manifested by general philosophers, not to mention by specialists in substantial fields such as the philosophies of science, art, or religion, is negligible. If even John Dewey's superb educational theories were ignored by most of his peers (however respectfully they considered almost everything else that he wrote), then surely comparable disregard of latter-day educational theorists remains at least equally the case. It is easy, of course, to reply that the bulk of articles and books spawned by philosophers of education are, at best, second- or third-rate elaborations of what academic philosophers have already developed far more ably.

And yet, returning to the sense of urgency mentioned above, I question whether such loftiness or aloofness can be a sufficient explanation of the relative indifference if not disdain manifested toward philosophic interpretations of education. I strongly suspect, rather, that these attitudes are traceable more basically to preoccupations with problems that strike most philosophers as more technical and intricate, hence more academically respectable, than are the cutting-edge, rough-hewn problems that education confronts as a struggling institution of culture. To say this much, however, is also to help explain why contemporary academic philosophers are also unresponsive, by and large, to the equally distressing problems of man-in-culture that intrigue some anthropologists. Nor is this reaction hardly surprising when one notes that education is part-and-parcel of culture itself. Neither education nor anthropology appears to challenge the conventional philosopher of this generation to come to grips with the perplexities that beset either or both fields.

In the degree that my general indictment is accurate (obviously there are important exceptions, some represented in this volume), I must take severe issue. Permit me, therefore, to highlight a conviction which is not distinctive, yet which is crucial to all that I now wish to discuss. This is the conviction that we live in a period of such frightening omens of global catastrophe that no philosophy of any sort—certainly no philosophy of anthropology and/or education—can afford the mere luxury of intellectual discourse for its own sake, however brilliant or penetrating. One need in no way denigrate the necessity of high-level scholarship, nor even impugn "pure" thought and "pure" research (question-begging terms though these are). What should be suspect, I maintain, is the casual and conventional posture of too many philosophers, too many anthropologists, and too many educators who continue to perform their rituals and routines as though nothing really unusual were occurring in the state of human affairs to warrant abrupt alteration in the more comfortable, respectable modes of their professional behavior. I regard these modes, on the contrary, not only as *out*moded but as thoroughly irresponsible. If academicians do not recognize, as several of our most acute observers of man's situation do recognize, that the culture-building animal is already well toward the distinction of becoming the final culture-destroying animal, then I suggest that they deserve very little claim to genuine respect by anyone—including their own peers.

These remarks, rhetorical though they surely sound, are perfectly capable of reinforcement from innumerable sources of authority and observation. But I shall bypass them with the hope that at least fellow theorists who agree with my premise of unprecedented crisis will be willing to consider some of its further implications. Of these the most imperative, by far, is the opportunity for radical renascence—a renascence of convergence among mankind as the sole species on earth capable of countering and even transcending the present destructive thrust toward human divergence that now threatens to destroy our own species and most, if not all, others as well. Whether mankind will, in the face of a shrivelling time-span, galvanize its latent powers in behalf not only of its survival but also of its advancement and rejuvenation is the most pressing of all questions of the climactic decades that remain before this century ends. I, for one, am extremely skeptical. Yet the human species does still have a viable choice. And the foremost task of an anthropological philosophy of education is to marshall its powers with the hope that man may yet make the right one.

II

The gross stages in my development toward the point of view which I have tried merely to anticipate may be reduced, in rough outline, to four.

The first stage began with my enrollment in the department of philosophy at the University of Chicago. As a graduate student, an initiate of twenty-four, I had somehow sensed after two years out of college (majoring in speech and literature) that my undergraduate education had been woefully feeble. Luckily, though, one or two elementary courses in philosophy had helped me to catch a glimpse of the notion that this vast discipline is, in one sense at least, simply a term for exceptional awareness of one's predicament toward oneself and toward the world. By sheer good fortune, moreover, the great humanitarian, Clarence Darrow, with whom I conversed while preparing for an international collegiate debate on capital punishment, was one of my first acquaintances to inspire me to seek further.

At Chicago, I discovered quickly enough that I was invading a territory far too overwhelming for one of my run-of-the-mill intellect and doubtless of more than average naiveté. But George Herbert Mead, James H. Tufts, Edwin A. Burtt, Max Carl Otto (as visiting professor), and T.V. Smith were among my fine teachers. Through several of them I also became exposed to the still vigorous "Chicago School" of pragmatism, upon which Dewey had earlier left so powerful a mark. Among these and other scholars, however, it was Professor Smith who became my mentor— so much so that I should like to share here a slightly edited reminiscence published under this title: "A Teacher's Influence."[2]

> I walked into his office one day in 1930 and sat down. Almost at once he said to me, "Ted, let me speak to you bluntly. You might as well know that your candidacy for the doctorate is hanging by a thread. We're not at all sure that we should continue you. It's not so much because you may not be able to meet our academic requirements; its because of you as a person. We're afraid you just haven't grown up enough. You seem superficial and yet arrogant about your superficiality. You'd better snap out of it, Ted."
>
> The man speaking to me was Thomas Vernor Smith (once known to thousands of colleagues and friends as "T.V."), Professor of Philosophy at the University of Chicago and Editor of the *International Journal of Ethics;* later Lieutenant Colonel and Director of Education, Allied Control Commission in Italy; state Senator and then Congressman from Illinois; author of more than a dozen books mostly in ethics; finally, Professor of Poetry, Politics, and Philosophy at Syracuse University.
>
> I mention T.V.'s record because it may help to understand why a scholar of already recognized stature, but with tremendous capacities still to be demonstrated as leader, could exert such impact upon one bewildered, lonely graduate student. I am, of course, paraphrasing his exact words, but I am not at all misrepresenting them. They

2. "A Teacher's Influence," *Theory into Practice,* Vol. 8, No. 5, December, 1969, pp. 296-97.

were too traumatic to forget. Yet I remember with equal clarity how I reacted. At the moment, I could only murmur my thanks and leave. Within a day or two, however, I knew that I had deeply needed this from someone like him—and from someone who cared, besides. I wanted to tell him so, and the only way I could think of was to give him a copy of the great novel, *Jean-Christophe*, by Romain Rolland, which surprisingly I had read but which he had not. He took it with him on an ocean voyage and wrote from Europe that he had read it with care.

The influence that T.V. exerted became compounded because of that first moment. For, as we drew closer together, it led to two further moments which somehow, in retrospect, fused into one life-confirming impression. Since I was still something of a maverick (T. V. liked to tease me by hailing me as "comrade"), I had mentioned a few months later that I was beginning to wonder about communist theory. . . . T. V. reached to a shelf above his desk and, pointing to the just published English collection of Lenin's writings, he said in effect, "Why don't you do a dissertation on Lenin's political philosophy? Maybe then you might really learn something about this stuff."

Well, I took him seriously indeed. With his approval, the dissertation was entitled "The Role of Acquiescence in Leninism." T.V. had also insisted most sternly that if I were to know about Lenin I had, of course, to know all I could about Marx and Engels as well.

And this leads me to the third moment. I had decided to write the dissertation all of a piece, not submitting it to anyone until I had it all down on paper. When it was retyped, I handed it to T.V., again in the same office where he had first borne down upon me. As he took it from my hands, he asked, "Is it any good?" And I still recall my answer. "Well, gosh, I'm not sure." Anyway, he read it almost immediately and when I returned, in terrible trepidation, I experienced the greatest single minute, I think, in my entire academic if not perhaps my personal life. "Come home to lunch with me, Ted. I want to talk with you about the recommendation I've already made to the University of Chicago Press: your dissertation should become a .book." In 1933, it did, and T.V. wrote the Foreword.[3]

Thirty-two years later, I published a book which is dedicated to his memory. Perhaps some of its "explosive ideas in education," discussing "culture, class, and evolution," reflect the influence of

3. See *A Philosophic Approach to Communism* (Chicago: University of Chicago Press, 1933).

that first venture. But what I really wanted to note is how Chapter One begins: "Professor T.V. Smith, one of the great American teachers of philosophy. . . ."[4]

Let me return now to the second stage. Upon receiving my degree in 1931, I became instructor in philosophy at a tottering institution, Long Island University (in Brooklyn). The offer had been made in the very depths of the Great Depression, and Professor Burtt may recall advising me not only to take the job but to consider myself extremely lucky. Despite no special ambition to live in New York, this break proved lucky, too: I was able to savor something of the radical ferment that was bubbling in that great city at a time of widespread suffering and economic shock, and also to meet a number of remarkable intellectual leaders—among them Max Eastman, Harold Laski (lecturing in America), and John Dewey. The latter, by the way, agreed to read and criticize part of my manuscript on the philosophy of communism, and later, when it appeared in book form, to review it with critical sympathy. I cherish that review very much.

Yet, during my first eight years in New York, I became increasingly restless as a teacher of classroom philosophy. To be sure, after L.I.U., from which I was very glad indeed to depart, my next appointment was in an almost equally shaky institution, Adelphi College, nearby, where as a one-man "department" I was able to offer a range of new courses mostly, I fear, for my own edification: besides ethics, logic, and the history of philosophy, I plunged into the philosophies of politics, art, religion, and even history. These enabled me to stretch my wings in ways that three graduate years never had, and I look back upon the Adelphi sojourn as my single richest opportunity to become semi-literate philosophically. Probably however, for temperamental factors as much as for others, I found myself more and more preoccupied with the sweeping events of those years of deprivation, patchwork remedies, and turbulence. The fact that, like countless others, I personally suffered from severe financial hardship (both L.I.U. and Adelphi stopped all faculty salaries for some time) surely provoked my mood. Still more relevantly, I had been strongly influenced by my own immersion in Marxian theory, so that I tended to interpret most of these events in a leftist, although never doctrinaire, perspective.

Meanwhile, very fortunately, I gradually came to respond both cognitively and empathically to the "social frontier" group of educators and

4. See *The Use of Explosive Ideas in Education* (Pittsburgh: University of Pittsburgh Press, 1965).

scholars at Teachers College, Columbia University, who were then attracting wide attention. Exceptional men such as Professors George Counts, John Childs, Jesse Newlon, Bruce Raup, Harold Rugg, Merle Curti, and William Kilpatrick not only were challenging education as a force for social change; they made me feel far more welcome as a newcomer from the Midwest than did the "pure" philosophers I chanced to meet in the East. And so, in the late 'thirties, I began for the first time to consider education seriously in terms of theory, even to the point of joining the Teachers College summer staff on two occasions. It was then that I also first knew Professor Kenneth D. Benne, with whom I have often since associated as colleague and kindred spirit. The most drastic consequence, however, was a new post I was invited to develop in educational philosophy at the University of Minnesota.

The next eight years, beginning in 1939, proved stimulating. Almost from scratch I had to learn what I could about the field of education. But, I also served as editor and co-author of the John Dewey Society 'yearbook on workers' education,[5] became involved in the same dynamic labor movement of Minneapolis which started Hubert Humphrey on his political career, accepted a vice-presidency in the then vigorous Progressive Education Association, and tried my hand at an experiment in secondary-school social studies which proved, in a sense, the germ of a self-fulfilling prophecy. In that experiment, I was first concerned seriously with "an educational exploration of the future of a democracy"[6] —a concern which has now reached the stage where I gladly identify myself with the burgeoning movement sometimes termed futurism or futurology.[7]

Nevertheless, whether wisely or unwisely (in backward glance, I think unwisely), I decided in 1947 to accept a professorship in educational philosophy at New York University. One of my reasons was a certain disenchantment with the pedestrian quality of education as encountered on professional levels. It was thus my hope that, at N.Y.U., I could rediscover some of the intellectual, moral, and social excitement that first intrigued me among men such as Curti and Counts. And while I did absorb a certain degree of that excitement (most conspicuously, through close affiliation with the N.Y.U. Center for Human Relations Studies and its exceptional director, Professor H. H. Giles), I was also compelled to

5. See *Workers' Education in the United States* (New York: Harper and Brothers, 1941).

6. See *Design for America* (New York: Hinds, Hayden and Eldredge, 1945).

7. See *The Climactic Decades* (New York: Praeger Publishers, 1970), especially Chapter 2 (originally presented as the Boston University Lecture for 1969).

conclude that what the liberal-arts people had been claiming all along often proved only too painfully correct. "Educationists" only occasionally measure up to standards of academic excellence that even rank-and-file scholars claim to approximate. On the whole, the School of Education at N.Y.U. differed conspicuously from Minnesota's in its gargantuan size.

Thus the third stage of my development occurred as much in spite as because of my N.Y.U. period. Notwithstanding my doubts about education as a profession, I by no means regretted my decision to specialize in the philosophy of education. I then believed—and I believe still—that close cooperation between the two fields can be of tremendous value. Yet I also reached the conviction that, as far as my own pursuits were concerned, a key link in the chain was missing—a conviction that had earlier begun to form from an unexpected invitation, while still at Minnesota, to undertake a research investigation of how representative school systems across the northern half of the United States were coping with problems involving minority groups. In this venture, then quite unprecedented, I tried to relate educational theory and practice to social, economic, and political patterns of urban communities. But gradually I realized, too, that anthropology, of which I still remained largely ignorant, would have to enter directly into analyses and prognoses of problems such as these if they were to be effectively resolved. By the time my interpretation of school administration policies in seven selected cities was published,[8] I had resolved to tackle anthropology head on.

Thus, at N.Y.U., I entered into a prolonged period of self-tutoring, always with special concern for anthropology in both its theoretical and practical bearings upon philosophy and education. Over a course of some years, I managed also to become acquainted with still another extraordinary group of scholars, all new to me but who befriended and encouraged me—among them the philosopher of anthropology, Professor David Bidney, and the greatest anthropologist, I think, that we have thus far produced in America: Professor Alfred L. Kroeber. I also knew, along with less notable figures, Professors Margaret Mead, Ashley Montagu, and Clyde Kluckhohn. In 1957, my book for which Kluckhohn wrote an insightful Foreword, was published as an "interdisciplinary exploration"—a fairly systematic attempt to merge the three major fields toward which I had long been gravitating.[9]

8. See *Minority Problems in the Public Schools* (New York: Harper and Brothers, 1946).
9. See *Cultural Foundations of Education* (New York: Harper and Brothers, 1957).

My fourth stage has grown out of the third. It began in 1954, even before the work mentioned just above was quite finished. During that time, I was appointed visiting professor at the University of Puerto Rico while on leave from N.Y.U., expecting to add a chapter of illustrative impressions. Yet I soon perceived, as practicing anthropologists well know, that no respectable interpretation of a culture can ever be achieved quickly. And so I remained in Puerto Rico for about three years; I wanted, if I could, to experience directly how an anthropologist goes about his field investigations. In my case, to be sure, I had no formal training. Besides, I really had no wish to become a "regular" anthropologist even if I could. For what fascinated me most was the philosophy or philosophies that underlie a living culture—in the sense, that is, of what Kroeber and others have termed its "ethos"—but I was also fascinated by how education, culturally interpreted, may transform an ethos into organized behavior. The book that followed in 1959 applies three principal overlapping categories in anthropological theory to the experience of real people—in this case, the wonderfully temperamental Puerto Ricans. I named these categories: "order" (structures and patterns); "process" (the dynamics of cultural change); and "goals" (the values and purposes toward which all cultures, invariably if clumsily, strive).[10]

Still another event occurred during this extensive stage. Instead of returning to N.Y.U. from Puerto Rico, I became professor of educational philosophy at Boston University. Here I sought not only to elaborate further the anthropological philosophy of education that was very far from satisfactory, but to develop a program in the almost virgin subdiscipline of "educational anthropology." Throughout a full decade, my graduate students and I invaded briefly but zealously some thirty or more subcultures, always utilizing anthropological and educational concepts as consciously as we could—subcultures ranging all the way from Italian, Negro, Yankee, Armenian, Jewish, and dozens of other clusters across New England, to French-Canadians in Quebec, Amish people in Pennsylvania, and Puerto Rican communities to which we, as an entire class, managed to fly.[11]

But my most gratifying single opportunity to metamorphose theory into practice began in 1962 when the U.S. Department of State asked me to serve in Asia as a "visiting specialist." During an exhausting schedule of several months, I was able not only to observe and lecture in various parts

10. See *The Remaking of a Culture: Life and Education in Puerto Rico* (New York: Harper and Brothers, 1959).
11. See "A Venture in Educational Anthropology," *Journal of Education*, Vol. 150, No. 2, December, 1967 (entire issue).

of Japan, as well as briefly in Korea and the Philippines, but to function in elementary fashion with the same organizing categories of culture previously adapted to Puerto Rico. The consequence of all this was a decision to return twice more to Japan for another full-scale research study, "retooled" to benefit by earlier weaknesses and blunders.

This investigation, extending again over nearly three years, required face-to-face involvement in the daily events of two subcultures viewed "from the bottom up"—*burakumin* (Japanese "untouchables") and *gyomin* (fishermen), with the close cooperation of a panel of regional leaders to provide a "top-down" perspective as well. The governing model of cultural order, process, and goals is developed further in the volume published in 1968.[12]

The fourth stage continues. After "retiring" from Boston University in 1969, I was presented, for the first time since 1939, with a new title: Visiting Professor of Urban Life (Springfield College, Massachusetts). To the extent that the title may have been justified, the pendulum has surely swung across a wide arc: from instructor and associate professor of "pure" philosophy all the way to the entirely "applied" assignment of how community education might attack literally explosive issues of the urban revolution. It is gratifying to suppose that a so-called philosopher of education, even if downgraded by the pecking order of Academe, might share in the struggles of a fairly average American city. As I found in both Puerto Rico and Japan, however, too brief cultural exposure is sure to be superficial and frustrating; hence I shall always regret my decision to leave the city and College of Springfield after but a single year—the only such abrupt change I have ever made. But the privilege of a visiting professorship in educational foundations at the University of Hawaii, where it may be possible once again to trespass upon frontiers of multidisciplinary theory and research, has been too captivating to resist.

III

How then is it possible to reformulate a point of view that has been galvanizing slowly through discernible stages? The answer, from what I have sought to recapitulate thus far, surely remains opaque. Almost nothing has been said, actually, of successive efforts to spell out my theoretical position more or less comprehensively, beginning in 1950 with

12. See *Japan: Culture, Education, and Change in Two Communities* (New York: Holt, Rinehart and Winston, 1968).

a book on education as "ends and means," continuing with two or three pseudo-popularized elaborations, and concluding in 1971 with a voluminous overview and interpretation of major "patterns" of educational thought.[13]

The latter, a substantially revised third edition, connotes from its subtitle ("divergence and convergence in culturological perspective"), that two modifications, for me at any rate, are momentous.

One of these may be epitomized by the bipolarity, "divergence and convergence." In sociopolitical terms, nationalism and imperialism have exacerbated divergences within the human race; yet precisely these same divergences compel man to recognize an unprecedented urge toward convergence—convergence as implemented in terms of world civilization and governed by cross-cultural interests and goals. This obligation is symptomatic also of my approach to current philosophies of education: earlier I was justly criticized for overstressing divergences and disparities among these philosophies. Today, granting important differences that continue to separate them, they are mandated by the necessity of sheer human survival, if by nothing else, to search for and to solidify a common ground on which to stand together in the face of the most monstrous enemy of all: human annihilation.

This search for convergence among educational philosophies certainly cannot, then, be encompassed sufficiently by the principal patterns that I first symbolized under the rubrics of four major outlooks, and that have been termed "perennialism," "essentialism," "progressivism," and "reconstructionism." To be sure, even though their meanings interweave with terms entirely congenial to his, none of these rubrics has ever been taken seriously by the "average" academic philosopher. Instead, the two movements of thought that have interested him most in the last quarter century and more are, of course, philosophic analysis and existentialism; it is these, understandably, that have preoccupied the attention of numerous educational philosophers as well. But I have contended that both movements—as well as such other less heralded ones as neo-Marxism, neo-Freudianism, and Zen Buddhism ("neo-" perhaps attaches to the latter as well)—are likewise germane to the overarching demand for world unity. Moreover, all of them bear in complex ways upon the four major

13. See *Ends and Means in Education* (New York: Harper and Brothers, 1950); *Education as Power* (New York: Holt, Rinehart and Winston, 1965); *Education for the Emerging Age* (New York: Harper and Row, 1965); *Patterns of Educational Philosophy* (3rd revised ed.) (New York: Holt, Rinehart and Winston, 1971).

patterns that I have just noted and that continue to have relevance for the 'seventies as well as, conceivably, beyond.

Now I must reiterate what has been underscored heretofore: no philosophic position of any consequence, however abstruse, can any longer remain oblivious to the crisis facing contemporary thought and therefore contemporary man. If this assertion is as defensible as I insist that it is, then each major pattern of educational philosophy must also search anew for ways not only to gain strength from among them but to consider how every one of the several "purely" philosophic positions (all the way from Zen Buddhism to philosophic analysis) likewise bears importantly upon and may enrich the conception of mankind that our common compulsions now demand.

The other modification implied in the subtitle—the term, "culturological"—is not at all adopted for the sake of novelty (in any event, it was popularized decades ago by the anthropologist Leslie White, and his followers, although with variant intent). A chief reason for utilizing it here is to compress the even more awkward term: "anthropological philosophy." Therefore one might now speak, more exactly, of the need for a "culturology of education." Nor is the more historic term, "philosophical anthropology," strictly preferable: the viewpoint here advanced is not, first of all, anthropological but philosophical. Anthropology provides the qualifying adjective: it is, above all, the science of culture that could help philosophy, really for the first time, to create and fructify the crucial demand for global unity that mankind can longer ignore at its supreme peril.

To enrich the significance of culturology a little further, what I am trying to suggest is that philosophy (as distinguished from the truncated meanings to which logical or philosophic analysts often like to constrict it), is perceived centrally as any symbolized pattern of beliefs that is more or less deliberately, explicitly acquired in order that any culture, and therefore individuals as the carriers of any culture, may strive toward reasonably defensible interpretations of, and guides to, its respective way of life. This is not to insist that every philosopher must become sophisticated anthropologically; many philosophers may continue in their own preoccupations to focus upon religious, scientific, political, esthetic or other phenomena. This *is* to insist, nevertheless, that when one carefully considers any of these preoccupations in the ubiquitous context of culture-building one must also recognize that their own significance and pertinence will be pervasively and often radically affected. For it is this culture-building which is, I contend, most indispensable to one's understanding of who we are, who we were, and who we can yet become.

That any fully mature and persuasive delineation of the concept of culturology would prove a herculean task is only too apparent. Equally apparent is that anthropologists themselves continue to debate endlessly over their own presuppositions, methodologies, and objectives. And when one compounds the task of relating culturology to education, about which both philosophers and anthropologists may also debate sharply both within and between their own fields, it becomes altogether too easy to conclude that maybe one had best relinquish the effort entirely. Still, it is worth reiterating—however trite this must sound to every veteran philosopher—that no philosophic theory is worth its salt if it does not continue to generate frustrations, disturbances, and perplexities. The normative criterion of any philosophic conception is then, I suppose, ultimately pragmatic: certainly, in the case of culturology, the question is whether it throws more or less light upon and thus provides more or less direction for contemporary mankind than do alternative conceptions. That it does throw much more rather than less light is one of my principal convictions.

IV

This conviction demands, at the least, one further central feature. In attempting to bear down upon education by way of culturology, one could well contend that such an attempt in no way requires you or me to "take sides" among the plural ways in which education has been incorporated by cultures. In one sense, the contention is sound; indeed, the history of education, if it were ever fruitfully interpreted by means of culturological theory, could illuminate both the necessary and sufficient conditions that affect varying patterns of educational authority, teaching and learning, and collectively desired directions either with or without the formal institutions of schooling.

But take the four dominant culturological viewpoints toward education to which I have referred. Each one—from perennialism on the "right" of the continuum to reconstructionism on the "left"—can now be interpreted not at all as self-contained philosophies of education but rather, when perceived through culturological lenses, as overlapping yet fairly discernible outlooks upon the modern world. Here, of course, a frank recognition of preference at once appears. I, for one, have been more or less identified by peers in my field as a "reconstructionist" who not only proceeds from culturological premises but reaches definitive culturological conclusions. One need not deny that a kind of circularity lurks in this process: a culturological perspective is drawn quite inevitably into the reconstructionist orbit; and vice versa. That elusive variables also lurk in such circularity is certain. Nevertheless, I see no justification in escaping from them if one is actually to "take sides"—certainly not if one recalls the major premise of worldwide disorder that pervades, in one sense or another, its every vital aspect.

In reaffirming the thesis of reconstructionism allow me, therefore, to paraphrase and adapt a statement prepared for the new *Encyclopedia of Education:*

Neither predetermined system nor monolithic doctrine, reconstructionism may be regarded as a malleable, ever-mobile perspective upon education. Hence, drastically unlike some "isms," it can no more be reduced to neat, polished categories than it can to a precise taxonomy of classroom routines and administrative skills. Nor is reconstructionism an original term of my own, having first been introduced by the educational philosopher, I. B. Berkson, who in turn had sought to extend it beyond both the thought of Dewey and the "social frontier" educators who functioned around him.

In any case, the term "perspective" is apt, but "posture" or "mood" is equally so. Reconstructionism aims to express a forthright approach to the crisis-culture of our age—a period that is beset by cyclonic events occurring on a planetary scale. Education, in turn, is viewed as integral to this alarming state of affairs even when many of its practitioners (or even most of its theorists) fail to concede or to act upon compelling responsibilities that the reconstructionist-oriented educator considers exigent.

Throughout prolonged attempts to formulate and test such an approach, I have also distinguished my interpretation from "social reconstructionism"—a term popularized in the 1940's and 1950's by a group of educational theorists at the University of Illinois. Reconstructionism, as perhaps most commonly regarded, is far from just a social philosophy of education; it is a theory of human "renewal"—a term made most famous by the eminent interpreter of planetary transformations, Lewis Mumford. "Social" is only one important "species" of a more inclusive "genus": renewal equally connotes the personal, political, economic, scientific, religious, esthetic, and certainly educational phases of man's inclusive, goal-seeking evolution. All of these phases are embraced by the term "culture" in the strict anthropological sense of the total environment that man constantly fashions and refashions.

The ongoing development of reconstructionist theory has produced applications in both the educational and community programs of various countries, although not always, of course, with frank allegiance to that term. One example is the internationally-oriented Friends World College which has at times described itself as a reconstructionist institution. An organization of younger educational theorists has also been launched in 1969 under the title: the Society for Educational Reconstruction.

Extending now the bifocal concept, culturology, reconstructionism regards education as the universal process of "enculturation"—that is, the process through which each successive generation of every culture enables the next generation to comprehend and behave in accordance with the beliefs, ceremonies, practices, and other characteristics of its own ethos. This includes, of course, every formal type of education. But it includes, too, those processes that may not be denoted formally at all—parental, religious, economic, and others. In both cases, enculturation embraces all those members who become initiated into a culture and who thus become its "learners," while those who do the initiating become its "teachers." If anthropologists agree about anything, it is that the existence and continuity of culture depend fundamentally upon this process.

Such a conception of education not only removes sterile notions from its conventional trappings and endows it with virile power; it also enables education to be brought into fruitful congruence with philosophy. For, again informally as well as formally, philosophy helps to refine and articulate whatever symbols are indigenous to cultural evolution, while education applies such symbols to the process of perpetuating and/or advancing that evolution. Neither precedes the other in temporal order, and neither can be adjudged as the cause of the other. To borrow a familiar term, philosophy and education prove to be "transactional" disciplines. But they become transactional within the embracing framework of culture itself.

Although anthropologists themselves dispute over its intent, the reconstructionist version of enculturation is, then, that it is neither univocal nor unilateral in its proper definition. That is, people learn variantly and teach variantly not only among hundreds of disparate cultures, but also even within each respective culture. Enculturation, in short, is a multivalent process varying according to vast ranges of need, opportunity, skill, and effectiveness.

Still, after conceding all such diversity, it becomes useful to group several major ways of enculturation that are observable both historically and contemporaneously in some, if not many, cultures of both East and

West. Moreover, they may be depicted, borrowing another helpful anthropological concept, as a spectrum of "value orientations" and hence especially in terms of axiology. These orientations although by no means all-inclusive, of course, may be termed the "restorative," the "transmissive," the "moderative," and the "transformative." That alternative terms might be chosen of possibly equal relevance, and that none is discrete or immune from the others, is indisputable. Nevertheless, when applied operationally (in other words, as concepts of interpretation rather than as reified structures), the enculturative process now functions predominantly if not always deliberately or consistently according to one or more of these major value orientations.

I select the restorative orientation first because it rightly claims the longest history. Its principal role is that of reestablishing explicitly basic beliefs and commensurate behaviors first matured in earlier eras of civilization—beliefs about reality, knowledge, and value that, in their inner core, are regarded as permanent and inviolable. More negatively expressed, the restorative orientation views our own civilization as beset by confusions, insecurities, and sinister warnings of disaster that are the result of having lost its bearings precisely because this core of permanence and inviolability has been shattered.

The second or transmissive orientation so frequently juxtaposes with the first that at once it highlights the danger of artificial separations. Even so, it also possesses its clearly differentiable qualities—qualities frequently considered, in the familiar language of social scientists, as virtually synonymous with "socialization." Certainly the transmissive orientation is far-ranging: it assumes that the primary task of teaching-learning is that of inculcating those culturally inherited attitudes, habits, customs, and skills that are essential to any given generation. The responsibility of education, and of philosophy as its symbolic rationale, rests predominantly in this task.

The third orientation, the moderative, implies that the enculturative process is capable of being resilient and pliable. Thus it maintains that cultural processes are not and need not serve exclusively as replicative or reinforcing; on the contrary, their very nature requires endless retesting and refurbishing that must come to terms with non-repetitive, hence novel and exploratory, aspects of culture.

The fourth, the transformative orientation, draws upon yet also deviates from each of the three others both in symbolization and in overt performance. Thus it stresses far-reaching, future-directing, and thorough-going redesigning and renewing of cultural dynamics as well as of cultural structures and cultural purposes.

The educational terms that could be attached to these several operationally defined value orientations have also varied at different times in history. I have earlier named them—respectively—perennialism, essentialism, progressivism, and reconstructionism. Only one of the four, however, is considered further here: the reconstructionist. For it is this, of course, that most fully symbolizes the transformative value orientation as a culturology of education.

Supported by perceptive and forceful interpretors, of whom Mumford is exemplary, the reconstructionist first of all reminds us of events that are verbalized *ad nauseam* but that are actually heard and acted upon only too meagerly. These include: severe imbalances in standards of health, living conditions, and education; eruptions of population with their Malthusian auguries of tooth-and-claw fury and starvation; sickening pollution of soil, water, vegetation, and atmosphere; proliferating national rivalries; racial conflicts and accompanying violence both between and within nations; entrenchment of cruelly blatant dictatorships, not to mention dozens of pseudo-dictatorships; deterioration of viable moral orders; finally, the technocratic revolution with its spawns of depersonalization, alienation, giantism, competitive space explorations, and atomic weaponry with the almost instantaneous power to liquidate much of life on earth.

Yet, virtually side by side with such shocking "achievements" of the first two-thirds of this century are the parallel achievements of almost infinite potentiality for a creative, fulfilling age of mankind—an age that could still be accomplished within the third that remains. These include: equitable living levels for every area of the globe, not forgetting the least developed areas; medical care and education to insure elimination of all scourges and, at the least, all pockets of illiteracy; regulation of population through effective, earthwide programs of family planning; conquest of pollution by cooperative, consumer controlled ownership of most natural resources in place of destructive and predatory corporate enterprise; world government superseding national sovereignties, with enforceable authority to prevent aggrandizing rivalries and their perpetual threats of war; replacement of dictatorial regimes by predominantly democratic ones; quest for and attainment of norms of human imaginativeness commensurate with an audacious vision of man as the only self-directing species that we thus far know in the universe; decentralized, popular

representative control of automated technology; interplanetary exploration as well as migratory occupations of the moon or beyond; total
liquidation of the arms race (above all, of atomic proliferation) in favor
of publicly, democratically managed atomic resources limited exclusively
to peaceful well-being.

In briefest compass, here then is one reconstructionist agenda. That it
remains an agenda (a truncated one, at that) is only too apparent.
Additional aspects of reconstructionist education both as policy and
program range all the way from cultivating esthetic originality on the part
of any growing child, to probing affective-cognitive depths of personality,
to group dynamics and sensitivity training (in far more normative compass than is typical), to militant participation as an educational requisite
of cross-cultural political and social action.

But reconstructionist theory recognizes that issues of theory and
practice are prodigious. It does not pretend in the least to "change the
social order" of or by itself; it can do so only in close-knit alliance with
other such life-affirming forces as politics and art. It demands, in addition, far more volition than hitherto to engage in patient, probing dialogue with proponents of divergent viewpoints, looking toward amenabil-
ities that are potential between the transformative orientation, on the one
hand, and, say, the restorative, transmissive, and/or moderative orientations, on the other. Certainly, too, if and as genuine, uncoerced con-
vergences emerge, these surely cannot rest upon intellectual grounds
alone; they must rest also upon the conviction among conflicting orientations that they, too, are entangled in a web of history from which, even
when they dream of doing so, they can no longer escape. That such a
conviction is already discernible may be well exemplified by those devout
spokesmen of the restorative value orientation (Pope John XXII, above
all) who so briskly promote the spirit of ecumenical communality.

Nor do I, for one, deny that the needed quest for convergence can and
should occur without relentless, vigorous debate not only between educational philosophers but also between academic philosophers, from whom
educational philosophers ought always to learn much. Because, indeed,
reconstructionists advocate a dialogue of opposition and reconciliation
that reflects, in turn, the endless transactions of nature and man, they
appreciate the need to learn from virtually every contemporary philosophic movement. They appreciate, too, that all paradigms, including the
fourfold one that I have tried to construct whether as educational
theories or as correlative value orientations, are bound to overstructure
and oversimplify. Their motivation, after all, remains an eminently practi-

cal one: the plea for convergence in behalf of a culturology of education appropriate to our precarious age.

At the same time, reconstructionist theory has directed attention to several more or less distinctive features of theory and action. One such feature may be termed "consensual validation"—a multiple and certainly controversial process of cooperative truth-seeking and value-crystalliza- tion. A second is "defensible partiality," delineated as a function of "practical intelligence"; this enables teachers and students to encourage and achieve legitimate convictions without falling into illegitimate traps of indoctrination. A third is "social-self-realization"—a deliberately dou- ble-hyphenated value that connotes unbounded human capacity delim- ited neither to individuality alone, nor to collectivity alone, but rather is conceived as a bipolaristic and reciprocal norm of optimal fulfillment. Finally, a fourth concept, "existential humanism," may be considered as an anthropological philosophy at once educational and religious. Its cardinal commitment is to both the transformable means and transform- able ends of an internationally empowered, democratically directed, future-centered, and cosmically conjoined community of mankind.

V

In retrospect, my brief excursion toward a "culturological autobiogra- phy," if I may label it that, has expressed a sort of awkward dialectic. In proceeding zigzag fashion from one large stage to the next, previous stages have been neither subordinated nor discarded. Rather, each succes- sive one has sought quite deliberately to incorporate preceding ones at the same time that it has sought further to transfuse its own import upon further planes of thought and action.

I am far from so presumptuous as to claim that these several stages thus tie into a neat conceptual package. On the contrary, as critics have amply pointed out, my writings suffer from inconsistencies as well as other obfuscations. Surely, moreover, one might speak just as sharply of my interpersonal behavior as of my professional conduct. Because I do not, for example, practice what I preach nearly as thoroughly or consci- entiously as I should, I have often generated doubts, frictions, and bitter hostilities. When these have occurred, the dialectic of my life has been disrupted at the cost of anxiety, even of profound anguish, both to me alone and to others very close to me.

One instance—this of only a semi-personal nature—must suffice. During the nightmare of McCarthyism, my radical views on society and education were often troublesome. Particularly in defending the right of Communists, real or alleged, to teach freely in the schools and colleges (but not to indoctrinate in them), I was attacked in campus newspapers and public forums not only by reactionaries but by extremely glib "liberal" intellectuals who at one point helped, intentionally or otherwise, to jeopardize my tenure. Unlike various victims, I happened to survive. Yet I am far from altogether proud of my own record. Not only did I almost unconsciously conciliate in moments of severe pressure; I feel now that I was just a little too eager to reassure the university Establishment that I myself was not a Communist (a fact that was and is perfectly true, of course, but what business, really, was and is it of theirs?). Nevertheless, personal and professional boycotts long continued to harass, if often surreptitiously.

But the scars that remain are more than healed by the dialectic of theory-and-practice to which I have referred as my "fourth stage." For here, with immense satisfaction, I have been able to operate persistently with my theoretical models in the laboratory of living cultures. To exemplify for one final time, the continuum of value orientations (please recall them as the restorative, transmissive, moderative, and transformative) is far from the exclusive product of philosophy, education, or anthropology; it has gradually matured likewise from the privilege of associating hour after hour, month after month, with everyday human beings. To drink *ocha* or *sake* while sitting, Japanese fashion, on the *tatami* of a shoemaker or fisherman; to engage in long discussion with Puerto Rican mountain *jibaros* troubled over *their* most serious problem—lack of running water; to play with school children, observe dozens of classrooms, share the struggles of teacher union leaders; to attend funerals and weddings (I was once even a "best man"!); to visit hot springs, pottery factories, Shinto shrines, night clubs, tobacco *haciendas,* festivals, sugarcane harvests; above all, to nourish such close friendships that even their most intimate concerns became at times my concerns as well—these, as devoted anthropologists so well know, are the discoveries that one effects only from frequent, prolonged "participant observation" and "observant participation."

Still, unlike a Hegel, who first made me aware of the "concrete universals" to which these simple experiences could point, but who also sought to prove that a final "synthesis" would be attained by the universal laws of history, my own shaping of the dialectic is far more reflective of a George Mead or an Alfred Kroeber than it is of him. For I, too, see no finality, perfect or otherwise, in the dynamics of human evolution. If, therefore, world civilization is to occur at all it must first be envisaged not as the culmination of, but rather as a magnificent prologue to, planetary convergence. Through the enculturative process, conceived in the perspective of an anthropological philosophy of education, I would like to contribute some part, however minute it must be, to the reconstruction of such a future.

Unfinishable Business

Harry S. Broudy

I have always admired men who fairly early in life concentrated their energies toward a single goal. Not only does such singlemindedness often result in outstanding achievement, but it also connotes clear-headedness and self-mastery, very important character traits. My own career, on the contrary, is a record of diverse enthusiasms, oscillations of interest, and a weakness for ventures that nobody with a clear head for his own limitations and even a modicum of self-mastery would have undertaken.

The ingredients for the potpourri of impulses are not hard to identify. To begin with, there was the circumstance that my father's rabbinical studies were aborted when he migrated from Russian Poland to the United States. Instead of actualizing his rabbinical potentialities in this country, he was persuaded by his relatives to go into business and sweep up some of the gold wherewith the streets of the United States were supposed to be paved. As matters turned out, he spent his life in America peddling dry goods in a small New England town, while Talmudic subtleties and voracious but indiscriminate reading became his avocation. I was the one chosen by my father to realize the rabbinical career he had abandoned, so that while my brothers and playmates were free to play in the early evening and on weekends, I was studying the Old Testament and commentaries under my father's tutelage.

A chemistry teacher in high school decided that I ought to attend M.I.T.; an English teacher thought I had a career in writing; the chemistry teacher had a more forceful character than the English teacher, so I enrolled at M.I.T. After about a year, I realized that chemical engineering was not for me—even though M.I.T. officials urged me politely but not too vigorously to continue, after my funds ran out. It was then that my father asked me to think about a rabbinical career. I did think about it while studying for an A.B. degree at Boston University, after earning some money as a newspaper reporter, but more about German literature of the Schiller-Goethe-Lessing variety—an enthusiasm for which was engendered by Professor M. J. Bailey—and about psychology of the Freudian variety as expounded by Wayland F. Vaughan. By the end of the junior year, Edgar S. Brightman's philosophy displaced my other loves. It submerged but did not obliterate all the previous penchants—an affection for the orthodox Jewish rituals and a strong aversion to the pressures of the small Jewish community for orthodoxy; an attraction to the romanticism of the Germans, and a profound admiration for M.I.T.'s technicians and theoreticians. To this day I have to force myself to question the Platonic dogma that mathematicians are at the top of the intellectual scale and to prevent it from warping my views on educational theory.

A sojourn at Harvard, after another stint at reporting, during the depression years of the early thirties did not reduce the heterogeneity of the motivational mix. There was the impracticality of working for a degree in philosophy at a time when, as Professor Woods, then head of the department, pointed out tactfully, jobs in teaching philosophy were scarce. Furthermore, he wanted to be sure that I knew that there were institutions that might hesitate to employ a Jew in such a capacity. "But then," he added cheerfully, "you wouldn't want to work at such an institution anyway," and we proceeded to map out a program of studies that presumably would lead nowhere.* However, going nowhere from Harvard was professionally better than going nowhere from almost any other institution.

At Harvard I was drawn with about equal force to the rationalism of Descartes and Spinoza; and to the anti-intellectualism of Bergson, James, and Kierkegaard. I marveled at H. A. Wolfson's erudition in all domains that he chose to study, but I enjoyed Bergson's animadversions on the

---

*I may as well confess while I am about it to a certain naïveté about anti-Semitism. Perhaps it was because I never lived in a large city, but I would be hard put to prove that I was ever the victim of anti-Semitic prejudice, although it would be almost impossible to convince me that it did not exist. After all, in those days, hotels were not backward about advertising their ethnic preferences in guests. In the pre-State of Israel days, I took it for granted that anti-Semitism was a fact of life like stormy days in November, and that submission to it was also to be taken for granted. In this spirit I was not very much surprised by Professor Woods' kindly warning and did not regard joining the academic world as more than a very remote possibility.

analytical dissection of the intellectuals just as much. James' criticism of Absolute Idealism forever prevented William E. Hocking from commanding my doctrinal allegiance. Hocking was kind enough to number me among his assistants, but much as I admired him as a man and as a teacher, I could never get over the feeling that Absolute Idealism misused verbal dialectics to paper over existential cleavages. For that treason, perhaps, when John Wild introduced me to Kierkegaard, I took readily to the latter's attacks on Hegel's speculative treatment of Christianity. The concreteness of individual experience, the reality of its sufferings, and its moral ultimacy constitute the one cluster of convictions that I have veered from least, morally, politically, and philosophically. Any view or proposal that sacrifices this arouses my suspicion and alarm. And yet, as I shall have occasion to remark repeatedly, when I ask myself what constitutes this individuality and why it has *prima facie* priority for our concern, there is so much that this individual being draws from non-individual sources that I become impatient with the worship of idiosyncrasy in politics or education. Granted the absurdity of much that we call human existence, one cannot base a theory of morality, art, or education on the absurd or any other surd.

It was under these mixed influences that I wrote my doctoral dissertation on "The Metaphysics of Personal Existence," based on the views of Bergson, James, and Kierkegaard, and to which nobody, so far as I know, has ever paid the slightest attention. The work on Kierkegaard antedated the interest in existentialism which was to flourish in this country with the publication of the translations of Kierkegaard's writings by the Princeton University Press, but I did not capitalize on that interest, aside from publishing a few articles and book reviews.

Although it was fashionable for graduate students to belittle professors, all the men with whom I studied at Harvard impressed me favorably. I admired Ralph Barton Perry for his dry precision and political liberalism; C. I. Lewis for his logical adroitness and philosophical sincerity; D. W. Prall for scholarly enthusiasm; Hocking for his wide learning and personal presence, and Otis Lee and John Wild for showing what I thought was some interest in me as an individual as well as for their intellectual stimulation. Wild's doctrinal enthusiasms were contagious. I mentioned my catching his interest in Kiekegaard, but I followed him also in reading Heidegger and later in his work on neo-Aristotelianism. His subsequent explorations in phenomenology I did not follow.

As for Alfred N. Whitehead, I took his courses without really understanding them. This, however, did not diminish my feelings of awe in his presence, but I suspect that his reputation as a mathematician occasioned this reverence more than his work as a philosopher. Above even this is my appreciation of his use of language. I am one of the few writers on education who does not quote Whitehead extensively. This is because although he made many wise comments on education, especially as it was accomplished in Great Britain, they serve more as illuminations of Education in the sense that we can almost equate it with the good life itself than of the more mundane problems of schooling in the United States.

My professional career was the resultant of many vectors, many of them adventitious. Among the latter must be counted the combination of the Depression of the early 30's and family circumstances that made it almost imperative for me to earn money rather than wait for an appointment in a Department of Philosophy. I suppose that had I been able to wait, such an appointment would have been forthcoming, as it did eventually for all my classmates at Harvard. As it was, I gravitated toward the philosophy of education.

It is idle to speculate on what would have happened had I joined the regulars in the teaching of philosophy. This I do know: increasingly, my professional life has been spent with people who do not teach or *do* general philosophy. I have tried, not too successfully, to keep feet in both general and educational philosophy at the same depth. My daily work has demanded writing and speaking to and conferring with school administrators, principals, and sundry professors, not more than a handful of whom hold membership in the American Philosophical Association.

Perhaps this inability to meld these fields accounts for my doubts about interdisciplinary solutions of such societal problems as environmental pollution, peace, poverty, and education. The inference from the fact that philosophy or sociology or psychology has relevance for problems of education to the conclusion that educators, philosophers, sociologists, and psychologists—not to mention economists, biologists, etc.—can form a team to solve problems of education unfortunately is more plausible than valid.

A field of study organizes its practitioners into a reference group to which the members look not only for the latest gossip on jobs, change of jobs, current writing and research, and the like, but also for prestige and psychological security. To ask these members to abandon their reference group and to make their way in a new one is expecting much more than most academics are willing to risk. One has only to wander by mistake into another group's annual convention to realize how socially disparate the enclaves of scholars really are. So unless the diverse groups already have considerable overlap in membership, the chances that a man can do equally well in both and be equally loyal to both are slim indeed.

The efforts to promote interdisciplinary activities on the university campus are themselves a measure of the difficulty in relating them logically. It is one thing for a biologist to look to chemistry for solution of some of his problems, because there is a sense in which chemistry gives a more general explanation than biology of the phenomena biology studies, and the same is true of the relation between physics and astronomy. Consequently, fields such as biochemistry and astrophysics emerge naturally and logically, and presumably the reduction of all sciences to physics progresses. We are not yet in the position of ordering the social sciences and the humanities in an analogous hierarchy of explanation. Ten disciplinary stencils applied to the same phenomenon, e.g., pollution of the environment, give us 10 possibly self-consistent analyses of the situation, but the task of translating the 10 into one is still not one of the 10. Multidisciplinary ventures enlarge the context of the participants and prevent hasty decisions, but they do not necessarily or even usually converge into a unified theory of explanation.

I have elaborated on this point because it is relevant to the problem of finding a scheme of general education that can function in an interdisciplinary way for the non-specialist; because it is so intimately involved with education for all the professions. The conceptual disparateness between the disciplines is institutionalized at the university and perpetuated by a division of labor that, however desirable and necessary, makes it virtually impossible for most people to work intensively in more than one discipline or field. Doing philosophy of education is one instance of the more general problem.

The mood of the educational philosopher is different from that of the general academic philosopher. Although both rank facility in dealing with ideas above vigor and expertise in action, the educational philosopher finds—sometimes to his dismay—that even if he does not act on the basis of what he says, others very well may. A philosopher or scholar does not really expect to have what he says taken that seriously unless he is talking to another scholar or a graduate student searching about for a dissertation topic. The current modes of doing philosophy do not encourage intimate conjunction between one's philosophical activity and other kinds. Moral philosophy, the sort Marcus Aurelius wrote, for example, and which once formed a part of the Humanities, did have the formation of character as one of its goals, and I am sure this sort of philosophy was included in the curricula of liberal arts colleges for a long time for the same purpose. This sort of "philosophy" today is more likely to be talked about in the departments of literature than in philosophy seminars. Certainly the determination of philosophy to deal with discourse is not without its benefits for linguistic behavior, which, in turn, has its reverberations in social action, but the causal chain is long and fragile. Existentialist philosophies, therefore, have pretty well pre-empted the field of action as far as philosophy is concerned, and to that extent, I would surmise, has made their claim to the title of philosophy suspect.

Philosophy of education also can concentrate on the analysis of discourse about education, and much of the writing in this field is of this sort, analogous to developments in general philosophy. It is beneficial insofar as talking nonsense about education is mischievous, especially if one does not realize that he has no logical right to be saying what he happens to be saying. One can, by confining oneself to rules and regulations of discourse, keep oneself well back of the front lines where the action really takes place—classrooms, meetings of the school board or boards of trustees, educational research and development projects, committees on curriculum revision, and meetings of the teachers' union.

However, there is a more proximate relation between philosophy and education. John Dewey noted that in a very real sense a theory of education is a proposal to apply or to test out a theory of truth and value. An educational theory proposes by teaching the tenets of the philosophy to produce the kind of individual and society that the philosophy advocates. Most Utopias from the *Republic* of Plato on, have incorporated an educational system. Some, like Plato's, were explicit transcriptions of a philosophical system; some were so implicitly.

Theoretically, the objection to this relation between a philosophy and an educational set of prescriptions rests on two kinds of difficulty: one is finding a non-arbitrary criterion for choosing among philosophies to implement; the other is that if the theory of truth or goodness is sufficiently general to be philosophically interesting, no single set of educational acts follows necessarily from it. Thus the ideal of liberal education could, for all we know, be realized equally well by a half dozen curricular schemes and by an indefinite number of pedagogical methods.

Practically, however, it would be difficult to deny that theories of truth, reality, and value do influence educational proposals. If one believes that science is the exemplar of truth and truth seeking, then the value judgment has already been passed and the educational imperative: "Study science!" seems to follow. I believe the Positivists are right in holding that all metaphysical descriptions conceal—I would say exhibit—

value judgments, for they purport to be the descriptions of value—facts which, I take it, the Positivists deny. But this denial, I would hold, is a methodological pose; actually, Positivism is itself a description of knowledge that also exhibits a value judgment.

If one examines educational theories, their relation to more general philosophical theories becomes fairly obvious. The influence of the Platonic-Aristotelian hierarchy of perfection—from the concrete, immediate, and the particular at the lower end to the abstract, theoretical, and universal at the other—on education has been enormous. It has held out successfully against recurrent rebellions mounted against it by anti-intellectuals of all stripes and varieties, ranging through the Christian attacks on the pagan intellectuals, the pietistic attacks on the Christian intellectuals, to that of the existentialists against all intellectuals. Perhaps this intellectualism does not deserve to survive; maybe it will not survive. The College Board Examinations are now trying to get away from its presuppositions.

It would be equally futile to deny that Christian doctrine had an influence on education; in our own times John Dewey's influence on educators cannot be explained without recourse to the promise of his theory that the method of scientific inquiry could free us (especially Protestant Fundamentalists) from the restraints of religious orthodoxy, the tyranny of authoritarian government, the arrogance of all absolutes while, at the same time, guaranteeing intellectual respectability to moral and social experimentation. For the multitudes of Americans brought up amid threats of fire and brimstone such a dispensation was welcome indeed. It followed, psychologically at any rate, that if only the schools could teach all children to think as scientists do—and they could—our problems would be solved.

The fact that educational action does actualize philosophical concepts—explicitly or otherwise—has influenced me in the direction of "taking a position" on the best philosophical grounds that I could find. Thus I find it difficult to justify a prescription that all youth should study a common curriculum of general or liberal studies without making explicit a belief in a teleological structure that at the species level, at least, regulates and explains human behavior. When I am told that this is an outworn Aristotelian notion not amenable to scientific discussion, let alone scientific proof, then I find myself at a loss for an adequate alternative justification. Cultural uniformity and uniformity of environmental demands are certainly not plausible justifications for common studies. Individual differences of interest, ability, and temperament also preclude the propriety of prescribing a uniform curriculum, unless these differences are grounded in a common nature of man. As another example, the problem of justifying the "imposition" on one generation by another that education involves seems to defy solution without some metaphysical assumptions about the nature of man, and some fundamental considerations about the criteria of truth.

At the moment I am less concerned with the correctness of these metaphysical and epistemological doctrines than to deny that they are irrelevant to educational theories and educational politics. For the fight for the control of education is political, involving as it does persuading the sources of power and money to move in one direction rather than in another. And that philosophy has a role in this struggle is clear when one examines the contending views about educational reform. When the rhetoric is sifted, sorted, and discounted, it comes down to this: Schools are bad when and because they do not reinforce the beliefs—sincere for the most part—about truth, goodness, and beauty that the critic cherishes. Educational reformers, when pressed for the reasons of their unhappiness with schools, sooner or later take their stand on beliefs about the kind of life they consider good. The junior executive thinking of his son's future in the economic bureaucracy, and the counterculturist accusing the schools of "murdering" children, oppressing them, destroying their creativity, will alike ground their last defence in a metaphysics. The role of philosophy of education is to make these roots explicit and overt, because they constitute the last chance for rational argument about education. Beyond this, only tests of power are possible.

What might be called the standard philosophical problems—the one and the many, the universal and the particular, society and the individual—keep the mind on a knife's edge. They have the wonderful property of perpetually inviting the mind to attack them yet resisting that attack successfully. This keeps philosophers in business, so to speak. I have wondered, at times, whether this peculiar quality of philosophical endeavor has not furnished society with an institution devoted to the postponement of action. The current attempts to involve academics in action in the social arena or even in the confrontation with campus activists make one think of chickens trying to fly; it never quite comes off. By natural selection, self-selection, or task selection, the academy draws into itself persons whose greatest skill and joy are in thinking about solving problems, not in getting them solved; the solved problem is no longer of great interest to your genuine academic. He is indefatigably active, Heaven knows, but not in the sort of action that makes up the process of existential change. He makes maps but is loath to undertake journeys.

Yet the standard philosophical problems have their existential counterparts, even in their dialectical ambivalence. Existence in its human form is predicamental, and while it is important for life to get oneself out of predicaments, it is no less important to remain in the tension of some predicament. In education this same delicate balance between process and consummation has to be preserved. Just as the statesman seeks the formula for maintaining a dynamic social equilibrium, so the educational philosopher and the educator seek a design for learning and teaching that does the same sort of thing for the pupil.

One form of this problem of balance is that of "imposition" to which reference has already been made. If the educating generation *conditions* the young into introjecting its own attitudes towards knowledge, reality, and value, then the self's autonomy is seriously compromised. The older generation—currently called the Establishment—imprints on the young a set of categories, a set of interpretational frameworks that acts as a cultural *a priori*. This *a priori* will affect, if not determine, the way in which the pupil will perceive and judge his world thereafter. In what sense, therefore, can one be both free and educated? On the basis of this argument, the Blacks and the Young have tried to defend their revolt against the white middle class. Yet what alternative to imposition of this kind does the educating generation—white or black—have? Each child cannot create his cultural world afresh. For one thing, he cannot begin with new ingredients. For another, if he could do so, what could he create for himself in a lifetime? Imposition is unavoidable, but does it have to be repressive and immoral?

One can escape from this dilemma via a theory of automatic internal development of the individual. One does not need to impose anything on the young; nature will guide the unfolding process toward its "natural" end. But all such theories hastily stipulate that the environment must be favorable to the "proper" unfolding; and it is the educating generation that is charged with managing the environment. The dilemma is not evaded by this ploy. Is there a way of imposing on the young that which will not destroy their autonomy but which, on the contrary, is the means to autonomy? There must be, because, if not, all educated men would merely reprint the thoughts and attitudes of the parent generation, and this, happily, is simply contrary to fact.

Yet citing the fact does not reveal the principle by which imposition can be defended. William Graham Sumner thought that social change, including progress, could be explained by the inexact transmission of the mores from one generation to another. Others, probably including Montaigne, relied on the clash of different cultures to reveal to the individual the dubitability of his own interpretational schemata. But surely change is not always so slow and gradual as Sumner envisioned it, and some people under the impact of a clash with an alien culture merely adhere more firmly than ever to their own.

There is really no mystery as to the answer. The rational powers of men are relied upon to become self-corrective, once they are fully developed. In this way one takes stock of one's inheritance, appraises it, and rearranges it; adds and subtracts, all the while relying on some form of intellectual validation for decision and commitment.

And so the problem in principle is solved: imposed rationality is not imposition. Unfortunately, when the principle is translated into an educational process, it has to be on some operative criterion of truth, of rationality. And whatever criterion is chosen has to satisfy at least the following conditions. One is that of universality; not that everything taught must be certain or claim to be true for everyone under all conceivable circumstances, but it must be universal in that it cannot be abrogated on the grounds of purely idiosyncratic factors, or factors that have no epistemic relevance to the validity of belief. The other condition is that in the scale of value, rationality as a principle is at the top. The two conditions, of course, are not unrelated. For education, the principle of rationality has to provide for the right of the educator to apply that principle selectively without self-contradiction. A parent, for example, might object to his child being taught certain truths: that his grandfather had been a thief and a profligate, or that his country had behaved badly in its relations with another state, or that the community tolerates much of what it professes to abhor. There are unpleasant truths in great abundance, and sometimes the objections of parents to what is being taught in schools is based on their belief that their children should be spared these unpleasantnesses—perhaps in the wistful hope that what children don't know they may somehow refrain from doing. I would not dismiss such an argument lightly. There are times when knowing the truth is neither necessary nor helpful. Obviously, at any given moment much of the contents of the *Encyclopedia Britannica* one can do without. Or when one is running to catch a plane, it is not helpful to be told that in

88 percent of the cases when one is late for a plane, it takes off on schedule. Or one may be too young, too old, too sick, too harassed to be told a given truth.

This type of objection is not based on the falsity of what is taught, but on the undesirable consequences of teaching it. The difficulty is compounded when the truth or validity of what is taught comes into controversy, e.g., the theory of evolution or Keynesian economics. When the judgment as to the literature, art, music to be taught as "good" is challenged, the school is vulnerable indeed. If what is acknowledged as true may arouse legitimate objection on moral or political grounds, what remains of the "right" of the school to teach what is not so acknowledged? There has to be a way in which the judgment of the school in these matters can be defended rationally.

If we applied the philosophical criterion of truth strictly, all an objector would need to show is a conceivable case in which the criterion might fail. None of the standard philosophical criteria of empirical truth can meet this criterion successfully—and propositions which qualify as necessarily true are not regarded as propositions about matters of fact. Accordingly, there is a fiduciary element implicit in all knowledge but in education this fiduciary factor needs to be made as explicit and as non-arbitrary as possible. In short, education needs a *rational* authority to make judgments about what is true, good, and beautiful as well as about when and how to teach them. If the authority is arbitrary, teaching can be repudiated as unjustifiable imposition. The authority of the law, the parent, tradition—all are arbitrary unless ultimately supported by the authority of truth itself. And so we have come full circle, because truth itself is not available as the source of authority. The circle can be broken by lodging the fiduciary grounds of truth in the canons that govern inquiry in various domains of experience, i.e., the intellectual disciplines.

All who carry on this inquiry systematically become members of an authoritative group within a particular domain of inquiry. This group develops rules for credentialling its members, and its judgment constitutes the consensus of the learned and the wise. The truth, on this criterion, is not that set of propositions C. S. Peirce said was destined to be accepted by everyone, but rather the propositions and judgments accepted at any given time by those credentialled to make such judgments. It is not *consensus gentium,* but rather *consensus doctorum.*

Whenever one proposes this criterion as definitive for the schools, one is showered by three sorts of objections. First and foremost, it is charged that this is a reactionary ploy to protect the status quo of the academy and the standard disciplines. Second, history is replete with reversals of judgments by the *experts,* and third, every domain is torn by controversies, so that consensus at *any* time is a myth.

The charge of reaction I shall pass for the moment, except to note its relevance for the problem of authority in general. If the basis for the accrediting process is not itself arbitrary and irrational, then the pejorative connotations of authority, i.e., authoritarianism, are undercut. But the criterion of the wise and the learned does not resort to irrational methods of credentialling. On the contrary, the criterion rests entirely on the method of critical reflection, without which the method of rationality cannot move thought beyond its initial intuitions.

As to the contention that the *learned* have been known to reverse their judgments from time to time, one might ask whether the changes were developmental or merely capricious. In the hard sciences successive changes have, on the whole, produced better science. Change has meant development. In the arts and humanities also changes in the judgments of the experts have not been capricious and have been defended on the grounds that the credentialled members agree are relevant and by modes of inquiry regarded by them as appropriate. To be sure, neither critics nor anyone else can account for tastes, but all of us, and critics especially, are expected to account for judgments of artistic merit.

Finally, the contention that the learned cannot agree among themselves at any given time cannot be taken simplistically. First, they do not disagree on everything. Astronomers may disagree on the origin of the cosmos, but perhaps not on the chemical constitution of the sun nor on what would count as evidence for one theory of origin as against another. In any field of study, there are non-controversial facts and theories and there are controversial ones. It is expected that all the accredited practitioners will have mastered the non-controversial elements so that they are qualified to carry on the controversy.

At the frontier, as Thomas Kuhn has observed, in his book *The Structure of Scientific Revolutions,* talented searchers may come up with an insight that reorganizes the whole field. Educationally, it is noteworthy that the "greats" in any field do not counsel omitting mastery of the non-controversial components of their field, nor do they regard such mastery as an obstacle to the creative genius; this sort of nonsense we hear only from bored or lazy students and schoolmen dreaming of royal roads not only to the teaching of mathematics but to creativity as well.

The criterion of the *consensus doctorum* operates wherever men are systematically concerned about distinguishing the true from false, the real from the spurious, the good from imitations of it. Good physics is what the credentialled physicists at any given time say it is, and a good baseball player is one who conforms to the standards of good baseball players as articulated by baseball buffs. In baseball as in physics, the right to participate in controversy—as distinguished from the right to have and express a preference—rests on the ground rules for accreditation to a community of connoisseurs. At any given time these rules are not themselves in controversy.

I have persisted in urging the use of this criterion for schooling despite the slings and arrows of relativism and the clamor for openness and freedom from imposition—qualities, by the way that I cherish no less than those who are making a good thing out of clamoring. I do so because, in addition to the considerations alluded to, I find no other criterion that differentiates as well between the educated and the non-educated man. I think that we can understand quite well what it means to say that he who is educated thinks, perceives, judges as do the learned. I am not sure that one can distinguish the educated man from the noneducated one by the other criteria ordinarily suggested.

The unschooled man can make money, love, and war about as well as the educated one can, the positive statistical correlation between schooling and income notwithstanding. The changes formal schooling bring about in the inward man nobody really knows; one retains remarkably little of the content studied in school. But engage a man in discourse on any significant topic, and it will be clear whether the modes of thought and feeling he employs have been shaped by the intellectual disciplines or not. But is having them so shaped a good thing? Perhaps one should leave this final decision to each man and not ask how "good" his decision is. If there is sense in asking whether his decision is adequate, to what else than some species of *consensus doctorum* can we resort for an answer? As with pleasures, our only recourse is to ask Socrates, not the pig.

Another reason for advocating adherence to this criterion is that I know of no other that will enable the school to defend its claim to intellectual autonomy with equal plausibility. Beset by pressures from every quarter, to what court can it appeal? The *consensus doctorum,* it seems to me, is the only one that in principle one can interpose against *vox populi.* I am convinced that most of the troubles schools get into are born when they grant the public the right—as a matter of principle—to make decisions about what is to be taught, and how.

Decisions by *vox populi* are not bad because the people or the students are making them. They may be based on sound belief and, in the long run, may prove as beneficial as any others, especially if what is at issue is to provide what the community wants. What makes the utterances of *vox populi* bad as the basis for decisions about schooling is that the welfare of the pupil is not necessarily what a majority of any given group may want. The nature of this welfare might also be a matter for rational inquiry. The longer the interval between the end of schooling and the assumptions of adult roles, the less likely does it become that a balancing out of diverse wants in the community will be able to define the character of schooling. Once the felt needs of diverse adult groups are accepted as grounds for building a curriculum or devising a method of teaching, all claims to objectivity and universality that one makes in the name of knowledge are undercut. Just as individual wishes are not evidence for the truth of what is taught in the school, so are collective wishes as to what the school ought to be not evidence for the truth about these matters.

In saying this I do not wish to make pretentious claims for a vast body of esoteric truth "about education" that a professional group guards from contamination by the layman. There is some useful empirical educational theory, to be sure, but more important is understanding the role of knowledge and the school in the social order, as well as in the life of the individual who must live in that social order. The intelligent layman knows the outcomes he wants from the school for his children; he is less likely to know whether a school can achieve these outcomes in the light of conditions that modern society imposes. Nor is he likely to understand the way knowledge acquired today will be used in a world his child will enter a decade or so later.

There is a sense, therefore, in which the important question today for education is not so much as to what knowledge is of the most worth or use, but rather whether knowledge itself, as the product of our best reflection on experience, can continue to exercise its authority over ourselves and our institutions.

The status of the intellectual values is important not only to education as a social enterprise, but also to the strategy of living in a modern technological mass society. I have tended to agree with Matthew Arnold that between the tyranny of social power of the collective and the anarchy of the individual impulse only what he called "culture" can mediate successfully. I am less sure of this now, or rather I am more sure than ever that simple juxtapositions of C. P. Snow's two cultures, of science and the humanities, will no more do for life in the modern technological society than a return to noble savagery in the form of hippie communes.

The modern technological mass society has not changed the generic formula of the good life for man, but it has imposed a radically different set of conditions for satisfying it. In the remaining pages of this essay, I would like to illustrate what I mean by this.

For example, one hears that in a mass technological society morality loses its meaning because the individual's control over events and his own life is severely diminished. The obvious fact of interdependence in a modern society has been used as an excuse for avoiding the moral judgment in social action. It is easy to point to the tangle of causes and to despair of finding moral agents to praise or blame for the troubles of the times. However, one does not have to identify individual villains or heroes in order to make moral judgments about the enactments of legislatures, corporations, and other institutions. One need only to identify the victims and beneficiaries. I believe that it is a reasonable moral principle to demand that a social measure shall be accompanied by a fair distribution of its benefits and costs, and in a modern society we can approximate the principle in practice. We cannot—even with such prescience as computers may afford—foresee all the consequences of a development such as automation in industry or the mechanization of farming or the effects of a given industry on ecology. Even when we do know that the effects will impose hardships on some of the citizenry, we may still have to choose this course of action for the greater good. But this is no excuse for shrugging off the fact that the costs of the change may fall unjustly on a luckless group—as we shrugged off the consequences of the transition from one kind of agriculture in the South to another.

In deliberating on any proposed social action, it is possible to ask: What can be done to compensate the innocent victims? How can we share the costs with them? And similarly with benefits. Laissez-faire individualism is morally compromised because the conditions of the competition, contrary to its assumption, are never fair after the first stride in the race. From then on the swift not only forge ahead, but also are shrewd enough to create conditions that make it impossible for the trailers to catch up. Since some variant of the Year of the Jubilee is apparently no longer feasible, the restoration of fair competition has to take place continually throughout the race. This rectification, while never mathematically perfect and almost never fully equitable, nevertheless is not impossible if we apply the insurance principle. Thus *before* a factory automates and throws 500 workers out of their jobs, it is just to demand that the community as a whole support the unemployed until they are re-employed and not be satisfied with consoling them that in the long run—say 15 years—the innovation will increase overall employment. It is not fair to ask the 500 to bear all the costs of the improvement when in fact, if it is really an improvement, the whole community will benefit from it. One can therefore hardly blame the Luddite who breaks up the "improvements" if he alone has to bear the cost of them. Every innocent victim of social action creates a moral claim upon the social group in which the action took place, and it is a claim that imposes in turn an obligation on the individual citizen.

Part of our horrible predicament, moral as well as social, with regard to minority groups, such as the Blacks, Indians, and Chicanos, is that we permitted ourselves the moral luxury of denying that as individuals we created the evil in the first place. That one's grandfather had nothing to do with the shameful history of slavery and exploitation does not relieve one of the obligation to redress the injury now being done an innocent victim—if there is a way of doing so; and in a modern society there is. Accordingly, although collective guilt is a knotty philosophical problem, collective responsibility for remedying it makes sense, because the innocent victim can be identified and social action to redress the injustice is possible.

Furthermore, once the possibility and desirability of correcting social injustice are acknowledged, one is obligated to exert oneself in finding and exercising the means for social justice. And here our problem takes an odd twist. Far from our being morally impotent, the volume of our moral obligation has been enormously enlarged by the potentiality for action that technology creates. The difficulty lies in a somewhat different quarter, namely, in the amount of knowledge needed to understand the context of social problems and actions. It is a fairly simple matter to identify the victims and even the circumstances that victimized them, but understanding the complexities of the possible solutions and their consequences is not a simple matter. Whenever I am tempted to think that it is, I set myself the task of determining as rationally as possible a taxation policy that would rebound to my financial well being. And if this presupposes knowledge about economics and finance that I do not have, how much more would I have to know in order to decide rationally about a tax policy that would do justice to the Blacks or the Indians?

Common sense and a decent intention are not enough—even when our general obligation is clear and the faith that something can be done is strong. Our great deficiencies, as far as making a better world is concerned, are not lack of freedom and power but rather a lack of the kind of knowledge that outside of our own field of specialization we are unlikely to have. The necessity for the "educated citizen" is more than mere rhetoric. A modern mass technological society with any pretensions to democracy can afford neither economic nor intellectual indigence; it is doubtful whether it can any longer afford the cleavage between an intellectual-literary education for the elites and occupational training and social docility for the masses.

Because so much of moral action in the modern society involves collaborating with others, a radical change occurs in the phenomenological aspects of the moral act. For one thing, because the volume of potential action is so greatly enlarged by technology, the areas of moral indifference are reduced. One finds fewer and fewer instances in which one can honestly say that one can do nothing to promote an ideal or to remedy an evil. Yet because the action an individual can take is often minuscule unless augmented by the co-action of thousands, this seems to diminish the significance of the moral act; it diminishes the vivid sense of the causal efficacy of the agent. The drama of the moral struggle slackens. Can Western man stop thinking of morality in terms of an individual wrestling match with the powers of evil? And if so, can he endure the dramatically impoverished notion of morality as a prudential calculus of choices and consequences?

There is also the matter of anonymity. It is one thing to do one's duty and to have others know it; it is another to do it without anyone else being the wiser, e.g., as when one makes a modest donation to a good cause—even at some personal sacrifice. Anonymity is even less satisfying than being positively misunderstood, because in misunderstanding, one's ego is affirmed whereas in complete anonymity it is not. Let us grant that the desire to be properly credited by our fellows is not the most admirable of motives, yet psychologically it is a powerful one, and accordingly enthusiasm for a mode of moral life devoid of drama played out in public is difficult to generate, especially in the young.

There is good reason for the current fear of alienation from and by others. It is not easy to regard individuals as ends in themselves when in fact most individuals are not very important or interesting. To concern ourselves about them as individuals becomes a matter of duty rather than inclination. But to be regarded as an object of moral obligation rather than being loved for one's gifts and charms is not satisfying either.

Technology and bureaucracy have not demoralized life, but they have de-dramatized the moral life by diffusing agency. Moral experience has to be turned inward to sense the subtleties of obligation, to defining one's duty and then doing it without the psychological rewards that ordinarily reinforce the impulse to do X because it is the right thing to do.

If one analyzes each of the standard virtues—courage, temperance, self-mastery, integrity—one finds that although they have lost none of their validity for the good life, the conditions for acting them out in the modern world have changed markedly. The potentialities for the good life exist in the modern mass society, but they have to be wrested from it by great cognitive competence, strength of will, and imagination. The new behavioral forms of the good life are not emerging from science—not even in science fiction; nor do the rituals of defiance promise anything more satisfactory.

I have looked more and more frequently to the arts as the *via media* between intellectualism and existentialism. Conceptualization, the heart of intellectualism, attenuates the particular for the benefits of knowledge. There is no science of particularity; hence there is no science of the human individual. I am not saying that statistical descriptions of human behavior are useless or even in bad form, but they are useful precisely insofar as we have to deal with men collectively. To the extent that insurance companies and other kinds of bet makers, educators, and lawmakers do deal with people collectively, to that extent knowing the facts about the characteristics of the group is common sense, and to act in ignorance of them is foolish. Humanly speaking, however, the individual version of the species' characteristics is more important than the species' characteristics as such.

The great lesson of Personalism for me has been the absolute claim upon the world that a personal mode of existence creates and imposes. This is the value-fact beyond which conceptualization cannot go cognitively, and beyond which it cannot be allowed to go morally. This claim asserts for every individual the right to resist annihilation in all its forms—intellectual, moral, and political—but from this I am not sure that a formula for what he as an individual can claim positively is derivable. For every such formula has to be translated into rights and acts that affect other persons, and so we are back with prudential calculation and the principle of insurance, whereby a rough form of social justice is the best we can do. This fact also blunts the right of the individual to push himself as his "project" regardless of consequences.

As to religious faith providing the individual with the shape of commitment and kindling an ardor in its behalf, I suppose this can never be ruled out. Those religions that seem least vulnerable to the rifle-fire of the intellectual are themselves so ethereal as to be little more concrete than conceptual systems themselves are. For me, at least—because of certain circumstances—the rituals of a religion are the operative factors in it. They provide images and emotions symbolic of more ultimate commitments. I recognize their anthropomorphism and discount their descriptive claims and historical pretensions, but I am aware of their power to move me. I am inclined not to attribute this power entirely to childhood conditioning but in part to the aptness of the image to the state of being of which it is the image.

These images, whether in art or in ritual, are the mediators, as so many aestheticians have argued, between concepts and perceptions; the perceptive image and the imaginative percept. Art, if not the truth, is the image of it.

For this reason, perhaps aesthetic education, or the shaping of feeling by the arts, especially the serious arts, has been the subject of much of my writing in recent years. If science provides technological means of augmenting the volume of our possible values, and if moral reflection is the way to appraise and criticize these potentialities, then art would seem to be the source for images of life that may serve as seduction to commitment.

In the nature of the case—or rather in the nature of art—one cannot predict what these life forms will be or which of them will enchant the coming generations. But the more sophisticated we are in the ways of art—all the arts—the more sensitive we can be to its probings and experiments with modes of feeling. These probes, I believe, are more sensitive to the disjointedness of the times than intellectual pulse takings of the culture.

In this connection I return to the circumstance that the ways of virtue in a modern mass society lack dramatic interest; whatever the benefits of cooperation, group deliberation, orderly parliamentary procedures, there is no way to make them dramatically interesting without conflict, and conflict is precisely what they are trying to avoid. If we reject the conflict of war, economic conflict, and political conflict; if we reject the religious conflict between good and evil by dissolving it in the sea of environmental influences, what shall be their substitutes? If there are no substitutes, are we confronted with a choice between a life that is boring and one that is evil?

To evade this dilemma, it seems to me, is the task of education and life in our time. Life in the modern society need not be a bore, because it offers a challenge to him who is willing to take on the task of self-cultivation, i.e., to be initiated into the consensus of the wise and the learned. Moreover, this self-cultivation—once the initial drudgery is over—is itself far from boring. By the means of this self-cultivation one may hope to remoralize modern life. Even so, the good life will be a struggle to extort freedom, individuality, and personal significance from a system that on the face of it denies all of them. This struggle neither entails immoral ruthlessness nor permits moral complacency. There is no lack of evil to be conquered, and the awareness that we have the power to remedy it disturbs any complacency we may be tempted to enjoy. This is a real, not a symbolic, struggle, for the outcome is not assured, and there is nothing allegorical or imaginary about the consequences of success or failure.

Toward a Philosophy of Philosophy

Edwin A. Burtt

When I began to philosophize several decades ago I took it for granted that anyone who devoted himself energetically to the task could work out a philosophical system which he would thereafter hold firmly and defend as persuasively as possible against its rivals. Minor changes would come from time to time, but no major revision would be needed. Other philosophers around me appeared to hold a similar assumption.

Something gradually happened, however, which undermined that assumption. My present philosophy has taken its form largely as the result of that undermining. It could have led to an abandonment of philosophy, and would have done so if I had continued to identify philosophizing with erecting a supposedly impregnable system. Instead, my concept of philosophy was transformed, and the transformation not only guided my own philosophical reconstruction but also led to a fruitful understanding—so it seemed to me—of the history of philosophy.

My initial way of thinking, reflected in my first book, *The Metaphysical Foundations of Modern Physical Science,* was a semi-Hegelian idealism which harmonized with the liberal Protestant orientation to which my religious searching had then led. This was slowly modified to make a place for the central ideas of Deweyan pragmatism, which was persuasively exemplified by my older colleagues at Chicago. When I came to Cornell in 1932, the Sage School was freeing itself from its earlier neo-Hegelian perspective and for a couple of decades several quite different philosophical standpoints were represented by its members. That situation encouraged in me a tendency, already gathering strength, to avoid becoming a disciple of any school and to develop whatever individuality I might be capable of. At that stage, however, I still assumed that it was the business of a good philosopher to concoct a system to which he could thereafter adhere, in its essentials at least.

One of the obligations I accepted when joining the Cornell philosophy staff was to teach a course in the history and comparison of religions—a field in which, despite my strong religious interest, I had previously been quite ignorant. The exploration of that field more and more intrigued me, and a pair of important lessons took form in my mind through that exploration.

I came to realize that a teacher of such a course is not filling his responsibility by merely acquainting students with external facts about the great religions of the world. Such acquaintance is needed, of course, but genuine understanding calls for something more. It requires a teacher to put himself as best he can inside each faith, realizing how the primary problems of life are met in its perspective and what form the structure of the universe takes in such a perspective. That proved to be a very significant and fertile realization, especially as the Eastern religions, notably Buddhism, became sources of spiritual inspiration along with my Hebrew-Christian heritage. This exploring venture not only led to a deepening interest in the Eastern religions which has continued through the years, but also to a broadening and enrichment of my whole experience. It gave me a clearer insight into the fundamental convictions that all faiths of civilized mankind share in common; it encouraged a sympathetic penetration of the distinctive genius of each faith, with the human aspirations thus expressed; and it made possible a profounder understanding of my Hebrew-Christian background than I had won before. To my surprise, I discovered that when a thinker interprets the faith in which he grew up solely through its traditional concepts and doctrines, the interpretation is inevitably a cramping one.

As an essential part of this rewarding quest I sought fuller understanding of the philosophies that had developed in the Eastern world, and naturally found myself comparing them with the philosophies of the West which I had already studied. The most important outcome of that comparative inquiry was that the concept of "presupposition" assumed an increasingly central role in my thinking. A presupposition is a hidden or tacit premise underlying any statement or question or piece of reasoning. And besides specific presuppositions behind this or that particular statement there are basic presuppositions—revealed, if one looks for them, in all statements characteristic of a given way of thinking. Before long I realized that, just as each philosophical school in the West was grounded in the basic presuppositions which distinguish it from other schools, so there are more general presuppositions reflected in the orientation of all Western schools and exhibiting (when brought to light) their difference from typical ways of thinking in India or China.

Further illumination came when, in this setting, I turned from Eastern modes of thought to reexamine Western philosophical schools in their difference from each other. I gradually became more interested in understanding them than in condemning those that diverged from my own current viewpoint and devising plausible strategies for refuting them. The concept of presupposition was an essential help in penetrating the core of any seriously proposed philosophy, so that I could grasp both its strong and its weak features and come to share whatever positive insight it had gained. It seemed clear that the responsibility of a teacher of philosophy is the same as that of a teacher of comparative religion—namely, not simply to expound the distinctive doctrines of this or that way of thinking but to help students realize how life and the universe look from its standpoint. As one thus comes to understand it, every philosophy can be seen to rest on a cluster of basic presuppositions, some of which such penetration will lead one to reject but some of which will convey an insight he does not want to miss. My fundamental orientation came to take the form naturally expressed in these questions: What are the basic presuppositions of this or that way of thinking? Which of them are acceptable as an addition to, or guide in modifying, my present philosophical beliefs? In the case of others, what revision is needed if their errors are to be wisely corrected? In this orientation I was more and more fascinated by the challenge to understand thinkers whose ideas reflect quite different ideological, religious, cultural, or historical backgrounds, and to seek a dependable method of bringing their positive insights together in a coherent whole.

The crucial consequence of adopting this approach to philosophy was that before long I realized that by the route thus followed I would never reach a philosophical system such as I had been eager to reach—a system to which I could thereafter confidently adhere. More insight always lay ahead, so it would obviously be impossible to erect a final philosophy. This meant that the conception of the philosophical quest which I had previously taken for granted came to appear undesirable as well as impractical. If that is what philosophy must be I would have to renounce it. My fundamental maxim now was "Keep growing!" and this clearly was a process to which there would be no end.

Might there be a way of philosophizing in which this would become the central maxim? Step by step an affirmative answer became persuasive. It led to a reconstruction of my own philosophy, and also to a transformed view of what has been going on in philosophical history.

Consider some features of that history which I found instructive at this point. I am well aware that to most of my colleagues they will at first sight look irrelevant to the essential concerns of philosophy.

Generally speaking, the philosophers who stand out in that historical evolution appeared to their successors as having championed a single system of ideas which in each case can be viewed as constituting his philosophy. Presumably he went through an early period of questioning and searching, but once he had found himself he could formulate a position to which thereafter he was able in essentials to stick. Most later philosophers, looking back at his work, would unhesitatingly think of that position as his philosophy and would teach it to their students as such.

There are a few disconcerting exceptions, but they have not been disconcerting enough to upset this picture of the philosopher's role. Berkeley late in life turned to a rather different orientation than the subjective idealism he had vigorously argued for in his youth, but that provocative idealism is still usually taught as his philosophy. The history of thought has not allowed him to change his mind. Schelling, to one who studies him in detail, obviously passed several times from one position to another, and this has posed difficulties to a teacher who feels that there must be a set of ideas which can be plausibly described as his philosophy. In fact, Hegel once made a remark about Schelling which beautifully reveals the presupposition dominating philosophical history in this matter. "He carried on his philosophical education in public." This remark was made as a taunt—the implication being that while a philosopher would presumably need a period of education in order to reach his mature position, he should reach it without spending too much time on the way, and once he had attained philosophical adulthood it would be a shameful weakness for him to change his mind. The taunt is especially revealing when one follows the course of Hegel's own philosophical development. He too carried on his education in public, to the extent of exhibiting the notable difference between his early philosophical writings and those which expound "the Hegelian system." The latter also are not wholly consistent with each other, but he would have been unable to admit any significant variation in them.

Kant is especially instructive on this topic. For twenty years or more he went through several changes in his basic orientation, some of them being rather radical. But when he published the *Critique of Pure Reason,* on which he had worked for a decade, he was sure that he had reached and organized a true system of philosophy.[1] However, he had too inquiring a mind to rest satisfied with the system he had expounded, and he could not help being influenced by the keen criticisms that the first edition of that book evoked. So, six years after its first publication a second edition appeared, which exhibited a number of changes in his basic doctrine. Of these changes he was rather ashamed, and his efforts to dissemble them in that edition make a philosophy already very difficult to master still more difficult. Toward the end of his preface to the second edition he says, after acknowledging changes from the first edition made "in order to remove. . . difficulties and obscurity,"

> In the propositions themselves and their proofs, and also in the form and completeness of the plan, I have nothing to alter. This is due partly to the long examination to which I have subjected them before offering them to the public, and partly to the nature of the subject-matter with which we are dealing. . . . The system will, I hope, maintain throughout the future this unchangeableness.[2]

The belief that it is a disgraceful sign of weakness to change one's mind, at least on important matters, still persists among philosophers. But in our day such a change is taking place more frequently than ever before. Among analytic philosophers, for example, there are many who have passed from the positivist perspective to that of the ordinary language philosophy; in fact, a few of them had begun their careers as adherents of the earlier analytic realism. And there is every indication that this readiness for change will continue and become more prominent.

Now in such a dynamic situation it makes a radical difference whether or not a philosopher has oriented himself in advance for a shift in his basic presuppositions. If he has not, he can hardly avoid distressing emotions when a shift takes place; it will seem very shameful, as it generally has in the past. And in that traditional orientation there are plenty of reasons why it should distress him. He will be aware that he has been trying to convert other people to ideas that he was not going to hold very long himself. In this poignant awareness feelings of guilt, resentment, and futility easily arise. He feels guilty because he has misled his students and readers—he has persuaded them, more or less successfully, to adopt a

---

1. That is, in its primary epistemological part.
2. Norman Kemp Smith translation, London, 1929, p. 33.

position that he now sees to be inadequate. He may be the prey of half-conscious resentment toward those who had induced him to believe the ideas he has now come to reject. This resentment can easily spread to the ideas themselves; he is moved by an urge to punish them for having maliciously deceived him. Gilbert Ryle provides a convenient example. He realizes that some readers of *The Concept of Mind* will be puzzled by his blunt summary of the Cartesian dualistic conception of man in the phrase, "the ghost in the machine." Hence in the *Introduction* he makes a frank confession: "Some readers may think that my tone of voice in this book is excessively polemic. It may comfort them to know that the assumptions against which I exhibit most heat are assumptions of which I myself have been a victim."[3] As for feelings of futility, when a radical change of position occurs late in a philosopher's career, it is hard to avoid a haunting sense that the main work of his lifetime has been in vain.

If, however, he has expected such a change and has oriented himself to what will be involved before it occurs, there is no place for these distressing emotions. To be thus oriented does not of course mean that he must keep silent about the ideas that seem to him sound. An active mind naturally expresses whatever position it has reached at a given time. But it is not necessary to do this in words implying that he thinks his philosophical education is complete.

Ludwig Wittgenstein occupies a unique place in recent philosophy when one views him in this setting. Many philosophers have been converted to the main presuppositions exemplified in his *Philosophical Investigations;* some have been concerned with the similarities and differences of method which it shows when compared with his earlier *Tractatus;* but so far as I know none have commented on the most instructive lessons that his philosophical career can teach.

Here is a thinker who, within his own adult lifetime, became a widely acclaimed prophet of two sharply different viewpoints in philosophy. His *Tractatus Logico-Philosophicus,* written fifty-odd years ago, became the major source and inspiration of logical positivism; and his *Philosophical Investigations,* developed fifteen to twenty years later, filled a similar role in relation to the ordinary language philosophy. Both books deal with the same provocative fact and problem: the fact that philosophers have sadly misunderstood the "logic of the language" they use, and the problem of how to correct that misunderstanding. But the solution proferred in the

3. Gilbert Ryle, *The Concept of Mind,* (London, Hutchinson's University Library, 1949), p. 9.

two books is radically different and the philosophies developed from them radically diverge. The correction proposed in the *Tractatus* is to replace the misleading way of talking into which philosophers have fallen by turning to a logically perfect language, which alone says accurately everything that can be said at all. The proposal in the *Investigations* flatly renounces that solution, maintaining instead that the language naturally used by people is correct as it stands, and the need of philosophers is simply to be reminded of the ordinary uses from which they have strayed.[4]

What now do I mean by "the most instructive lessons" that his career can teach us? They are naturally suggested, I think, when we remember that he died soon after he had developed, as fully as he presumably could, the important ramifications of that second solution. Let us ask: If he had lived longer, would he have adopted a third viewpoint, as different in its basic presuppositions from the *Investigations* as the latter is from the *Tractatus?* Quite possibly he would. He was evidently capable of facing serious weaknesses in the ideas he had championed and was open to alternatives that might be more adequate. But the psychological forces at work in such a situation are complex and may conflict with each other, especially when a philosopher is habituated to feel shame at the need to abandon a viewpoint he had publicly defended. Wittgenstein might feel this shame sufficiently to say (unconsciously, of course) to himself: "Well, I had to change once from my early philosophy, but to change again would be too undignified to endure." In that case he would be driven to defend the view in the *Investigations* even more vehemently than he would otherwise.

How helpful it would have been to students of his philosophies if in the Foreward to the *Investigations* he had not only acknowledged grave mistakes in the earlier book (which he forthrightly did)[5], but had also pointed out the major respects in which his orientation underwent no change and had indicated why the new philosophy appeared to be the needed correction! To do this, however, is very difficult for any philosopher. A minor reason is that he usually grows into the new viewpoint step by step, not all at once, so that the differences do not stand out clearly together. But the major reason is that in defending his former viewpoint he has very likely said, as Wittgenstein did in the *Tractatus:* "The truth of

4. This is not to deny the presence in the *Tractatus* of a few statements which seem to anticipate the viewpoint of the *Investigations*.
5. Page X^c of the *Philosophical Investigations* (Anscombe trans.), Oxford, 1953.

the thoughts communicated here appears to me unassailable and definitive. I am therefore of the opinion that the problems have in essentials
been finally solved."[6]

This survey of recent philosophical history seems to show that to pass
in the midst of a thinker's career from one set of basic ideas to another is
now taking place more frequently than in the past. The main change still
needed is to leave behind the haunting sense that such a passage is
somehow shameful, and to form the habit of offering one's present
viewpoint to the world, not in terms implying that it provides a final
solution of the issues dealt with but in the frank expectation that it will
need to be revised, quite possibly in fundamental as well as in minor
matters.

Once philosophers are habituated to the idea that transition from one
orientation to another is not a humiliating weakness but the normal and
sensible thing at any period of a thinker's life, a wise view of philosophy's
future can be gained and much in its past history becomes easier to
understand. Glance briefly at Descartes and Spinoza in this connection.

The "Cartesian circle" has often perplexed students of Descartes. Early
in his *Meditations* the criterion of truth that he adopts is a "clear and
distinct idea" of whatever reality is involved. Resting on this criterion, he
demonstrates the reality of God and the assurance that God is not a
deceiver. Once that is accomplished, the reader finds him saying that
because God is real and does not deceive we can trust our clear and
distinct ideas. When these two pieces of reasoning are put together, it
would seem that nothing at all has been proved—each main premise
depends for its power to convince on the conclusion drawn from it. But
look at his reasoning in the context of its presuppositions, and the
possibility that there may be a shift from one set of presuppositions to
another. Initially, the assumed perspective is that of the determined
doubter, who can consistently doubt everything except his own doubting.
Later, when the implications of the idea of a Perfect Being have been
traced, employing the same criterion by which he saw that he could not
doubt his own doubting, another perspective is established. In it, what is
most certain is not one's clear and distinct perception but the reality and
perfection of God. A thinker's own existence, with whatever ideas take
form in his mind, has now become derivative rather than primary.
Whatever capacity anyone has to think clearly and distinctly comes, as he
will now humbly acknowledge, from God. But this could not be asserted

6. P. 29 of the *Tractatus*, London, 1922.

before the reader has become convinced of the reality of a God perfect in goodness and truth. If this interpretation is correct, there is no "circle"; the illogicality arises from the gap that is left between two sets of presuppositions. Presumably Descartes expects an alert reader to make that shift with him, and thus to bridge the gap.

In Spinoza's case there is no illogical circle, but a shift in basic presuppositions is nonetheless apparent when one looks for it. In the first part of his *Ethics* the philosopher demonstrates that nothing in the universe happens teleologically; reality is a system bound throughout by mathematical necessity. Hence there is no freedom. But by the time he comes to the fifth part, teleology is tacitly reinstated and a way to win rational freedom is revealed. Through knowledge of the universe, and especially knowledge of his emotions, a man can achieve liberation from bondage and realize the union with God in which true blessedness consists. The paradoxical aspect of this teaching is vividly disclosed by putting the gist of it thus: Through understanding that there are no goals in the universe, the supremely important goal can be attained. How could an unusually clearheaded thinker like Spinoza fall into such a contradiction? The answer, I think, is that the contradiction disappears when one realizes that a shift of basic presuppositions has occurred. The first part of the *Ethics* presupposes that no understanding of reality is possible in terms of the Jewish-Christian faith in a providential deity; a faith of this kind must be replaced by the recognition that every happening in the universe is inexorably determined. The fifth part presupposes that this deterministic understanding of reality has the value, not only of satisfying our cognitive quest for truth but also of guiding us toward the blissful union with God in which our whole being finds fulfillment.

Other illustrations of an important presuppositional shift will appear when one looks in philosophical history for them. Hegel's significance, I would suggest, is that he impressively exemplifies the attempt to make a rational dialectical process out of this dynamic passage from one set of presuppositions to another.

What kind of enterprise would philosophy become if it were generally assumed that the normal thing is not for a philosopher to round off his system and then defend it against all critics, but to keep growing—to hold even his basic ideas as revisable in the light of new insight which might at any time be gained? Philosophical history at large—to personify it for a moment—takes this open-endedness for granted; it welcomes the infinitely varied sets of ideas that are proposed from time to time. It never commits itself to any particular set, but keeps responsive to all of them and receptive to whatever value they have. Also, of course, it refuses to be limited to the sets that happen to be available at any given period, but always leaves room for new insights leading beyond the horizon drawn by the systems of the past.

My recommendation is that each philosopher identify himself with this inclusive historical process, instead of with the particular cluster of ideas that happen now to appeal to him. Why not welcome continued revolution in his philosophy, to be fostered under conscious guidance instead of reluctantly submitting to it when a change is thrust upon him by accidental forces? No matter how satisfying or successful his present way of philosophizing appears, will he not be in a better position if he realizes that it is always capable of revision in the direction of greater adequacy? What would be lost in such a dynamic orientation that ought not to be lost?

But a reader who has followed me thus far might feel that what has been stressed simply affects the attitude in which one philosophizes and has no bearing on the substance of his thought. I would agree at once that what becomes important from this viewpoint is a way of philosophizing rather than any particular system of ideas. But a fuller answer is called for.

First, this difference in one's way of philosophizing is by no means negligible. The same kind of achievement would doubtless be won as has been won in the past history of philosophy, but more rapidly and efficiently. Militant polemics would disappear; they would be replaced by sensitive collaboration between philosophers. To spell this difference out a bit: New insights would be gained more easily than they can when thinkers dogmatically cling to their present presuppositions, and those who propose a new insight would do so tentatively, without any need to make presumptuous claims or to defend it with anxious heat. Other philosophers would feel no urge to whip that disquieting idea off the stage, but would welcome its challenge. Its champions would be free from any irrational assurance that they have at last found the key to philosophical truth, and its opponents would be free from any irrational longing to remain in peaceful bondage to their own pet systems. All participants in the debate would combine their resources in an endeavor to discover and unfold the promising possibilities in that new insight—drawing the distinctions needed so that its systematic bearing on problems in every field of thought can be explored. It is at this point that progress requires the talent of analytic philosophers; they, more skillfully than others, can dissect complex ideas and reveal in detail what they imply.

In brief, when this orientation is generally adopted, whatever is unsound in the presuppositions of a new philosophy would quickly be laid bare and left behind, while the enduring contribution it makes would be clarified and find its happiest articulation. The arena would still be noisy with rival schools, but instead of trying to annihilate each other they would compete to see which can contribute best to the more adequate philosophizing of the future. In this sense there would exist in the forum of discussion a single unfolding movement, rather than a medley of warring philosophies.

These differences, however, involve no change in the content of one's philosophizing. So the second part of my answer is needed. In what way would the content of a philosopher's system be affected?

My conviction is that in this orientation one's philosophy would be unified to a degree that on current presuppositions is very difficult, and that the unity thus realized would take a definite form. Let me elaborate.

When a philosopher is open to his own basic presuppositions and receptive to the presuppositions of others, expecting to keep growing at that deep level, he will naturally bring together whatever insights come from these varied sources. He seeks to envision a total perspective in which the positive value of each can find its appropriate place. This can be done only if he recovers a sense of the wholeness of human experience and takes it as his task to offer a coherent interpretation of that wholeness. But since he sees clearly the impossibility of a final system of the universe he will not be tempted into some of the bizarre claims of traditional metaphysicians.

However, interpretations of the wholeness of experience will inevitably vary. Which interpretation is superior to all others, and how can we tell?

The answer is that from this viewpoint such a question does not arise. In a dynamic and receptive orientation a plurality of philosophical visions is not a vice but a virtue. Where one has a blind spot another can be enlightening. It is good that all are available, so that a seeker for fuller understanding can profit by any way of thinking that he finds fruitful. A philosopher will naturally aim to reach conclusions that will ring true to the experience of others as well as himself. But he will know that his own limitations have not been overcome; his conclusions are inevitably relative to them.

Are we left then with an unrelieved pluralism in the philosophical arena? To respond to that question and reveal more clearly the kind of unity that can be won by this route, consider the relation between science and philosophy. The scientist has a method by which he can overcome the relativity due to the "personal equation" of different investigators and reach conclusions on which other scientists will agree. Would philosophy, as pursued in the above perspective, be hopelessly unscientific?

That might easily seem to be the case. But reflect a bit. Perhaps this perspective is just what is needed to bring out the fundamental harmony of philosophy with science. Let us remember that science has a history—not merely in the trivial sense that it reveals a succession of discoveries which add to our knowledge, but in the more important sense that it reveals a succession of theories about what science intrinsically is and about the form its observations and explanations should take. Always, of course, the scientist seeks some regular order in the objects and events that make up the world he investigates. But many patterns of order can be discovered. The most instructive lesson that emerges, as in this setting one surveys the history of Western thought, is that at any given time science presupposes the special kind of order that needs to be disclosed if it is to realize the values which thinkers at that time are eager to realize.

Consider the broad difference that stands out when the conception of science generally taken for granted in ancient and mediaeval times is compared with the modern conception. Ancient and mediaeval thinkers, almost without exception so far as I know, took it for granted that science and metaphysics form a single body of knowledge, whose detailed regularities constitute what would now be called the scientific part while its ultimate structure was provided by metaphysics. It was confidently believed that through the unifying metaphysical principles that body of knowledge can become a final explanation of the universe and all that it contains.

What widely accepted value was reflected in these presuppositions? A very plausible answer is that it was man's longing for security in an insecure universe. When everything that happens is explained by a cognitive system thus constructed, thinkers feel that they are winning intellectual security through the demonstrable and potentially complete knowledge which appears to be established, and such an achievement provides the needed support for the emotional security they also seek.

What is the essence of the change that occurred when this conception of science was outgrown? The fundamental answer seems to be: Modern scientists are more ambitious and self-confident. They have come to believe that by verified knowledge, organized in a different pattern, men can increasingly control toward their chosen ends the processes going on in nature. Instead of security, ever growing mastery of the environing world is the dominant value of modern science, and its investigators presuppose the kind of orderly pattern that makes realization of this value possible. And what kind is that? Instead of an order grounded in metaphysical principles that are supposedly eternal, it is a network of causal and functional relations so conceived that thinkers can predict the future effects of forces now at work and can make them serve desirable ends wherever the causal conditions necessary can be controlled.

The most decisive contrast between this orientation and its ancient and mediaeval predecessor is that successful prediction must be recognized as always relative, never absolute.

A supposedly final metaphysical explanation naturally poses as absolute truth, but not an explanation in terms of predictive order. Nature obviously assumes no obligation to confirm the predictions of thinkers about her behavior, and in a dynamic universe new events take place that could not be predicted in advance at all. The radical consequence is that while continued progress is possible in making more successful forecasts and taking account of new data, the conclusions reached are never final. They are always capable of being improved, and the need to revise them may become apparent at any time. So the aim of establishing final truth, which dominated pre-modern science, has had to be abandoned. Scientists sometimes still describe their work in terms reminiscent of that aim, but when one looks at their practice it is evident that continued progress toward further truth is what they really take for granted. And not only can new truths be discovered, but their incorporation into the body of science may require a significant change in the knowledge with which they are incorporated. So science is now viewed, not as a quest to uncover the changeless structure of reality, but as the endless process of revising and improving what at present passes for knowledge. Many of the revisions thus appearing are minor, but every once in a while a major revision comes.

How about philosophy, when it is viewed from this thoroughly dynamic standpoint? What does it need to become, if it is to be scientific in the way that is now relevant and possible?

Look once more, with this question in mind, at its past. It was expected, in its metaphysical branch, to provide the foundation principles and the final capstone of the whole structure of knowledge. Were that the only role it could fill, its function would now be over. But what it actually contributed, I believe, was something different, and that contribution is needed today as much as ever. The greatest philosophers were, in fact, prophetic sages. They envisioned, and expressed in systematic form, a comprehensive picture of the universe such that for many centuries after them the work of science could hopefully develop under the guidance of its basic presuppositions. Aristotle is the outstanding example of a prophetic sage in the ancient period; Descartes came close to filling the same role in the early modern period—at least, in his vision of what the physical world is like when conceived as a dynamic mathematical order. If it is difficult to see him in these terms, the difficulty may be due to the fact that all thinkers now take his main contribution for granted, and when they look back at him what catches their attention is apt to be some specific theory—such as his ontological argument in theology or his vortices in astronomy—which has been largely or wholly abandoned.

Will not this prophetic function always need to be filled? If science undergoes revision from time to time, in its pervasive presuppositions as well as in its detailed truths, it is ever calling for geniuses who can be sensitive to newly emerging needs in the enterprise of explaining nature and can envision novel possibilities in the way physical or social science pursues that task. Many such visions will prove to be blind alleys, but a few—so one can justifiably expect—will achieve the same degree of success that the greatest philosophers have achieved in the past.

It may be that in the future this particular function will be filled more by theoretical scientists than by philosophers; the former are familiar with the firing-line of the quest for knowledge while the latter are not. However, in such a situation a great task that can only be performed by men of philosophical talent becomes visible and is more challenging than ever. Intellectual progress calls for the vision of thinkers who are sensitive to the whole panorama of human experience, and respond to new possibilities opening up in the realms of religion, of art, of ethics, and of social statesmanship as well as of science. The universe that challenges our quest for inclusive understanding is much more than an extrapolation from the data and theories of current science. Thinkers are needed who can perform the arduous pioneering task of envisioning the whole that includes all these realms and detecting how the constructive role of each can be pursued in harmony with the constructive role of the others. Such a task is not impossible and the reward of success is great. The geniuses who perform it, whatever they may call themselves, are philosophers.

One more question remains. What kind of unity can a philosophy realize when it is developed in this dynamic and inclusive setting?

I see only one plausible answer. It is the unity that can be exemplified by a philosophy of man. Such a philosophy emerges in this perspective as all-encompassing; every other branch becomes a distinctive part of a wise philosophy of man. Of course man would not be dealt with in isolation. He would be viewed as interacting with the surrounding physical, social, and metaphysical universe, and ever growing beyond any horizon that might seem to limit him. Philosophy thus pursued would be mainly concerned with his basic presuppositions and values, as they take form from time to time in this or that limited group and in the quest of mankind as a whole to realize lasting fulfillment. The familiar branches of philosophy would fill their natural place in such a perspective. Metaphysics becomes a search for the most general features that can be delineated in this dynamic interaction. Ethics becomes a clarification of the most dependable and widely shareable good for man that can be envisioned. Logic becomes a quest for the most trustworthy pattern of inference from any set of premises to a conclusion. In each of these branches a wise philosopher will respect the hard won deposit of past thought, while always being open to its revision.

In the course of modern history, science, psychology, and social thought had to break away from philosophy, largely because the latter had become enclosed in a rigid shell unable to provide for their free development. That break has been very constructive. But the continued separation of these enterprises from philosophy means that in our day promising visions of man in his wholeness are both exceedingly difficult and more than ever needed. The thinkers who are overcoming this separation, however inadequately—Arnold Toynbee, Buckminster Fuller, Lewis Mumford, Marshall McLuhan, Abraham Maslow, Barbara Ward, Teilhard de Chardin, to mention only a few—come closer to filling the main philosophical role today than most academic philosophers. But presently prevailing assumptions among the latter will not last forever, and in their own fashion they are contributing to an understanding of man. Philosophers are men, and every way of philosophizing reveals something significant about those who follow it and the values they are seeking to realize. Such values are shared by many other men.

It may be pertinent, however, to suggest a change of label by which to refer to the ways of philosophizing now popular in university circles. Are not those exhibited in the English-speaking world ventures on the border-line between philosophy and mathematics, or philosophy and linguistics? This way of referring to them would have the virtue of reminding us that there are other borderlines that have been exemplified in the past and doubtless will be in the future—such as the borderline between philosophy and theology, or psychology, or history, or social thought. Ventures in each of these borderlines have their special value; they enrich our understanding of man and the universe. But this way of labelling them would make it easier to see their relation to the all-embracing venture that is obviously philosophical.

No Pot of Message

Herbert Feigl

Complying with the flattering invitation to write in a rather personal vein on what I believe, I have taken the liberty of sketching an autobiographical background to the development of my philosophical point of view. I did this in the hope that it might be of some interest, if not of some slight use, to young "budding" philosophers.

After half a century of studies, searchings and reflections, philosophy still strikes me as a highly questionable enterprise. The Scylla of absurdity and the Charybdis of triviality seem forever to threaten. Or, to switch to a more homely metaphor, philosophy—especially in its more ambitious form of "systems"—is like a blanket that is too short: if you pull it up to your chin, your feet get exposed (and vice versa). Complete "coverage", it seems, can be achieved (to use yet another figure of speech) only by means of verbal sedatives. Moreover, as Bertrand Russell has remarked, the solemnity of some philosophers merely conceals humbug. In what follows I hope to discredit and diminish the "prophet motive" so typical of philosophers throughout the ages.

Having had the advantage of an early and thorough training in the "exact" sciences (mathematics, physics, chemistry, and astronomy) I could only heartily agree with Kant that (especially) metaphysics is a "groping in the dark". Yet, Kant's own "critical" philosophy seemed to me peculiarly musty and dogmatic. My teen-age idols were the philosophizing scientists Ernst Mach and Wilhelm Ostwald. But even then I objected to their (rather anachronistic) negative attitude toward the atomic theory. In this issue I agreed enthusiastically with the realism of

Ludwig Boltzmann and Max Planck. At the age of about sixteen I would wander through the wonderful, extended pine forests of my homeland (i.e. the Sudentenland in northern Bohemia) and visualize electrons, atoms, and molecules in my physical environment. While pure mathematics and geometry were of great interest to me, the fields of study that fascinated me most were theoretical physics, physical chemistry, and astronomy.

As far as I can tell I was one of the first two scholarly-minded persons in the German-Bohemian-Jewish Feigl and Beck families from which I originated. The other one was a second cousin, two years my senior, Arthur Beer, who became a well-known astronomer (astrophysicist and spectroscopist) later in Cambridge, England. It was he who helped me toward a better understanding, especially of the mathematics, of Einstein's general theory of relativity (differential geometry and tensor algebra). I had happened, at the age of sixteen or seventeen, upon an article by an able (I think his name was Emil Abel) Viennese physical chemist in an Austrian chemistry journal. This was, I believe, in 1918 when Einstein's name and fame were still completely new to me. I found this article on the special theory of relativity extremely challenging. My first reaction was the suspicion that the theory must be in error. Promptly I set about to refute it. But in trying to do that I learned a great deal of physics and mathematics and, of course, found out after a few months of diligent work just who was wrong! My attitude then changed completely and Einstein became my number one intellectual hero. Indeed, in 1920 (when I was 17 years old) I made the 60 mile trip from my hometown to Prague where I heard Einstein's lecture on relativity on the first evening and a thrilling discussion of Einstein with some of his critics on the following evening. Einstein's Olympian calm and superiority, coupled with his humility and great sense of humor remain unforgettable to me. It was in 1923 that I finally had the courage to visit the great man in Berlin. He advised me on further studies in theoretical physics; he was also quite outspoken about his philosophical predilections—and aversions. It was not until 1954 (one year before his death) that I was privileged to spend another afternoon in conversation with Einstein in his Princeton home.

After I had read (as did two or three of my classmates in high school) parts of the works of Kant, Schopenhauer and Nietzsche, I happened (in 1919) upon Moritz Schlick's little book on *Space and Time in Contemporary Physics*. There I found a reference to the first edition (1918) of Schlick's great masterpiece, his *Allgemeine Erkenntnislehre* (General Theory of Knowledge.) Schlick soon became my favorite philosopher. I was also impressed with the book by Alois Riehl on contemporary philosophy. Riehl, whose work I still think was more important than that of the other Neo-Kantians, never received the recognition he deserved. In addition to many other important contributions and clarifications, I was immensely pleased with the sort of critical realism and its supporting arguments I found in both Riehl and Schlick. Impressed as I was with Mach's insistence upon the immediately given (his "elements") as the ultimate basis of all factual knowledge, I had of course realized that my physicalistic orientation urgently required a coherent and tenable solution of the mind-body problem. The place of mind in nature, with the corollary puzzles regarding the freedom of the will, exercised my curiosity and my imagination. Partly prepared by Schopenhauer's metaphysical approach, the mind-body monism explicated and defended by both Riehl and Schlick struck me like a thunderbolt. (It was many years later that I learned of Bertrand Russell's similar but independent solution, fully expounded in his book *Human Knowledge* of 1948.) Those very early influences and experiences left a permanent mark on the development of my philosophical thought.

Perhaps I should also mention that at the age of about eleven to thirteen I had read ardently most of the science-fiction novels of Jules Verne and Kurd Lasswitz. I "identified" with Captain Nemo of *Twenty Thousand Leagues Under the Sea* and of *Mysterious Island*. I was thrilled with Lasswitz's *On Two Planets* and with the intellectually, technologically and morally superior Martians described in that story. Very naturally then, physics and chemistry (and to some extent the French language) became my favorite subjects in the *Realschule* (secondary school, age 11-14) of my hometown Reichenberg (in what was then Austria-Hungary).

My two grandfathers had been simple, but moderately prosperous businessmen. My father, having escaped from school at age thirteen, began what was to become a meteoric career, first as a weaver (working 12 hours a day, six days a week in a small town of Saxony). Soon his great technical talents were recognized. He was a skillful and highly ingenious textile designer. He also invented important improvements for the weaving looms of that time. My father was the first in Europe to use rayon patterns in the weaving of woolen fabrics. (He also was among the first few automobilists in Austria.) In the course of the few years before the first world war, he became a leader in the Austrian textile industry, and after 1920 was for a few years the General Director of "Textilana". This was perhaps the greatest textile manufacturing (spinning, weaving, and dyeing) corporation in continental Europe. Only the English industry could successfully compete with Textilana. My father's interests lay exclusively on the technical and organizational side. (He left the financial aspects to his associates.) For a few years he was a "man of property and affluence". But the (delayed) effects of the business depression did catch up with him and his enterprises, too. Thus he retired from his position and moved to Vienna in 1927. That was the year in which I received my doctorate in philosophy from the University of Vienna. Also in 1927 I began teaching—first astronomy—and later, various courses in philosophy, especially in the philosophy of science at the *Volkshochschule Wien*, i.e., the People's Institute of Vienna (for adult education). Many of its instructors were also faculty members of the University of Vienna.

During his active years my father had hoped that I would become an industrial chemist and thus join the scientific staff of Textilana. But already during the four years of my studies at the excellent vocational high school of Reichenberg (major field: chemistry) my interests shifted strongly toward pure and theoretical (rather than applied and technological) science. The high seriousness of a superb teacher and devoted scientist, Paul Artmann, who had returned to our school from the war in 1916, very definitely influenced my studies, interests and aspirations.

My father, a very practical and extremely energetic man, was at first quite disappointed. But as he watched and recognized my success in school, he reconciled himself with having a budding scholar for a son.

As I see it now, psychologically (if not psychoanalytically), it was necessary for me to find a kingdom of my own in order to obtain the approval of my father. This extremely powerful and successful man expected from his children similarly great achievements. But because in contrast to my father I lacked practical and manual skills, and was of a more contemplative nature ("dreamy" my father used to say), it had to be the realm of ideas in which I could hope for any measure of success.

My father was socially and politically highly alert. He was on excellent terms with his workers; he provided them with adequate and pleasant housing, and though his attitude was somewhat paternalistic, he never suffered the adversities of a strike. To be sure, he had no patience with the Communists, but his mind was open in regard to a humane socialism. My father was clearly a typical "self-made man". He would, no doubt, also have been extremely successful in America had he chosen to migrate there. He was an outspoken atheist—this made my own emancipation from Judaism (at age eight) quite easy.

My mother was an excellent spouse and counterpoise for my father.

She had a lifelong interest in the arts, literature, and music. Her religion—if it can be so called—was that of a Spinoza-Goethe-type pantheism. Since she played the piano with great understanding (but without technical virtuosity), it was from her that I received what I still consider my life's most precious gift: the love of music and some knack for improvisation on the piano. Even before I reached age ten I asked my mother to play one or the other of the many Beethoven sonatas for me—again and again. And when at the age of ten I heard a performance of *Die Meistersinger* I became for at least fifteen years an ardent admirer of Richard Wagner's music. Having succumbed to that magical spell, it was not before I reached the age of thirty that I began fully to appreciate Bach, Mozart, and Schubert. During my student days in Vienna (1922-27), however, my greatest musical experiences were the symphonies of Anton Bruckner and Gustav Mahler. I have remained faithful to these two Austrian composers, as well as of course, to the classical and a few contemporary ones. Thus I must avow that I consider truly great music *the* supreme achievement of the human spirit. In keeping with the well-known aphorism of Ludwig Wittgenstein ("whereof one cannot speak thereof one must be silent"), I am inclined to think that music expresses (even more than poetry) what is inexpressible in cognitive and especially in scientific language.

My social and political interests were most dramatically and rudely aroused by my experiences (1921-22) at the University of Munich. Twelve years before Hitler's rise to power, the anti-Semitism in Germany was already quite noticeable. My cousin Arthur Beer and I encountered a curiously vicious circle when we tried to become students at Munich's University. In order to enroll at the University we needed a permit of residence from the police (we were, as Czechoslovaks, after the revolution of 1918, "foreigners" in Germany). But in order to obtain the permit of residence we would have to be admitted as regular students by the University. Both my cousin (by then already known for some contributions to astronomy) and I were politically quite innocent as well as rather ignorant. But the rejection by the University stung us into action. After a long, adventurous, and often distressing fight against the bigoted authorities at the University and the Police we finally won. An elaborate letter of complaint, endorsed by a liberal lawyer, went up through several levels of the Bavarian bureaucracy. After two months of our protestations the Minister of the Interior of Bavaria himself signed our permits of residence. By early March of 1922, however, i.e., at the end of our first semester at Munich, the new regulations excluded even non-Bavarian German students. There was no possible recourse against this. Hence we moved to Vienna where mathematics, physics and philosophy promised to equal, and were soon to excel, the qualities of the University of Munich.

I had learned that Moritz Schlick (whom I had thus far known only as the author of two superb books) was going to accept the famous chair (earlier held by Mach and Boltzmann) in the Philosophy of the Inductive Sciences at the University of Vienna. Thus I was fortunate to become a student of this truly great philosopher, and later even more fortunate in being favored with the friendship of this superbly kind and generous man.

Another event proved of the greatest influence upon my work and philosophical development. Browsing in a bookstore in Munich in early 1922, I came upon Edgar Zilsel's *Das Anwendungsproblem,* a book dealing with issues of probability of induction. It had been published in 1916, but perhaps because of some flaws in its logico-mathematical aspects had not attained the recognition it so richly deserved for its brilliant and challenging originality. Five years before the publication of John Maynard Keynes' *Treatise on Probability* (and two years before C. D. Broad's first essay on the subject) Zilsel formulated in an extremely stimulating manner the problems that are even today unsettled and subject to intensive disputes. After writing (in 1922) a prizewinning (but unpublished) long essay on the philosophical significance of the theory of relativity, I turned my attention increasingly to the topics of determinism, indeterminism, induction, and probability. I still remember the fever of excitement that gripped me in the spring and summer of 1925 when I began making copious notes of the ideas that whirled in my mind. "Chance and Law; an epistemological analysis of the roles of probability and induction in the natural sciences" was the title of my doctoral dissertation (finished early in 1927). Much of this early work of mine has, of course, been superseded by the rapid subsequent developments. Perhaps the most glaring defect was that I was unable at the time to discuss the indeterminism of quantum mechanics. The theories of Heisenberg, Jordan, Born and Schrödinger were formulated precisely during the period in which I wrote my thesis. I could not possibly have penetrated and interpreted those truly revolutionary developments. All I can say for myself in this connection is that I dealt with the issues of determinism vs. indeterminism as judiciously as my lights then permitted. The early quantum theory of Planck, Einstein, and Bohr had already suggested to me that theoretical physics may have to countenance a concept of absolute chance. Still, my (emotional?) preference was the one to which Planck and Einstein tenaciously held throughout their lives, i.e., that of a "rock-bottom" determinism. In such a conception of the world there is room only for *relative* chance; and the exploration and explication of relative chance formed one of the more original parts of my dissertation. Schlick (who had hardly helped with advice or supervision) was extremely pleased with my work, and proposed publication in the *Schriften zur Wissenschaftlichen Weltauffasung* (edited by P. Frank and M. Schlick, Springer, *Wien*). Yet, in view of the new turn in physics I decided to revise my dissertation thoroughly. But I had underestimated the task. The interpretation of quantum mechanics has remained an intricate and highly controversial matter to this day.

A small part of the ideas of my thesis did get published in the first volume of *Erkenntnis*. The title of that article was "Wahrscheinlichkeit und Erfahrung". Having favored the frequency interpretation of probability, I was nevertheless (I believe) the first to point out its logical difficulties. I had realized that such notions as (i.e., R. von Mises') limit of relative frequency is not definable in terms of convergence criteria such as are used in the pure mathematics of infinite sequences or series. The dilemma in the case of probability is to say either nothing empirical (i.e., the limit of frequency lies in the closed interval between 0 and 1) or something that is (almost) bound to be false (by stating a definite form of convergence). I suggested a pragmatic solution for this problem as well as for the "grand" problem (Hume's problem) of induction. I was greatly pleased by the approval of my ideas by R. Carnap, and (with some qualifications) by H. Reichenbach.

My dissertation was written during the first two years of the activities of the Vienna Circle. My friend and mentor, Friedrich Waismann (ca. six years my senior) and I had—I believe in 1923 or 1924—suggested to Schlick the formation of an evening discussion group. Philosophically interested mathematicians and scientists, together with mathematically and scientifically trained philosophers, were to discuss issues in the logical and epistemological foundations of mathematics, physics, and occasionally also of biology, psychology and the social sciences. The subsequent development is by now an important and well-known chapter in the history of recent philosophy. Along with other ("advanced") students I enjoyed the great privilege of being a member of the Vienna Circle from the time of its inception in 1924 up to the time of my emigration in 1930. Besides Schlick, who was its rather self-effacing leader, the Circle comprised such mature and outstanding scholars as the mathematicians Hans Hahn and Kurt Reidemeister, the sociologist and economist Otto Neurath, the philosopher Victor Kraft—and after 1926 its most contributive member, Rudolf Carnap. Among the younger participants were R. Waismann, and a little later Karl Menger, Kurt Gödel, and Gustav Bergmann. There were also stimulating visitors such as Philipp Frank, C. G. Hempel, Eino Kaila, Alfred Tarski, *et al.* During my last year (1929-30) in Vienna, a young American student, Albert E. Blumberg, joined the Circle. He worked on his doctoral thesis under Schlick, and I helped him with the German language as well as philosophically. It was Blumberg who got me interested in American philosophy and encouraged me to visit (and possibly to settle in) the United States. Even before that I had the pleasure and good fortune to get acquainted with Dickinson Miller who was a visiting member of the Circle in 1926. A year later I received from him a charming and generous invitation to join him and his friend Professor Emeritus C. A. Strong in Fiesole (in the hills above Florence, Italy). Both gentlemen spoke German quite fluently so they did not have to suffer my (then) rather poor English. We mostly discussed matters of epistemology, and it was my task to report on developments in the Vienna Circle. I accepted another such invitation to Fiesole during the following year (1928). I cherish a copy of C. A. Strong's *Theory of Knowledge* which he personally inscribed with a friendly dedication to me.

My studies in philosophy under the guidance of Moritz Schlick, Robert Reininger and Heinrich Gomperz; of theoretical physics under Hans Thirring; mathematics under Hans Hahn; psychology under Karl Bühler— together with the tremendously exciting experiences in the Vienna Circle and the continuing private discussions, especially with Waismann, Carnap, Gödel and Natkin, helped in shaping my philosophical outlook. By 1929 we had become convinced of our philosophical mission in the world. The first Unity of Science meeting took place in Prague in the summer of that year. This was also the first public joint effort of the Vienna Circle with the Berlin Society for Scientific Philosophy, led by H. Reichenbach and R. von Mises. I also participated in the even more fascinating second meeting in Königsberg in 1930. Present at that meeting were also Werner Heisenberg, John von Neumann and Arend Heyting.

Ludwig Wittgenstein whose *Tractatus Logico-Philosophicus* was the subject of many extended and lively discussions in the Circle, never joined our group during the two years (1927-29) of his architectural activities in Vienna. Schlick and Waismann, however, managed to per-suade this brilliant but highly eccentric man to meet with them and often also with me, either at Schlick's house, or in cafés. Occasionally Wittgen-stein also came to tea at my fiancée's home. I remember that on one occasion he read some poetry by Tagore to us. Wittgenstein was at that time very reluctant to discuss philosophical matters. When asked about one or the other cryptic passage in the *Tractatus* he said he couldn't reconstruct any more just what he meant when writing it. But on a few rare occasions we witnessed his most impressive and highly intuitive approach to various philosophical problems. As a person of great seriousness and ruthless intellectual honesty and self-criticism he remains, next to Einstein, certainly the most fascinating thinker I ever encountered. Schlick and Waismann quickly became ardent disciples of Wittgenstein. To my chagrin Schlick ascribed to Wittgenstein philosophical ideas that he (Schlick) had already expounded much more lucidly in his 1918 book on epistemology. I was also disappointed with Schlick's compromise with positivism (phenomenalistic version)—and the abandonment of his critical realism as "metaphysically suspect".

As all the world knows, Wittgenstein's return (in 1929) to Cambridge and the development of his later point of view—or method of philosophizing—exerted a tremendous influence in English, American, Australian, and most recently, even in German philosophy. In complete agreement with Bertrand Russell and Karl Popper I find little of genuine importance in the work of the later Wittgenstein. In my opinion it must have been the almost hypnotic power of the man that created a coterie of disciples around him and that rendered his "ordinary language" approach so fashionable for a good many years. A truly brilliant mind and independent, honest searcher for clarity, Wittgenstein still suffered from (I think) a typically positivistic phobia of metaphysical issues, especially of the quandaries of transcendence. Thus he tried to restore the world view of commonsense by describing the uses of words in common speech. This whole approach seemed doomed to sterility to me, mainly because it (largely) ignored the importance of concept formation and theory construction in the sciences. Given my own education and predilections I still consider knowledge at its best, most reliable, and most fascinating in the more advanced sciences. Moreover, the ordinary language analysis can resolve philosophical problems only if they arise out of rather obvious equivocations, ambiguities or syntactic-semantic confusions. The more profound issues of traditional philosophy, such as the nature of truth, the validity and scope of knowledge, the mind-body problem, the problem of universals, etc., etc., can only be repressed, concealed or glossed over, but not solved by the rather lazy and cavalier "Oxbridge" type of procedures.

As I have indicated above, my "formative" years were those devoted to the study of the sciences, and later the scientifically oriented philosophical work in the Vienna Circle. Schlick and Carnap, and to a much lesser extent the early Wittgenstein, but also the many discussions with Neurath, Kraft, Gomperz, Zilsel, and later with Reichenbach, decisively influenced my philosophical outlook. It was not before 1929 that I came to know and soon became a friend of Karl Popper's. To him and to Reichenbach I owe a great intellectual debt. Although I had been in the "loyal opposition" in regard to the positivism of the Vienna Circle, I had a hard time maintaining against them the sort of critical realism that I had originally learned to adopt from Schlick's own early work (also from Planck, Boltzman, and from Oswald Külpe's *Realisierung,* and from Alois Riehl's *Der Philosophische Kritizismus,* etc.). The first impact and shock came to me from Carnap's *Der Logische Aufbau der Welt* which I studied in typescript (it was larger and even more technical than the book published in 1928). Under the influence of Carnap and the early Wittgenstein, Schlick and Waismann were converted to a sort of phenomenalistic positivism during the middle twenties. Their brilliant and powerful arguments overwhelmed me temporarily. But encouraged and buttressed by the support of Popper, Reichenbach, and Zilsel, I regained confidence in my earlier realism and developed it in my first book on *Theorie and Erfahrung in der Physik* (1929), and later in several articles written during my academic career in the United States. That first book received much cherished comments, not only from my friends and colleagues in the Vienna Circle, but also in letters from Albert Einstein and Wolfgang Pauli. I had been able to deal briefly (though I think now only rather inadequately) with the philosophical aspects of quantum mechanics. In addition I expounded ideas of the level structure of scientific explanation, and the hypothetico-deductive method in theory construction generally. In this regard I anticipated in my very informal way some of the views developed more fully by C. G. Hempel and Karl Popper in later years. But I was not aware of William Whewell's work at the time.

Encouraged by Albert Blumberg (and also by those two magnificent American philosophers, Strong and Miller) I applied for an International Rockefeller Research Fellowship early in 1930. It was my great good luck to receive such a fellowship. I had submitted very favorable recommendations from Einstein, Schlick, Carnap, Thirring, and several other Viennese physicists and philosophers. So, immediately after the Königsberg meeting in September of 1930 I made my first voyage to the "New World" where I stayed for about eight months at Harvard University. My main first contact there was the physicist-philosopher, P. W. Bridgman, the originator of the "operational" approach in the logic of science. I also became acquainted with A. N. Whitehead, Henry Sheffer, C. I. Lewis, R. B. Perry, Susan Langer; and among the younger scholars or graduate students, Paul Weiss and W. V. O. Quine. On the advice of my Harvard friends I began looking for a teaching position in the United States (by Spring of 1931). I enjoyed a reunion with Albert Blumberg during the Christmas season of 1930 in New York. It was there that we wrote our well-known article, "Logical Positivism: A New Movement in European Philosophy." We thus provided the philosophical outlook of the Vienna Circle with its internationally accepted label. Our article (published in the Spring of 1931 in the *Journal of Philosophy*) started "the ball rolling", and for at least two decades lively controversies ensued regarding Viennese Positivism. Although I quite openly expressed my critical opposition, especially to the phenomenalistic reductionism, I did behave myself rather aggressively as an antimetaphysician throughout the nineteen-thirties. My role in the United States was thus similar to that of Alfred J. Ayer in England. I still regret that early manner of mine, especially when I remember how cordially and generously I was received in the many academic institutions that invited me for lectures or colloquia (often entire series of such). Since I have told the story of my experiences and impressions in the United States in my memoir in the book *The Intellectual Migration* I shall mention here only how grateful I feel to this country, and especially to the deans and presidents of the State University of Iowa and the University of Minnesota, where I found a peaceful haven well before hell broke loose in Europe.—I now turn to

WHAT I BELIEVE

Space permits only a very brief and condensed survey of whatever philosophical conclusions I have reached. While I feel quite strongly about some of them, the terse, dogmatic tone in which I shall present them is merely due to the brevity demanded on this occasion. The attitude of open-mindedness is the only fruitful one in our age of science.

1. *The Task of Philosophy.* In producing a lucid and coherent account and analysis of human knowledge and valuation, the aim is to make explicit the presuppositions or basic assumptions, to clarify the pivotal concepts and methods of cognition and valuation. The most successful way of doing this still seems to me the procedure of logical reconstruction. The question "What do we mean by the words and symbols we use?" should precede the questions of justification. The tools of modern logic should be employed wherever they are genuinely helpful. But

formalization and axiomatization is needed only for the more exact and exacting purposes. "Half-way stations" toward ideal language formulations are often quite sufficient for the solution of problems in the general theory of knowledge, moral philosophy—and even in the philosophy of science. While it would be most desirable and commendable if professional philosophers could contribute (on the side of conceptual revisions and innovations) to the progress of the sciences, it seems that only a very few philosophers nowadays have the scientific training to collaborate helpfully with the specialized scientists. The tasks of clarification and understanding are already extremely demanding and ambitious for philosophers in our time.

2. *Language, Meaning and the Demarcation of Science from Metaphysics.* Critical reflection in these regards have shown that philosophy traditionally has suffered from the burdens of conceptual confusion and of the (related) "disease" of demonstrationism. As already strikingly exemplified in Plato, the necessity of mathematical truths, the conclusiveness and exactitude of mathematical reasoning and proof have been perennially shaping the aspirations of philosophers. Thus we find that exaggerated conception of knowledge—as contrasted with mere opinion—and the conviction of the rationalists that genuine knowledge must either be self-evident to the "natural light" of human reason, or strictly deducible from self-evident premises. But ever since David Hume's sceptical arguments at least the empiricists have considered all factual knowledge claims as at best highly confirmed (by observational data), and as always in principle open to revision, if not refutation. Thus responsible scientists hold their theories as "true only until further notice", such notice being given when discordant evidence turns up. Pure logic and pure mathematics, however, rest on postulated premises—which need not be self-evident. I realize I will be considered quite an inveterate and "reactionary" logical empiricist. But I remain unconvinced by the clever arguments of Quine that are intended to show that there is no sharp line of distinction between the purely formal truths (e.g., of arithmetic) and the factual truths (e.g., of physics). I retain the distinction between the purely formal and the factual type of meaning. But I do not object if the formal type of meaning is regarded as the "null case", or extreme lower limit of factual significance. The tautologies, i.e., the logical truths, or statements whose form—once *definienda* have been replaced by their *definientia*—boils down to logical truths do not require observations for their validation; certainly not observations of the sort that are indispensable in the factual sciences (natural or social).

If purely formal and factual meanings are the two types of cognitive significance, then cognitive significance itself must—for the sake of clarity—be distinguished from pictorial, emotional and motivative significance of words or sentences. Only in regard to cognitively significant statements is it appropriate to ask whether they are "true or false". And while in common communication cognitive and non-cognitive significance are often combined or fused, it is of the utmost philosophical importance to avoid confusing emotive with cognitive significance. Many of the "guaranteed 100% unsolvable" puzzles of traditional metaphysics rest on exactly this type of confusion. For example, the metaphysical ideas of space, time, substance, causality, vital force (entelechy), soul, etc., are peculiar combinations of absolutely untestable notions with empirically testable concepts. Once the confusion is disentangled, the scientifically meaningful and fruitful core can be separated out.

The much debated and often revised testability criterion of factual meaningfulness seems to me useful and, even, indispensable. Unless some of the concepts appearing in our statements are connected, no matter how indirectly, with some data of immediate experience, those statements would at best have formal significance but they would be devoid of factual meaning. I think the enormous amount of debate and quibbling that concerned the meaning criterion has been largely a waste of time and energy. The logical empiricists (especially Carnap) had an extremely important point there.

According to the liberalized criterion much of traditional metaphysics and even of theology is perfectly meaningful. But, of course, empiricists should never forget to ask as to whether there are any good reasons for accepting the tenets of those speculative and/or intuitive (or purely dogmatic or kerygmatic) doctrines. In my opinion nearly all reasons traditionally given are no good reasons at all. I think that the beliefs in a personal God, or in the metaphysical Absolutes (space, time, substance, etc.), are motivated by wishful or pictorial-emotional thinking. And since I—against the current vogue of obscurantism—maintain that there is a fundamental difference between the subjective motives and the supporting objective reasons (i.e., justifying grounds) of beliefs, I reject as false (or as extremely unlikely) all those "transcendent" (but meaningful) assertions.

There are, however, fairly clear cases in which the meaning criterion has to be invoked. If a metaphysician or theologian makes his beliefs absolutely "proof against disproof", and thereby (usually unwittingly) renders his problems absolutely unsolvable, then it is proper to ask as to whether his syntax, semantics, or pragmatics is in good order, or as to whether he is the victim of a misuse of language—be it through simple equivocations; violations of formation rules; or lack of connections, ultimately by ostensive steps, with the data of direct experience. I think that despite its metaphysical-theological framework, Leibniz's arguments in the famous correspondence between him and Clarke regarding Newton's notions of absolute space and time are a classical anticipation of the pragmatist-positivist critique of the "perniciously" transcendent metaphysics. "A difference must make a difference in order to be a cognitive difference"—this is the way I keep paraphrasing what is common to the views of C. S. Peirce, William James and the Logical Empiricists. The difference between an assertion and its denial must in principle be open to at least partial and indirect observational test, otherwise there is no factual meaning present in the assertion.

3. *The Scope and Validity of Knowledge.* The liberalized meaning criterion allows for hypothetico-deductive tests (i.e., confirmations or disconfirmations), for inductive interpolations and extrapolations, for analogical conceptions and inferences. Hence I think that a critically realist position is justifiable. The epistemological puzzles about the "external world", "other minds", the past and future of the universe, the reliability of memory, the occurrence of unconscious mental processes, the existence of unobservable entities (subatomic particles; nuclear forces, etc.) can be resolved affirmatively. In these matters I feel I am closer to the outlook of Reichenbach and Popper (their differences are irrelevant in this connection) than to Carnap's position. Nevertheless, Carnap's distinction of "external" and "internal" questions, i.e., questions regarding the categorial frame and questions within the frame, is well conceived.

My own distinction between two types of justification ("vindication" and "validation") is an exact counterpart of Carnap's distinction. Since in the justification of knowledge-claims (and for that matter also of moral or aesthetic evaluations) we must obviously avoid both the begging of questions and infinite regresses, validation must terminate with premises (basic assumptions, presuppositions) which in the given context are not susceptible to further validation. But these "ultimate" presuppositions of validation are neither arbitrary conventions, *nor* unquestionable a priori truths. They are susceptible to a different type of justification, or "vindication" as I call it. The vindicative argument can show that the adoption of the validating premises will achieve the ends we pursue in the given context. Or, as in the clearly weaker case of the justification of inductive inference or of the hypothetico-deductive procedure, it can at least show that if any method or procedure yields the desired results (correct explanations, predictions, retrodictions, etc.), the usual application of the scientific method will do the same. This idea can be made more plausible by considering observation and experimentation as a sampling procedure, i.e., as the attempt to obtain representative samples of the regularities (deterministic or statistical) of the—possibly limitless—universe. There can, of course, be no guarantee that a given sample is representative, and without special assumptions of background knowledge, there cannot even be any estimates of the probability of the "fairness" of the sample. Nevertheless it is clearly *rational* to assume—until further notice!—that the given sample *is* representative. For to assume that it is not representative would open the flood gates to limitless possibilities. This would amount to a complete capitulation to scepticism or cognitive pessimism. David Hume has shown once and for all that neither rational nor empirical grounds (nor any combination of the two) can justify the ultimate presupposition of inductive generalization. Hence he maintained a purely psychological view of habits of expectation (later labeled by Santayana as the doctrine of "animal faith"; even B. Russell at one stage of his philosophical development spoke of "physiological induction"). Karl Popper, deeply impressed with Hume's arguments, abandoned all efforts toward a justification of induction; he even denied the importance, if not the very occurrence, of induction in the growth of knowledge. But, as perhaps the first to criticize this view of Popper's, I asked the crucial question why we should put our trust in (or "place our bets on") laws, hypotheses and theories which, despite severe tests, have thus far not been refuted. To this question Popper has never given a satisfactory answer. He used to (and perhaps still does) call such theories that have successfully survived searching criticism "well corroborated". But since Popper himself refuses to identify corroboration with confirmation, he does not provide any reason whatever for the generally accepted practice of using a well corroborated theory as a guide for further research or, in its practical application, for our expectations and actions. Nevertheless there is an important lesson to be learned from Popper's views: Practically all our knowledge-claims are based on background theories. Only within the frame of assumptions about space and time; about the place of experience in the world of nature; about the mechanisms of perception and observations; etc., etc., can we examine (test) all knowledge-claims, be they fully specific descriptions, or very general hypotheses. Science is (contrary to classical positivist dogma) not a compendious and economical summary of experience, but an attempt at understanding (explaining) the facts of nature by means of laws, hypotheses and theories.

In the light of this conception of scientific knowledge (which I wholeheartedly accept) my view of the justification of induction can be more fully and adequately formulated. The experimental samplings of "nature" are to be considered as confirming or disconfirming pieces of evidence for *theories;* and it is the extrapolation of the (e.g., spatio-temporal) scope of those theories which is genuinely inductive. Thus while no guarantees can be given for even the "probability" let alone certainty of theories, the only reasonable ("rational" in one of the several senses of this slippery term) procedure is to stick, until further notice, to those theories which have "proved their mettle" under severe scrutiny, and for which impressive positive evidence is accumulating.

4. *Mind and its Place in Nature.* As I mentioned before, beside the issues of induction and of scientific explanation, the mind-body problems have held my attention ever since my adolescence. I am now inclined to proceed according to the "divide and conquer" maxim. It seems helpful to distinguish at least three major issues in the cluster of mind-matter problems: (1) sentience, (2) sapience, (3) selfhood. While it is not advisable to disregard the interrelations of these three features of mind, I think the sentience aspect has engendered more profound bafflements than the other two. In any case I have been primarily concerned with this first problem. I have tried to steer clear of the reductive fallacies of materialism and radical behaviorism; but I have equally shunned the seductive fallacies of the mental-substance (let alone of an indestructible soul) doctrines. It is obvious that in regard to this central problem of modern philosophy we still have to combat the tendencies of simple-minded (or tough-minded) as well as muddle-headed (or tender-minded) thinking. The occurrence of immediate experience, as well as the physical structure of the universe and of the human organism and its processes have to be assigned their proper places in a scientifically as well as philosophically tenable account of our world. Fortunately the battle against "crass" materialism is now as obsolete and unnecessary as is the battle against (subjective, or objective) idealism. What is wanted is clearly a view in which conscious experience is understood as the subjective aspect of certain processes in the central nervous system, perhaps primarily in the cerebral cortex. Of course this formulation is metaphorical and hence needs to be replaced by the straightforward result of a logical analysis. Just this, however, is a difficult and highly controversial task.

First of all nothing significant can be achieved without close attention to the best established results of the sciences, in this case of psycho-neurophysiology. If we dismiss on scientific grounds animistic, vitalistic and dualistic-interaction views, we seem to be left with a choice between doctrines of emergent evolution and psychophysiological parallelism or of a materialistically slanted epiphenomenalism. Mind as a product of emergent evolution is still a favorite among some philosophically untutored biologists. Although I think this view could be made (in fact has been made) philosophically more sophisticated and respectable, I am inclined to repudiate it in favor of a more plausible theory. Starting with parallelism, i.e., with a view of a one-one, or many-one correspondence of the physical to the mental, a more incisive reflection upon the meaning of the concepts on each side of the relation leads to a gratifyingly simple, though on first sight, unconvincing solution of the puzzle of the relation between sentience (immediate data and qualities of consciousness) and brain processes. This is the identity theory, currently hotly debated. In an early attempt I conceived of this theory along the lines of a simple translation of mental into physical terms. But since the correspondence (one-one; or many-one) is clearly a matter of empirical investigation rather than of logical synonymy or equivalence, a more adequate solution seems to be suggested by a twofold approach or twofold knowledge theory. We have knowledge of the phenomenally given (the "raw feels" of sensation, desire, emotion, mood, intention, etc.) by direct acquaintance; whereas our knowledge of physical objects (including our own brain) and the processes in which they are involved (or, if you will, of which they consist) is indirect; it is what B. Russell called "knowledge by description". Such knowledge is "structural" in the sense that it concerns the logico-mathematical network of relationships only; and that the qualitative content (as in the case of our knowledge of other persons' mental states) has to be conceived and inferred by analogy to our own immediate experience. Within the physical (scientific) conception of the world the qualities of direct experience are indeed "homeless", unless they are "attached" or "introjected" by analogical reasoning. I keep an open mind (and continue to work) on the best formulation of the identity theory. In a long essay of 1958 I argued for a theory of co-designation; i.e., the view that mentalistic (phenomenal) terms designate the same events or processes that are also designated by the terms of the physicalistic (brain-physiological) language. Currently I prefer to put it as a matter of two "perspectives" (of course this is still metaphorical) namely the egocentric and the intersubjective account of the world. The files are not closed on this intricate problem. Both the approaches of science and those of logical analysis are still far from finished. There is the problem of the complete reducibility of biology (via biophysics, biochemistry, and molecular biology) to basic physics. Much as I am impressed with the progress in this direction, there are on the other side some scruples about the adequacy of the neo-Darwinistic and genetic explanations of evolution. Furthermore, as an empiricist I even have to (at least) go through the motions of an open mind in regard to parapsychological phenomena (ESP). While these strange "facts" (if they are not products of deception, illusion, delusion, etc.) need not necessarily militate against the basic physicalistic program of science, they might yet force upon us incisive revisions of our total theoretical outlook on mind and nature.

I confess that my outlook is still somewhat "Victorian" in that I favor the view that mental processes are part of nature. But I admit, nay insist, that the world conception of modern physical science, impressive as it is, can hardly be final. As to whether there is a "rockbottom" of nature, and if so, as to whether it conforms to strictly deterministic laws (as conceived in classical physics from Newton to and including Einstein) or as to whether there is an ineluctable indeterminancy (à la Heisenberg, Bohr, Born, von Neumann, et al.) must—in principle—remain undecidable. Still, the experimental evidence of quantum physics makes it rather plausible that the physical theories of the future will have to countenance an element of absolute chance. Perhaps (to use Einstein's famous phrase, but contradicting him) God does play dice with nature!

There is, however, no solace to be derived from the micro-indeterminism for the traditional problem of free will. Absolute chance cannot be the basis of free choice or action. As Hume, Mill, Sidgwick, Schlick, and Hobart already very clearly realized, the sort of moral responsibility that presupposes free choice, is not only compatible with determinism. It would be outright impossible if it were not for a fairly large measure of lawful determination of human volition and action. Only if we are the doers of our deeds, i.e., only if our deliberations, intentions, decisions, etc. are causal consequences of our characters and personalities (and are not forced upon us by external or internal compulsion), can we be justly considered praiseworthy or blameworthy for whatever we will or do.

A Few Remarks on Ethics, Religion, and the Problems of Human Affairs.

Although I feel strongly about all these matters of "Practical Philosophy," I have a little to add to what many other recent thinkers (for example, M. Schlick and B. Russell) have said much better than I could possibly say. I repudiate the "naturalistic fallacy," i.e., the attempt to derive moral value judgments from facts about human-nature-in-the-social-context alone. All the strenuous and tortuous sophistry that has been applied to the contrary has left me unconvinced. Without basic commitments even the most thorough and complete knowledge of matters of fact does not and can not yield moral imperatives. The Hippocratic oath that young medicos have to swear is a good illustration of the point at issue. Without firm resolve to help rather than to harm his patients the doctor could use his medical, psychological (and even commonsense socio-psychological) knowledge quite "diabolically"—i.e., to the detriment of those whom he treats. Quite generally, what we *ought* (or ought not) to do cannot be inferred from what *is* the case (or from a knowledge of what happens under what conditions) alone. To be sure, factual information concerning the likely consequences of various courses of action is indispensable, and always of the greatest importance. But without commitments to basic aims or values (and/or to basic rules regarding "right" and "wrong") we could never justify our morally relevant decisions or actions. "Saints" as well as "Scoundrels" can make use of factual information. The difference between them is not intelligence, but the presence or absence of good will.

For anyone with even a minimum of training in logical analysis it is a ludicrous and pathetic spectacle presented by countless philosophers who invariably beg the question by either presupposing tacitly some moral valuation, or by (what really amounts to the same) using persuasive definitions of human nature. Thus, if it is argued that the "real nature" of being human involves the capacity for being fair, just, helpful, kind, and self-perfecting, then this simply conceals the exhortatory character of this persuasive definition. It seems to me intellectually more honest to state quite explicitly the nature of our moral-social commitments.

I, too, believe (with Aristotle) that man is a "rational animal". But I feel that on the whole mankind has made deplorably little use of the capacity for thinking and acting rationally. As Strindberg put it so poignantly in *Dream Play:* "It is a pity for mankind". We are now well on the way to ruining the planet we inhabit, if not to exterminating ourselves by overcrowding, or by environmental pollution, or by a nuclear holocaust. Quite generally our social behavior is barbarous, in many respects closer to that of ferocious beasts than to the ideal that philosophers and the founders of the great religions (Buddhism, Judaism, Christianity, etc.) delineated. Of course, in our age of science, orthodox or dogmatic religions are no longer intellectually acceptable. If I am to label my own outlook it is that of a scientifically oriented humanism. This is best summarized in Bertrand Russell's sentence: "The good life is one inspired by love and guided by knowledge". As to whether mankind can grow up toward genuine humane-ness, as to whether we can stop being crude and cruel blunderers in the art of living together (individually, racially, nationally, and internationally) seems questionable now. As a humanist I do not wish to deprive persons of their religious faith if it is an indispensable support for them and if it does help them to love their fellow human beings. But I entertain only a cautious hope that a truly enlightened mankind will be able to achieve a permanent peace and a harmonious way of life.

In regard to the question concerning the "meaning of life", I can do no better than to quote Wittgenstein (*Tractatus* 6.521): "The solution of the problem of life is something one becomes aware of when the problem vanishes". A life that is conducted in accordance with the ideals of justice, kindness, brotherhood, freedom, love and self-perfection is the only one (for normal human beings) that promises genuine satisfaction, perhaps even a measure of joy and happiness. There is abundant advice (by wise psychologists, economists, sociologists, etc.) as to how to improve *la condition humaine*. While I have given a good deal of thought to these matters, I do not know of a cure-all for the many evils that beset us.

A Concluding Remark

I may not be a "philosopher" in the commendatory sense of that word. It would be arrogant and largely unjustifiable for me to designate myself as a wise man. Even after many years of honest searchings, I can only claim to being a lover of wisdom—which is, after all, the original, etymologically genuine meaning of "philosopher." I have also sufficient insight into the sources and factors of my intellectual development to realize that my views are largely the outcome of my deep involvement with the scientific outlook. Other philosophers owe their point of view to very different sources of inspiration. Aware of all this I must admit the present essay is indeed no more than a *confessio fidei*. Hence I am far from confident that I could offer a "message" that would be acceptable to any but kindred spirits.

Philosophy After Fifty Years

Charles Hartshorne

It is really more than fifty years that I have been doing philosophy. In 1918, as an orderly in a military hospital, I thought out the basis of the philosophical doctrine I still hold. At that time I had read a few philosophical writings and had heard one lecture in a class formally devoted to philosophy. The writings were: Emerson's essays (on the edges of philosophy here and there), Coleridge's *Aids to Reflection,* Royce's *Problem of Christianity,* James's *Varieties of Religious Experience,* Augustine's *Confessions.* None of these were particularly in my mind as I reached three basic convictions.

I.   Experience is essentially emotional and social. Sensation is the objective side of emotional experience; it is feeling, but feeling that is one's own only derivatively. Primarily it is feeling to which we respond, rather than feeling by which we respond. (I did not then put it in these words.) Ten years later Whitehead's "feeling of feeling" neatly expressed the point. There is a given emotional unity in all experience, but there is a duality in this unity. It is social or participatory, not merely egoistic; public as well as private. In 1925 the study of Peirce acquainted me with rather similar ideas. He identifies sensation and feeling as forms of Firstness; and his Secondness and Thirdness, as well as his doctrines of agapism and synechism, affirm the social unity in the duality or plurality.

II.   Even the totality of human and animal wills is plurality in unity, a unity which in principle is directly experienced. Human purposes are given as overlapping in many ways and degrees. Here Royce's discussion of "community" was probably an influence. Motivation is not reducible to mere self-interest and there is no wholly distinct self. Here, too, monistic and pluralistic extremes are both wrong. There is a many in one. The inclusive oneness I interpreted as deity.

III. Because of (I) there is no need to limit the divine unity to living things, leaving the nonliving world outside, as H. G. Wells (in *Mr. Britling* and *The Bishop*) at that time proposed to do. A dualism of mind or will as opposed to mere insentient matter contradicts the very structure of experience as throughout participation in sentience or feeling other than one's own.

It is clear that, with these positions taken, my philosophical task had from the outset considerable focus. Any hard dualism or materialism was only a curiosity. But so was any mere spiritualistic monism, such as Bradley's. *Plurality* in unity seemed as truly given as plurality *in unity*. So Bradley's challenge, when I came to it, was for me merely technical: where did his critique of relations beg the question or commit a logical fallacy? But equally R.B. Perry's or Russell's unmitigated pluralism, like Hume's, must conceal a blunder somewhere. I thought I could see where the fallacies were.

Many questions remained, however. One was, What are the primary subjects of the objective feelings, those only secondarily or by participation one's own? I had no idea of the answer in 1918. Troland's form of panpsychism, later Peirce's and Whitehead's, and the monadology of Leibniz, helped me to an answer. The subjects are chiefly microentities, especially (judging from current science) cells or living subhuman individuals in one's own body, but involving, in less distinct fashion, the very atoms or molecules of which the cells are composed, and also more or less indirectly the active individuals composing matter in the environment. At this point the divergence from the Berkeleyan subjectivism (which I used to find it amusing to defend) became definite. We do not experience mere ideas, even divine ideas, but rather subjects having ideas—or at least feelings—of their own, subjects on countless levels other than either the divine or the human. What we feel in sensation is how these other subjects feel. Whitehead is by far the most explicit on this point of all the philosophers I have read. But Peirce did write, "consciousness is a sort of public spirit among the brain cells". (I should say, nerve cells in general, with probably the peripheral sense organs—rods and cones, say—included.)

Another question concerns the temporal relations of subjects. Is the "I" in "I feel" something strictly identical throughout the life of a human animal, something already there before the infant can possibly say or understand "I"? Or is the actual subject doing or suffering the feeling something that comes into being with the feeling, to be superseded by a new—though closely related—subject with new feelings the next moment? On this point I am indeed Whitehead's disciple (though James had already taken the position). *The Concept of Nature,* and Northrop's enthusiasm for this book appealed to me (about 1922), and later *Religion in the Making* and the metaphysical works, plus the discovery that the Buddhists had thought in this way for two thousand years, reinforced the conviction. I came to think that the West, until Hume, James, and Whitehead, had failed to think through the relativity of self-identity, had made it into a false absolute. Strawson and Shoemaker exhibit this incomplete analysis once more. They perhaps succeed in refuting certain alternatives to the traditional substance view, but not all alternatives.

A third question concerns the interpretation of the cosmic unity of life and experience as deity. By the principle just set forth, a divine subject should be momentary, destined to be superseded by other divine subjects. (I shall not here discuss the puzzling question how this is to be related to relativity physics.) Rather oddly it was Hocking, before I knew anything of Whitehead, who prepared me to accept this implication. For he led me to break finally with the medieval (in a later version Roycean) view of the divine experience as a *totum simul* spanning all time once for all, leaving no future really open for God. I don't recall ever quite accepting this view; but it was a discussion with Hocking, who on this point sided with James against Royce, that brought my thinking to an explicit conviction. A merely immutable deity I have long regarded as an empty abstraction, just as Fechner and Pfleiderer (as I eventually learned) had long ago said it was. On this issue I am an Hegelian: the merely infinite, or merely absolute, could not be a concrete reality. God must be finite and infinite, relative and absolute, mutable and immutable. In spite of Hegel there need be no contradiction in this, since there is a distinction of respects. The absolute side is an abstraction. There is no law of logic forbidding a thing to be immutable, say, in some abstract aspect, but mutable in its concrete fullness.

Still another basic question concerns the causal structure of the cosmic process. Do the initial conditions of a process and the causal laws strictly and completely specify the process (classical causality), or do the conditions and laws specify the process only incompletely or statistically, rather than absolutely (neoclassical causality)? I was early convinced by William James and Hocking that classical causality cannot apply to human actions. Subsequently, Peirce, Whitehead, Heisenberg, and still others led me to the clear conviction that the classical principle, rather than merely falling short of universal validity, is universally invalid, applying strictly to nothing whatever. It is an artificial simplification or exaggeration, a typical case of absolutizing an essentially relative principle. Always the initial conditions and causal laws restrict the possible outcome, but they never specify it with absolute precision. Not because of our ignorance. Saying that it is because of ignorance that we must formulate the laws statistically is itself but an expression of ignorance. No one knows that nature is classical in its causal structure. All attempts to prove it have failed, from Spinoza down. Peirce showed, long before quantum mechanics, that (as Maxwell had hinted) a classically causal world is, as such, an unknowable world. Peirce showed more than this. Before Bergson and Whitehead, he argued cogently that a satisfactory world view is possible only if we admit creativity (his word was "spontaneity", but he meant about what Bergson and Whitehead have meant by the other word) as universal principle, inherent in concrete reality as such. Causality is then the way in which any given act of creativity (and this is the same as any given unit of concrete reality or becoming) is influenced or made possible, but yet not fully determined, by antecedent acts.

What limits freedom is simply earlier cases of freedom—otherwise nothing whatever. "Limit" does not mean absolutely determine. To ask "Why may not the antecedent cases completely determine the given case?" is to show that one has not grasped the meaning and pervasiveness of creativity or spontaneity. To create is to determine the otherwise undetermined, particularize the otherwise and antecedently unparticularized, and thus add to the richness of reality. As Peirce saw, particularity is in principle arbitrary. It cannot follow either from any universal necessity or from antecedent particularity. Each new particular is a new dose of arbitrariness, of causally transcendent freedom. Laws are universals, and they cannot, even in combination with antecedent particulars, generate or fully specify subsequent particulars. Peirce and Whitehead between them have, to my satisfaction, proved this so far as anything philosophical can be proved.

Heisenberg's famous paper of 1927 was shown to me by a young physicist friend almost as soon as it was published. I showed it to R. B. Perry, who didn't seem to like it. Since I had already bade farewell to the classical causal concept, I saw in it the dawning of a new day in science. During the forty-three years since then numbers of philosophers have persisted in reacting defensively to the new principle. They have explained it away, hoped it would be reversed by later experiments and theories, and argued that it left the philosophical question unchanged. In a sense it did, but what was the philosophical question? For a Peircean or Bergsonian, for Whitehead or Dewey, the question was, what is the logic of the causal concept? There are two views. On either view, causality is real possibility: the initial conditions and laws limiting what can happen in a particular situation. Any sane philosophy grants so much. It remains, however, to decide whether what can happen has all the specificity of what then does happen, or whether instead antecedent causal or "real" possibility is less specific or particular than the actual subsequent event. There is paradox in the first view. For if what can happen is the same in character as what does happen, then the distinction between possibility and actuality seems to be nothing definite at all. Further, if nothing different from what can happen could happen, then real or causal possibility coincides with causal necessity. Thus modal distinctions collapse. This alone should make us suspicious. There are many other conceptual reasons for this suspicion. I am entirely persuaded that unqualified determinism is a mishandling of concepts.

The philosophic issue in its purity is indeed not changed by quantum mechanics, but only because the philosophically perspicuous position was nonclassical all along. Yet something has been changed, and significantly so. This is the cultural position of philosophy relative to science. In the days of Hume and Kant, scientists and philosophers alike thought in classical terms, and no one had the imagination to anticipate a probabilistic science. To take science seriously was to take classical determinism seriously. True, Descartes was an indeterminist regarding the human will, and so were Locke and Crusius. But their view of science had no integral relation to this doctrine. Thus philosophers faced the dilemma: either a blind dualism of causal concepts, or a universal determinism. This situation is gone forever. We now know that science can be done in nonclassical ways. From now on determinists must assume full philosophical responsibility for their view, without appeal to the prestige of science. And the philosophical case for determinism has been as thoroughly explored as any topic, from the Stoics and Spinoza to Kant, Schopenhauer, De Broglie, and many others. I say that the deterministic project has failed. Qualified determinism, yes indeed; every animal must live as though the initial conditions limited future possibilities. But no animal must or even can show by its actions that it takes the future as absolutely determined. Life is devoid of any such absolute, whether absolute order or absolute disorder.

There is one ambiguity in the present scientific situation. Quantum uncertainty seems negligible on the macroscopic level of animal organisms, where the statistical probabilities may be so high as to amount to virtual certainties. Heisenberg's calculations allow a human being, according to most competent judges, virtually no leeway, given the initial conditions. But here again a philosophical issue is involved. As some physicists have argued, formulae designed to explain systems in which no quality of experience or thought corresponds to a system as a whole may not apply, without qualification or "supplementation" (Heisenberg's word in this connection) for a system which has a unity of feeling, thought, and purpose. As Wigner puts it, the presence of consciousness must make a difference, and since quantum mechanics says nothing as to what difference it makes, the laws it proposes cannot be accurate for the whole of nature. A philosopher is no more obligated to accept the absolute adequacy of quantum mechanics than Kant was obligated, though he seems to have thought he was, to accept that of Newtonian mechanics. But the one way in which quantum mechanics will not be superseded is by a reinstatement of classical physics. As a chemist friend said to me once, "whatever we do we're not going back to those fleshpots."

Becoming is creation. It is not the mere exhibition of something whose specificity has been already created. This has immensely important theological applications. For one thing, it disposes of the classical form of the argument from evil. For this argument takes divine creativity to be the only efficacious creativity, capable of determining once for all every particular. But the creationist view denies that this is so much as conceivable. God could not determine all particulars; for particulars must be in some degree self-determining. Why then is there evil? This question should be paired with the really more fundamental question, why is there good? For if each particular entity is selfdetermining, how can there be harmony between the entities? I hold that the best answer is in terms of eminent Creativity, universally influencing but in no case determining all non-eminent creative acts. In this way limits are set to discord, to frustration of creatures by creatures. But within the limits it is a matter of chance and not of providence just what goods and evils ensue. That there is supreme creativity explains how there can be good; that there are lesser but genuine forms of creativity explains how there can be evil.

Consider a floating object in a narrow river. Because the river is narrow, we know much about where the object will be so long as it continues to float. But the wider the river the less the location of the banks tells us about the future location of the object. To eliminate all uncertainty by making the width of the river infinitesimal is to make it impossible for any significant object to float in it. This is the dilemma confronting a world creator. If there are to be significant happenings, there must be appreciable scope for creaturely selfdetermination. But this means appreciable scope for unfortunate conflicts as well as for fortunate harmonies. Make the risks trivial and you make the opportunities trivial. I really believe that the dilemma is rigorous. A harmless but rich and vital scheme of things, a pure utopia, is a contradiction, or else mere verbiage.

Unfortunately the problem of evil is not the only, or for me the most puzzling, difficulty in the theistic view. I remain a theist, but I do not claim to have lucid solutions for all its problems.

I have now sketched my position, as it has been for much of the fifty-year period in question. Now I ask myself, what have the cultural changes during that time taught me as to the significance of such a philosophy? Is it still relevant? What will the philosophical future do to its fortunes?

The cultural changes are considerable. Fundamentalist Protestant and Jewish religions seem much less influential, and Roman Catholic fundamentalism much less dominant. We have the search for purified religion, and the search for some non-religious yet if possible adequate world-view. More or less definitely Marxist conceptions have become more widespread. In technical American philosophy the New Realism is forgotten and Critical Realism as such is scarcely to be found, unless Wilfrid Sellars in his ingenious, complicated way is to be considered as in this tradition. Pragmatism is no doubt influential, but usually merged with other trends. The idealism of Royce, Bradley, or Hegel has but a few scattered defenders. The "linguistic turn" is much in evidence, and so is the influence of symbolic logic. Specialization is a notable feature. A philosopher today is primarily an aesthetician, or a meta-ethicist, or a logician, or a socio-political philosopher, or a philosopher of science, or an historian of philosophy, or perhaps a philosopher of religion. My own specialty is easier stated negatively: I am not a logician, though I try to make some use of modern logic; I am not a meta-ethicist, though a few basic ethical principles are important for my whole philosophy. I am not a philosopher of science in the sense of having competence in the technicalities of mathematics, physics, genetics, or evolutionary theory, though I think a good deal about the philosophical bearings of natural science and psychology. Aesthetics and metaphysics, including the global history of the latter, and one branch of ethology (the study of animal behavior) are my specialties, though I have published little on the first.

The decline of fundamentalist religion in some ways favors the acceptance of the philosophical values I treasure, in some ways perhaps disfavors it. For example, consider the belief in "personal immortality". (I use quotes because there are two quite different possible meanings for the phrase.) The "neoclassical metaphysics", as I call my view, gives no support to the most usual form of this belief. Until recently this meant a serious conflict with religious sentiment. But how serious is the conflict now? Neither Tillich nor Niebuhr is clearly committed to the conventional idea of immortality. Do most church members really live to get themselves (or others) into heaven or avoid getting into hell?

All readers of Whitehead know that there is another view of immortality which seems, for some at least, able to do the real work of the conventional view. True, one can no longer try to scare would-be villains into tolerable behavior by threats of everlasting torment. But how well did this method ever really work? Is it not a deplorably ignoble method of trying to influence people for good?

I can see a sentimental appeal in the idea that we shall meet our friends again in the hereafter, but I think it is more wholesome to think that what we wish to do for our friends must be done in this life. As Frost has it, "Earth's the right place for love, I don't know where it's likely to go better." This is at any rate where I stand on that issue. Can we have a humane culture on that basis? If not, can we have a humane culture?

There is the objection that many have no fair chance in this life and should have another and better opportunity elsewhere. But on the creationist view, there will, in any sphere, be chance and good and bad luck. Moreover, since self-identity, as I shall argue presently, is secondary, and the basic motive is precisely not one's own long-run advantage, the demand for justice, to each according to his deserts, is not an ultimate axiom, valid cosmically or metaphysically.

That many persons have needless luxury while many others have deeply impoverished lives is tragic. The remedy, however, is not heaven, but better social arrangements and better conduct on all our parts. "Voluntary austerity" needs to be adopted as an old yet new virtue. In this I agree with Denis Goulet. It is foolish and almost wicked to indulge in dreams of an economy of abundance for the entire world. No such thing is in sight as a sober political prospect. To will luxury for all is, practically, to will misery for hundreds of millions, or even billions. There are large pockets of fantastic abundance and large pockets of terrible deprivation. The former are more obvious in this country, the latter in Asia and South America. But both are almost everywhere. The old rich-poor contrast is not going to disappear by everyone's becoming rich. This is wishful thinking. The best we can hope for in the foreseeable future is that the class of neither rich nor poor will grow relatively to the other two classes (especially the second) and that the renunciation of riches will become more voluntary. Earth's resources are finite, and man's population expansion, which shows no sign of ceasing in the near future, guarantees that the world economy will not be one of abundance. Man will press against his resources in any future we can reasonably predict, and the question of distribution will remain critical. The justice we need is on earth, not in heaven. The gospel suspicion of riches is not irrelevant, but more relevant than ever. Here the clergy may have much to repent about. (Still more their rich parishioners.) Have they dared to preach on this point? Have the hippies had some insight into this?

Because self-determination and hence chance is pervasive, any justice anywhere will be rough, not exact. But the degree of injustice in the historic treatment of blacks, for instance, is indefensible. The point is not that the universe owes each of us this or that, but that the rational aim for each of us can only be the general good and that it is not for the general good that individuals should be grossly disadvantaged by irrelevant criteria such as color. Slavery and its lingering fragments and consequences are basic causes of present unrest and disillusionment. We have sown the wind and need not be surprised by the whirlwind. It is, however, a tragic truth of history that such whirlwinds often injure the very persons whose grievances are their causes.

I mentioned a non-conventional view of personal immortality. This is the Bergsonian-Whiteheadian doctrine of the cumulative nature of becoming, or "the immortality of the past". It is our earthly lives that are imperishable, our actual experiences. They persist as background content, memories, perceptions, through all future experience. True, these memories and perceptions are mostly, in ordinary cases, very faint. But according to theistic philosophy there is also the extraordinary or "eminent" case, divine perception and memory. Thanks to it, the full vividness of our experiences can "live forevermore". Is this personal immortality? If one's actual concrete experiences are not personal, I do not know what would be. They represent all that one actually is. Beyond our actual experiences our personalities are simply potentialities for experience.

Those who want to "wake up" in heaven are not asking for the preservation of their earthly actuality; rather they ask for the actualization of additional possibilities. I hold with Whitehead that actual occurrences, experiences, are the concrete entities and that all actual value is in these. If immortality is preservation of the already created, Whitehead's view furnishes it. If it is opportunity for further creation of ourselves by ourselves, the view does not furnish it. But we should know what we are asking, whether preservation or additional creation. Before Whitehead, what great philosopher has been clear about this distinction? Perhaps Fechner was. The future of religion will depend in no small part upon whether people can realize that preservation of what we create in ourselves and others suffices to give life a lasting meaning, and that to ask also for endless further self-creation is not easily distinguishable from asking that we should be God, who indeed is endlessly self-creative.

The feeling that death is wrong, in principle an evil, or the evil, rests on several confusions. (1) There is the confusion between the concrete and the abstract. Preservation of an animal organism means not that something concrete and actual remains in being; for what the animal actually is now it will in any case not be the next moment. Rather, something of what it potentially is now it will actually be the next moment, and what it actually is now will belong to the reality of the past, and only so far as remembered or perceived will it belong to the reality of the new present. What is preserved in animal endurance is something abstract, the identical form or pattern of the animal. But its present experiences will belong to the past. The basic preservation of the actual is not through this abstract continuance. The animal instinctively strives to maintain itself; however, this self, an abstraction, is but a link in the more abstract continuance of the species, and the still more abstract continuance of life in general on earth. Animals sometimes instinctively risk death to preserve their young. Self-preservation is not an absolute in nature.

(2) There is the confusion between the failure of one's own consciousness to continue in new experiences and the failure of consciousness in general to continue. This latter failure would indeed be monstrous; nay more, it is, I hold veritably inconceivable, as some say their own failure to continue is inconceivable to them.

(3) There is, for those of us who are theists, the confusion between ordinary and divine experience. It is not my death, but God's that would make my life a mere absurdity. (But the idea is itself an absurdity.) For all of life is, wittingly or not, an offering to the divine life. Death, and

even more than death, the way each of our experiences vanishes into the (humanly speaking) largely forgotten past should convince us that we are not the final reapers of the harvests we sow.

In my opinion, held now for 52 years without encountering a shadow of reason to alter it, self-interest, i.e., interest in one's own future adventures, fortunes, misfortunes, and death, is in no sense whatever *the* rational motive for action. It is a rational motive in exactly the same sense as interest in the future of another person is rational. It is merely stupid to find only one's own future appealing or interesting. The present actual self enjoys aiming at future consequences, whether upon one's own future life or another's, and this present enjoyment in aiming at future consequences needs no guarantee that the same animal individuality will always benefit by what it now does. One's future selves are interesting, so are the future selves of others; and not to be interested in the interesting is the essence of ignorance or irrationality. Self-identity of the single empirical individual through change is not *the* key to motivation. Every Buddhist has known this for two thousand years. Whitehead knew it. How many in the West have not known it? As Whitehead said, one weakness in both Buddhism and Christianity is the way each has protected itself from the other. Millions of Christians have mouthed the words, "love they neighbor as thyself," and yet have more or less definitely accepted a metaphysics which implied: "I love myself because I am myself; I am not the other person, hence I cannot love him as myself." This is a scandal in nearly all western philosophy of religion.

There is still another confusion in the feeling that death is wrong. Death coming too early, before one has actualized one's essential potentialities, is of course an evil. I do not see such deaths as providential but as unlucky tragedies. Human life has a basic pattern: infancy, childhood, adolescence, the prime of life, old age. Each brings basic novelties that furnish refreshing contrast to previous experience. Each in fortunate cases lasts long enough so that the variations on the theme of the stage in question are not tediously numerous, yet numerous enough to bring out the value of the themes. I seriously propose the aesthetic analogy here. A theme is worth a finite, not an infinite number of variations. A human individuality is a theme, a subtly complex one, to be sure, but still a theme. It can stand many variations. But the conventional idea of immortality implies infinite variations. I deeply disbelieve that my individuality could stand an infinity of diverse expressions, except so far as it is God, rather than myself, who enjoys the variations. God will, I take it, recombine his memory of me with an infinity of other objects of his experience. But this amounts to saying that the only theme worthy of infinite variations is deity. I go on record here and now as not claiming for myself any such infinite inexhaustibility.

There is then nothing evil about death simply as such. It is only a boundary, establishing the definiteness, the distinctiveness, of each non-divine theme. That in all these centuries of philosophizing the points made in the previous paragraph have rarely been expressed seems strange. No wonder people are confused. They do not even have a decent theory of death. The other animals need no such theory, for they do not know that they die. But man does need it, for he does know.

Giving up dreams of heaven and nightmares of hell should make it easier to focus on our actual problems of helping one another to live nobly on earth.

Contemporary youth is exacting in requiring that views be "relevant". I should like to mention one way in which the doctrine of creationism is relevant. The deterministic bias, whether in the theological or secular form, easily leads to the idea that life could be completely non-tragic, harmless but beautiful, devoid of conflict but full of vitality. Perhaps the First Cause could arrange such an ideal scheme of things, or human ingenuity and determination could do it. The initial conditions once perfected, everything would be ideal and according to everyone's desire. The philosophy of creativity banishes these dreams. All the utopians unwittingly imagine an absence of creativity. Self-determined beings only by good luck fulfill each other's purposes entirely. I decide X, you decide Y, what ensues is X and Y, and this neither of us decided. Introduce deity, eminent decision, and still you and I must be in some degree self-decided, so that there will be an XY which not even God has decided or intended. Nor was it causally predetermined. It just happens. The familiar practice of scornfully deriding chance as having nothing to do with freedom misses this point as if by magic. Chance intersections of self-determining purposes are inherent in the very idea of a plurality of genuinely active individuals, if "chance" means, not intended by anyone, and not the only causally possible occurrence, given the initial conditions. Accidents will happen in any scheme of things, and some of them will be unpleasant.

The impossibility of utopia does not mean that all reform is foolish. The real aim of reform is not to bring us closer to heaven but, under the given conditions, to optimize the ratio of risks and opportunities. With the changes inherent in science and technology, customs and institutions lose their previous fitness, so that without reform not only do we not move closer to heaven but we do move closer to hell. Obviously pollution of our environment is a worsening of life; we will be lucky to slow down the deterioration. Heaven is not the end of this road.

The early modern view of science as chiefly increase in man's power for good tended to make far too light of the truth that man's power for evil is similarly increased. All freedom is dangerous; science magnifies the consequences of man's freedom, and in some ways the freedom itself. On either count it magnifies the risks, already great, in the human mode of animal existence. It should have been taken for granted all along that immense care would be needed to keep the new risks from outweighing the new opportunities. Purely non-tragic views of life are woefully inadequate. Deterministic philosophies are partly responsible for such views. Theological determinism first, secular determinism afterwards, both are bad and their consequences are still with us. I have known kind persons who thought that the poor were so only because they deserved to be; for, after all, God, who arranges everything, is just. There are secular versions of the same sort of cruelty. And all utopians indulge in it. They imply that there is or could be a right scheme of things: if it exists, misfits deserve little sympathy; if not, it should be brought into existence and all who stand in the way are to be brushed aside. But social arrangements do not exist to eliminate all risks; they exist to mitigate the possible unlucky consequences of freedom and favor the lucky ones. They do not exist to eliminate luck, good and bad, for this cannot be. And the unlucky are also fellow human beings. A federal commission has reported that our present economic arrangements virtually guarantee not only considerable unemployment but pitifully low incomes for substantial numbers of those employed. Considering the waste and frivolous luxury which we also have, it cannot be held that this is the best we can do. But raw violence does not seem the most promising way to persuade the more fortunate or influential groups to make the needed changes.

The anarchistic trend noticeable today reminds one of the saying of Ortega, a true philosopher of creativity: "Anarchism is a social disease." Coherent social action is a wonderful creation. It is at least as amazing how much good human beings do to each other as how much harm they do. The problem of cooperation to maintain a city, or even a family, is not simply how those with good intentions, or even good intentions and good intelligence, can prevail over the wicked or stupid. Good and intelligent men use their creativity in various ways which only by extremely good luck can prove entirely harmonious.

What is wrong with "bourgeois" ideas or ideals is partly their non-tragic, deterministic faith in the absolute goodness of some actual or possible form of social order. But anarchistic revolutionaries also have a form of this faith. It is hard to admit that in any society there would be evils for which no one was wholly responsible. I understand the impatience of the victims of racism, that centuries-old wickedness and folly. But no establishment, and no absence of an establishment, will make life on a high level easy, or enable us to dispense with patience for our own fate and charity for our fellow creatures.

It should not be overlooked that accelerating technological change is bound to make parts of our tradition dangerously inadequate. The challenge of Marx at this point was more relevant than most of our ancestors admitted, and so was the challenge of Malthus. Indeed technology has accentuated the threat to which Malthus pointed. Scientific hygiene has made the easy answers to this thinker even less convincing than they otherwise were, and scientific studies of genetics and of environmental, especially family, influences have made it even more obvious than before that racism is a doctrine resting upon quarter truths. More and more its defence implies ignorance or dishonesty.

All freedom has risks, man has the most freedom, scientific man the most of all. From freedom come all dangers as well as all opportunities. People who accept cars and television, but expect social routines to continue as they were in their own youth, when the understanding that made these things possible was not yet in being, are deceived. It may not suit our convenience that novelty cannot be limited to mere gadgets, but it cannot. We shall have to create socially as well as mechanically and electronically. Creativity is the ultimate principle.

I believe, however, that one ancient truth remains, and it is clear that some of our restless young are aware of this, the truth that love also is ultimate. Indeed, creativity and love are two aspects of one principle. We create out of creations by past selves, including our own past selves, and we create for future selves, our own future selves in no absolute sense having the primacy. All life is socially dependent, socially contributory, as well as in some degree, self-determining. Each person may do "his own thing", but only by participating in the lives of others; each acts for the present joy of acting, and beyond the present looks to the joys of those who come after. While life lasts, one is oneself among those who at least may come after, but this is not guaranteed and, if one faces the centrality of death in life, it is not the main point. The present appropriates the past and (at best) willingly serves the future. Man is the one animal who can conceive the universal; his privilege and dignity is that the individual can see himself as one pebble on the beach. Ultimately, taking the entire future into account, it is the total content of the beach that matters. For me it is only a clearer statement to say that it is God, the fully immortal being, who finally matters. He alone is the reaper of all harvests. For us is the joy of the planting, for him the joy of the reaping. This is what it means to me to say that the meaning of life is the glory of God.

Reason and Commitment

Glenn R. Morrow

"I am and always have been one of those natures who need
to be guided by reason, whatever the reason may be that
upon reflection appears to me to be the best."

"The unexamined life is not fit for a man to live."

These words of Socrates, as reported by Plato in the *Crito* and the
Apology, have always seemed to me an epitome of the philosopher's
creed, and the creed not merely of the philosopher, but of every person
who takes life seriously. Therefore in contributing to this volume a
statement of "the things that matter most," as I see them now towards
the end of my philosophical career, I can only reaffirm this lifelong
conviction. The things that it seems to me most important to assert today
are, as always, the recognition of reason as the essential element in human
nature, and the necessity for its use in human affairs. To many of my
own generation this statement may appear so obvious and banal as not to
deserve reaffirmation. Yet the present philosophical climate is decidedly
unfavorable to such a declaration of faith. The words of Socrates have
not been, nor are they likely to be, expressly repudiated; but the winds
today are quite contrary, and their violence at times threatens to sweep
us off our feet. Indeed their near-hurricane force is even welcomed in
some quarters because it promises to do just that—to make a clean sweep
of the past and leave mankind free to write, it is hoped, a new charter of
freedom and humanity. Faced with problems of unprecedented magni-

tude, so we are told, whose solution we must be about at once, we are impatient of reflection and want action. "Don't think! Do something!" seems to be the motto of our impatient rebels, who must have action and commitment, even though the action be direct and the commitment hazy.

Unfortunately this mood is fortified today by influential currents of philosophical doctrine. Our age has been called the age of analysis, and so it is perhaps for the professionals. But for the general public it can be more appropriately called the age of existentialism. Perhaps it is because professional philosophers have devoted themselves so wholeheartedly to analysis that it has fallen to the existentialists to provide a philosophy for the non-professionals. The truth is, existentialism, if taken as an attempt at a reasoned philosophy, is rather a ramshackle construction and few philosophers take its logical pretensions seriously. Yet its revolutionary but profoundly pessimistic temper, and its preoccupation with the actual, the here-and-now, to the discredit of the abstract essences of conventional philosophy, have had a great influence upon artists, literary men, psychologists, and many others in the general public who are serious and concerned. It is not often observed, however, that its revolutionary temper is so pervaded by its pessimism that the revolution it prepares us for is a revolution of nihilism. I think it will repay us, therefore, before considering the positive part of my statement of faith, to review briefly the foundations of this powerful cross-current of thought.

Existentialism gets its name from its basic premise that existence is prior to essence.[1] By existence we mean the here-and-now-ness of a man or a thing; by its essence we mean this being's character, its nature or structure and all the other general traits that are involved in it. Now if we start from the essence of a thing, we have already, to some extent at least, predetermined its role and limited the range of its action. The action of a falling stone—or, to use Sartre's example, the root of a tree—differs from the action of a man, since its nature precludes it from doing the varied things that a man can do, and vice versa. Hence to make essence primary is to limit a being's being. Only if we take existence as our starting-point is a man, or any other being, free to be. Thus the existentialist who asks

1. On existentialism see particularly Jean Paul Sartre, *L'Être et le Néant*, 1943 (English translation, *Being and Nothingness*, 1956), *L'Existentialisme est un Humanisme*, 1946 (English translations *Existentialism*, 1947, *Existentialism and Humanism*, 1948); Marjorie Grene, *Dreadful Freedom*, 1948. Some passages in the later part of my essay are adapted from my article, "The Philosophical Presuppositions of Democracy," *Ethics*, April 1942.

"What am I?" can only answer "I am I," i.e. an individual distinct in my existence from all others, a center of action and commitment without any character that would limit me to this or that action or commitment. In this way my freedom and integrity are assured. Having no character to determine my action, I am free to make my own character through my action. But this freedom turns out to be, according to the testimony of the existentialist himself, a "dreadful freedom" indeed, as Marjorie Grene has so effectively shown us in her book with that title. He confesses to being filled with anxiety, to being appalled by the abyss of nothingness over which he is suspended; and these experiences he thinks reveal to him the heart of being. His plight is assuredly a pathetic one; but it is of his own making. For in eschewing essence for mere existence he has barred the way to finding any role for himself other than action *qua* action. And even this role he can assume only in defiance of his starting-point. For why should a bare particular, as he asserts himself to be, act at all? Inaction would be perfectly compatible with its characterless existence. Thus in emphasizing action and commitment the existentialist has deserted his own premise, and in trying to find a direction for his commitment he becomes a pathetic particular in search of a character which his professed principles forbid him to find.

To be sure, few men who call themselves existentialists operate from such a barren and self-contradictory starting-point as this. Sartre himself, as we have seen, insinuates action and freedom among his primary data, though without any manifest justification for doing so. Others have smuggled in other assumptions to relieve the starkness of their basic premise. Some have introduced God, or a shadowy Thou, among the elements that the I finds in its self-awareness. The addition of these and other factors logically extraneous to bare existence leads to a great variety of existentialist philosophies. But they clearly belong to a single family. Common to them all is an obsession with the actual, the here-and-now; a reliance upon action and commitment as the fundamental way of affirming one's existence; and a dismissal of all general principles or traditions that might give perspective upon the actual and define the course of the self's commitment. The reigning traditions in theology, in philosophy, in moral and political science, even in natural science are thrown aside, not always because they have been examined and found wanting (such examination would be inconsistent with the existentialist's contempt for abstract principles), but often because the existentialist shirks the task of mastering them, or is simply tired of them. He confesses to feelings of boredom and nausea when he looks at our society with its bourgeois morality and technological efficiency, or the institutions of organized religion with their apparent lack of concern for personal piety, or the systematic philosophies of the schools entangled in the irrelevant intricacies of logic. Many an existentialist painter or musician likewise, I suspect, is merely bored by the traditional discipline of his craft and rejects it chiefly because he feels incompetent to master it. Existentialist productions indeed often reveal the emptiness of the artistic self that insists on going it alone without benefit of tradition. In short, the past is irrelevant, just as the future is uncertain. All that counts is action now; and since the world in which the existentialist acts is, like himself, without form or structure, such action is inevitably hazardous and in the last analysis futile. Its futility, however, is emotionally redeemed somewhat when we make it as emphatically as possible a repudiation of tradition, e.g. by an act of treason or matricide, as Sartre suggests.

Yet Sartre declares that existentialism is a humanism—an assertion of the integrity and freedom of the human self despite the irrational forces that surround him. But such a humanism, like the world against which it asserts itself, is irrational, however dogged and heroic it may be. There is admittedly a romantic kind of heroism in going it blind; dogged persistence in a hopeless task is admirable, in a Quixotic sort of way; and the intoxication of action may provide for the actor a kind of surrogate for the confidence that accompanies reasoned action. But for the rational man this kind of satisfaction is not enough, and that so many of our contemporaries find it enough is profoundly disquieting. A humanism that discards Prometheus and takes Sisyphus as its hero can hardly be a humanism that can serve us in these critical days. And should it really be called humanism?

The crisis of our times shows that there is much in our traditions from which we need to be emancipated. For traditions do undoubtedly bind us. They explain our past, our failures whose consequences we are now reaping, as well as our successes of which in easier times we were wont to boast. But traditions that have been advantageous in the past may become a handicap if they are taken uncritically as prescriptions for the future. And many of our conceptions of the nature of man have always been of dubious value. We have been taught, for example, that man is a lustful and acquisitive animal; and thus the right of private property is not only explained but justified, even when it claims power over irreplaceable common resources and even (God help us!) over human beings. Or that man is a power-seeking animal (a beast of prey, as Spengler put it); and wars of aggression become a natural and inevitable expression of human nature. These are only a small sample of the traditions regarding the nature of man that have constricted our thought and action, and we must challenge them, as the existentialist counsels us, if we are to face the future adequately prepared.

But to challenge a particular tradition, or many such traditions, that we believe to be false is not to challenge the whole of tradition; and here the existentialist becomes incoherent. His program of making all essences secondary and irrelevant looks like a policy of overkill. If it were successful it would make the challenge itself illegitimate; for if it is a part of the nature of man that he should challenge and reject what he considers to be erroneous views of his own nature, the character that leads him to question and challenge would fall under the universal proscription. It is clear that neither Sartre nor any of his followers intends this. The inescapable implication, therefore, of the protest and the agony of the existentialist is that man is a being capable of reflecting on his nature and of rejecting a policy or an action that he thinks incompatible with his freedom.

So much of the essence of man, then, we find implied by the very protest of the existentialist. Having admitted so much, cannot Sartre also go further, with Socrates, and not merely reject what he finds unacceptable but also commit himself to what he finds best? Only an obstinate persistence in discrediting essence stands in his way; and this obstinacy can not itself be taken as a part of the nature of man in general. For common experience shows that it is a part of human nature not only to reject what is unacceptable, but to choose what is acceptable, and in the case of open alternatives, to choose what is the most acceptable.

To illustrate this obvious point I shall turn not, like Socrates, to the actions of the baker or the cobbler, but to another equally commonplace situation, one familiar to all of us who live in a suburban community. A man on his way to keep an engagement in the city finds that he has missed the train that would get him to his destination at the proper time. He immediately thinks of alternative ways of getting there, such as the bus or a taxi; he weighs the considerations for and against these or other alternatives, and eventually selects that one which seems to him upon reflection to be the best. This is probably, to the existentialist, too commonplace for serious consideration. But so much the better for our example; it shows that we may take it as a typical case of human choice. There is here nothing that is unusual; it merely describes the way in which we naturally expect a human being to behave. Even a man who lives in a culture without railways, buses, or taxicabs has problems analogous to this which he meets and solves, more or less successfully, every day of his life. If, then, this is taken as typical of human behavior, we can see that the essence, or nature, of man contains some remarkable capacities. Our commuter thinks of alternatives to his customary way of getting into the city; he traces in imagination the consequences that would follow from choosing one or other of these alternatives; and he does this by recalling his knowledge of how and where these alternative means operate. To think of alternatives, to have knowledge available for recall, and to deduce consequences from the knowledge available—these features make his choice a rational one, in at least a minimal sense of this term.

Of course the man in our example, being human, does not have perfect imagination and infallible information; he may not think of all the alternatives that are really available, and his knowledge of those he considers may be incomplete or erroneous. His reflection may after all not be successful, and he may decide that he can best telephone his partner that he will be late. What he certainly does not do, if he is a normal man, is to spend his time cursing his luck or beating his breast for his carelessness in not consulting the train schedule. Nor will he commit himself to walking, or flying, to the city. In other words, his actual situation is one that has a structure and a context, and he imaginatively recalls elements from the institutions around him that will suggest a course of action within his power. In possessing these capacities and in utilizing them when the actual occasion requires, he is a rational man and is acting in a rational manner.

The commitment in this case is a relatively trivial one, when viewed from a cosmic perspective or when compared with the momentous social problems that face us today. But there is no dearth of examples of far more complicated problems that man has met and solved with the same basic equipment exhibited in the simple example just described. Some twenty-five years ago the United States Treasury, with a vastly increased national budget as a consequence of the War Against the Axis Powers, and relying almost solely on the income tax for revenue to meet this budget, found itself facing a difficult problem of tax-collection. When the citizen's obligations were computed at the end of the taxable year, most citizens found that the taxes due were larger than they had anticipated and had made provision for, and in a large number of cases these obligations could not be collected. An imaginative person in the councils of the Treasury, Beardsley Ruml, conceived an alternative to the time-honored method of collecting at the end of the year and devised a plan for collecting during the year in which the taxable income was being earned, through the withholding of taxes by employers and other salary-paying agencies. The effectuation of this plan required approval of the Congress and the cooperation of business men and directors, who had to introduce complicated new methods of bookkeeping and disbursement. There was grumbling and dissent at first, but the plan was generally accepted after a short time; and its smooth operation during the succeeding years and its effectiveness in solving the problem with which the Revenue Service was confronted have made Ruml's pay-as-you-go plan an outstanding example of political imagination. Its acceptance is likewise an example of rational commitment—this time by a community, not an individual—to an imaginative new idea, violating custom and involving the derangement of established habits of business men and citizens, but winning general acceptance, even by those whom it seriously inconvenienced, because of its reasonableness.

These examples illustrate the capacity of man to solve a problem by transcending it, i.e. by getting above it through understanding its elements and utilizing knowledge of himself and of his environment to obviate factors that obstruct action. It is this capacity that alone provides the freedom which the existentialist so uncompromisingly demands. For freedom in the concrete, not in some absolute metaphysical sense, consists in the ability to evade or remove obstacles to what we want to do. An obstacle that is merely felt and not understood is likely to remain a hindrance to our action; whereas when we understand its nature, and our own, we can sometimes devise a way of eliminating it by removing the conditions of its occurrence, or a way of evading it by changing our habits. No amount of loud assertions of our Freedom will make us free of a here-and-now hindrance, nor will any arbitrarily chosen commitment in assertion of our freedom enable us to evade an obstacle, except by a happy miracle. The making of our own character, on which the existentialist insists, is subject to the same inexorable law. Only by transcending one's nature through understanding the faults that one wishes to correct, and invoking corrective factors in oneself or the environment, can one get free of them. But in order to do this, a man must have a nature to begin with, a nature that includes this capacity to transcend oneself through intelligent analysis and understanding. So far has the existentialist missed the way; he can only counsel us to beat against the bars of our cage, to cultivate Anxiety, or contemplate the abyss of Nothingness that so fascinates him.

The predicament of the existentialist has been worth examining, for our examination has shown how arbitrary and factitious it is, and how it can be avoided by a recognition that the nature of man is to be rational, in the sense described—a nature which the existentialist has in part admitted, despite himself, but has in the main ignored. But can we today seriously reassert this time-honored Socratic doctrine? It is obvious that we not only can but must do so, in some sense, if we are even to be existentialists. But "reason" and "rational" have been used in various senses in the history of thought, and we must choose our meanings carefully. It is hardly possible for us to maintain today that man is rational in the Cartesian sense, the possessor of an angelic intelligence, infallible in its intuitions and infallible also in its deductions, if only it uses the proper method. Nor can we maintain, like Descartes, that reason in man is only casually connected with bodily parts and passions. This is the classical rationalism, and its psychological and metaphysical difficulties are familiar to us all. The classical rationalism claimed both too much and too little for human reason. It claimed too much in the way of control over conduct. The function of reason in our experience is less august, but on the other hand more effective, than the classical rationalism assumed. The examples we have considered, which could be supplemented at will from the history of the race, show that man does have the capacity of solving problems by intelligent analysis and manipulation. He is not always successful. The reason with which he is endowed is a human reason, a capacity limited in its range and uncertain in its exercise, more evident in some of us than in others, and in all of us more active at some times than at others. Nevertheless this capacity is remarkable both for its past achievements and for its possibilities. This constitutes the essence of man, an essence which even the existentialist, if he is aware of the conditions of the human problem, cannot logically ignore. The fact that existentialists usually do ignore it indicates their preference for considerations other than logic.

But enough of existentialism. Let me now develop briefly the implications of this broader humanism that has appeared in our examination of the so-called humanism of the existentialists.

We have seen that this capacity for free and rational commitment depends upon the ability to transcend a problem by intelligent analysis and manipulation of its elements. The word "transcend" is deliberately chosen, for it literally expresses what happens when a thinker rises above his problem to view it as an object for analysis, and when his imagination roams in the realm of possibilities in search of a solvent factor. Though his thinking is stimulated by the particular situation that confronts him, it is not bound by the actual; indeed if this were so he could never arrive at a solution. In the process of reflection, he is in a real sense a member of two worlds, the actual which frustrates him, and the imaginary which may hold the means of his liberation. In imaginatively exploring this other world he is moving among possibilities, not actualities. A possibility is something that at first sight seems very peculiar. It is not an actuality, for it is merely thought of; and yet it is not unreal, at least not all possibilities are, for we distinguish between real and unreal possibilities. The best that we can say provisionally is that a real possibility is something that can be made actual. This means that if a possibility is to be more than an airy castle in the imagination it must itself have a structure that makes it capable of being grafted on habits and processes in the world of actuality. This is the wonder of creative thought, whether exhibited in the solving of relatively trivial problems of private life, or in the more imposing creations of science and technology: the thinker, during the process of invention, is living in another world, exploring its implications, fashioning and refashioning the ideas suggested by his imagination until he has a conceptually consistent structure that will mesh with the the concrete conditions of our world so as to make a stable addition to it.

This other world in which the creative thinker is immersed is, as every inventor learns through his failures, not merely a world of airy dreams and enticing phantoms; it is a firmly articulated cosmos, a world of laws as inexorable as anything in the realm of actuality. When Wilbur and Orville Wright dreamed of making a heavier-than-air flying machine, they found that they could make their dream an actuality only by discovering and utilizing the laws of aerodynamics; and every advance in aeronautics since their simple biplane has come about through further exploration of this hitherto unknown region, with its complicated equations governing thrust, lift, drag, airflow, and the rest. These factors and the equations that connect them are not the creations of imagination; they are a hard reality that must first be found and when found reckoned with and utilized. In the same way the principles of the reflection, refraction, and diffraction of light underlie the structure of the lenses in our telescopes, microscopes, cameras, binoculars and dozens of other optical instruments that we take for granted today, and the inventors that made into working realities their dreams of such instruments had to learn and apply the intricate laws of this world of light. We call this other world in which the creative thinker penetrates a world of thought, but it is a world as real in its way as the Rock of Gibraltar, and only because it is thus reliable is it useful to the creative thinker. This order as conceived by the thinker is certainly different from the realities of actual and sensible experience, for it is an abstract world of universals that are apprehended precisely only by the thinker in his thought. But it is assuredly a more august world, for it enables him to understand and control the world of sensible realities that first confronts him.

How can we be sure of the truth and validity of these principles uncovered by the imagination of creative thinkers and invoked by them to solve the problems with which they are concerned? The answer is that we can never be completely sure. For the reason in man, even that of the greatest of creative thinkers, is a human reason. It is not infallible, and it sees at best a part only of the vast intelligible world. But the successes of our science and technology afford ample evidence that knowledge, accurate knowledge, is often within human grasp. These discovered principles, therefore, acquire a certain validity from their very success in solving the problems to which they are applied. In the realm of science and technology the authority of these principles is further buttressed by empirical tests, of varying degrees of precision. But since these tests are themselves applied by human beings, and since from the nature of the case they can seldom if ever be perfectly precise, their authority ultimately rests upon the scientific community that accepts them. Such acceptance does not, as we now know, guarantee their permanent validity. The revolution in physics that has occurred since the beginning of this century shows that principles universally accepted at one time may be questioned, revised, and perhaps rejected because of later advances of creative thought. The intelligible world in which our thought moves is constantly surprising us by revealing unsuspected quirks in its structure that force us to remake our hard-earned conceptions of it. But the history of science gives us a reasoned confidence that the human race is on the right path in exploring, through the intelligence with which it is endowed, the indefinitely vast world that is as yet unknown.

The history of mathematics is a still further buttress to this reasoned confidence in the powers of the human mind. There is no region of human thought that at first sight seems further removed from the actualities of our experience. Though mathematics began in the need to solve simple problems of calculation and land measurement, its connection with tangible experience became progressively more tenuous with the advance of analysis, abstraction, and generalization, until today the mathematician is generally thought of as living in a world of his own fancy, and the very name of his science is likely to strike terror in the mind of the undergraduate student, and arouse uncomprehending wonder in the average layman. Yet again and again in the history of science one of the beautiful but airy productions of the pure mathematician has been found to have important application in our here-and-now world of things and events. Apollonius developed in elaborate detail the theory of the conic sections by exploring the logical implications of his imagined figures and curves, apparently with no inkling of their empirical applications. Today the equation of the parabola, a Cartesian restatement of a theorem of Apollonius, is essential for the construction of the automobile headlight, and many other instruments in common use requiring the concentration of beams of light upon a limited target. What is even more striking, the world of nature apart from human contrivance has a similarity of structure to the systems of pure mathematics. It is astonishing, for example, to see how often we encounter the logarithmic spiral not merely in the pages of textbooks in higher mathematics, but also in the structure of living things, that follow the law of this spiral in the pattern of their growth. "God geometrizes" is the old-fashioned way of stating the surprising fact that the human mind, in its excursions in the intelligible world, guided only by the logic of its own nature, quite often lays bare the structure of things in the larger cosmos which it inhabits.

In the solution of social and moral problems, human reason by virtue of its capacity to apprehend another world than the actual, exhibits a function analogous to what it has in the area of science and technology. I have cited earlier Ruml's pay-as-you-go plan as an example of imaginative political invention and its success in solving the particular problem that confronted the Internal Revenue Service. Another example of wider import that will occur to us all is the framing of the American Constitution, unquestionably a new form of political structure, requiring the renunciation of sovereignty by the several states and their union into a larger sovereign body. The framers of the Constitution, like the inventors of the telescope and the flying-machine, solved their problem by applying principles of political theory that had been elaborated by eighteenth-century thinkers. In the area of social and moral problems, the validity of the principles invoked cannot so easily be established as in science and technology; time alone can show whether they will be effective in solving the difficulties to which they are applied. Yet before they can even be put to this test they must be adopted by those who are to live under them; and this adoption requires something like an act of faith in hitherto untried principles.

But this acceptance of hitherto untried principles reveals another trait of human nature that is often overlooked, viz. its willingness to accept the authority of general principles. Nothing would be more incompatible with the character of the existentialist's stubborn particular than that it should give way to other particulars in the assertion of its being. But this willingness to subject himself to a rule that applies to others as well as himself is a character of the human being that we can observe every day, if we have eyes to see it. Let us assume a simple case of a dispute between two persons over the ownership of a certain property. Most such disputes are settled, and settled amicably. The principle that resolves the issue need not be a dictate of absolute and eternal justice, such as would satisfy a philosopher or a divine intelligence. What is necessary is that the principle be accepted by both A and B as having authority on the basis of their insight. It may be a rule which has authority for them primarily because of its age or its source—for example, some long-standing custom, or some principle of the common law. To the philosopher it is often astonishing to observe what authority some nondescript but ancient precept, such as prior occupation or prescription, has over the ordinary man once it is brought to his attention. But it ill becomes the philosopher to ignore the fact that such rules do possess authority and that it is by such rags and tags of moral principle that many of our day-to-day conflicts of interest are resolved. Or the principle that resolves the conflict may be a formal one: B admits the justice of A's claim because he sees it is the sort of claim he would think justified if he were in A's position or the sort of claim that he has himself made in similar circumstances in the past. Or the reconciling principle may be a procedural one, such as the resort to arbitration: A and B may agree on the justice of having their claims settled by a third party, for example by a majority of the voting members of the community or by an assembly of their elected representatives. Or the procedural principle may be that of compromise: A and B may agree that it is just, under the circumstances, for each to abate his claim and settle for half a loaf. In all these cases the disputants have reached a position from which their conflict of interests is capable of a solution on principle, i.e. from a perspective from which one's private claims can be viewed objectively and judged by a standard that is acceptable to others as well as to one's self.

This appeal to principle is an appeal to reason, and the frequency of its use in human affairs is but the counterpart and consequence of our reason's capacity to apprehend another world, a world recognized as superior to our here-and-now world and authoritative over it. It is this other world that stimulates and nourishes all our efforts to enlarge the range of our knowledge and increase our understanding of this one. Having recognized so much, it is natural for us to suppose, as wiser philosophers than I have done, that this world by which our thoughts and reasonings are nourished is itself a larger mind, continuous with our own, manifesting itself in the structures in nature that our mind finds itself adapted to comprehend, and exerting upon our thought a mysterious but powerful pressure for greater range and consistency in our understanding. However imperfect our capacity is to apprehend that world, it is of profound importance in the development of human history, enabling man to transcend any present achievement and elevate himself to higher levels of knowledge and action. This is the conception of man that I think correctly represents his nature as we know it, "a creature," as Milton said,

> "not prone
> And brute as other creatures, but endued
> With sanctity of reason."

As one looks at our past one can readily share the romantic interpretation of Lessing and Herder, that history is the story of the progressive education of the human race. We cannot so readily share today their eighteenth-century optimism that man's progress is inevitable. Yet it ill becomes us, in these moments of crisis, to despair of the prospects of a species of being so highly endowed and placed in a world so fittingly arranged to stimulate and enhance his powers of understanding and action. It is possible that we will not solve the problems that now confront us. But if we fail, it will be because we have not properly used our powers; and I cannot believe that the failure, if it comes, will be irretrievable. My long experience as a teacher has shown me that a student of ability cannot ever be hopelessly delinquent. He may fail a term test, but he has it in him to finish the course with honor. And so it is with humanity, I firmly believe, in meeting the tests that we are undergoing today.

Ideals in Retrospect

Stephen C. Pepper

For as long as I can remember I have had a consuming desire to know about things, about what they really and truly are, and about what makes some things and acts good and others bad. Of course, at first I learned what to think about things from my parents and close surrounding relatives. The answers were direct and authoritative and there was little or no wondering on my part about certain inconsistencies with approved behavior shown by some persons outside the family. Grandma's hired servants, for instance, went to church early in the morning and to a different church from the rest of us in the family.

The first vivid awareness I can remember about possible complexities in the true and the false and the good and the bad came at the age of eight. I had been a rather solitary child. My father was an artist and between the ages of two and eight, except for several visits back to the homes of my grandparents in Maine, I was brought up in Paris. My father was studying there in the art schools. When I was eight my parents returned to America and took up residence in the town of Concord not far from Boston. Then for the first time I was sent to public school and had to learn to get on with a lot of other children.

From my years abroad, I must have seemed a little strange to the other youngsters. There were three little boys in particular who laid for me as I passed by their school building on the way to mine. One evening near tears I told my parents about it. Sweet Aunt Louise was visiting us at the time. My father listened to my troubles and remarked, "Why don't you fight them?" To which Aunt Louise exclaimed, "Oh dear! Oh dear! Oh dear!" This came to me as a perfectly astonishing idea. "But what do I do with my books?" "Put them down on the ground and go for the boys," he said. And he showed me how to double up my fists so as not to sprain my thumb.

Well, this was a totally new insight into the nature of good and bad. I thought I had learned that goodness was the same as kindness. But apparently it was good to be unkind to another if he were unkind to you—and this on father's own authority. This puzzle made a deep impression on my mind. And, let me say, it still does. It unfortunately appears to be a real true ethical principle.

Next morning I went out and put it to test. I happened to be a rather big boy for my age. When the three little boys came out to have their usual fun with me, I laid down my books, clenched my fists (and no doubt my teeth) and prepared to hit them. To my astonishment they disappeared and never bothered me again. Father's principle had worked.

From then on I became more and more critical about more and more things. I found that even the grown-ups did not agree completely about what was really true and good. I had quite a struggle with religion, even though my parents were unusually liberal considering their background. For my grandfather on my father's side was a minister and I admired him greatly as everybody else did. And he had been president of Colby College. But even with all that authority I finally in my college years at Harvard broke away from religious dogma and the church. It just could not be true, and if not true, it could not be really good.

It was not by chance but inevitable that when I discovered philosophy I wanted to make it my profession. For here was a profession whose aim was to find out about the nature of things—the marvelous coincidence of coming upon a job for which I would be paid for doing just what I had the greatest desire to do. It was George Herbert Palmer in my junior year who introduced me into philosophy through his course in ethics.

He was a great teacher. His example in this course contributed to strengthen another deep desire of mine which grew out of my close childhood environment. This was to grow up to be of service to man. All my close relatives were filled with this ideal and were fulfilling it in lesser or greater ways according to their lights. They were all of them more or less involved in the northern Baptist church, and my grandfather, a model to me, had given his whole life to the service of men as minister and teacher and administrator. The ideal of service to men was part of the air I breathed. It was rarely spoken of explicitly. It was assumed by all of us. My father as a painter was carrying on this service in his devotion to all things beautiful and in his desire to create beautiful pictures for the delight of others. To be creative in the production of things beautiful and true was the highest imaginable service to man.

Palmer through his example as a creative teacher, not only in his illumination of the study of ethics, its theories and the data that supported them and the errors and corrections made, but in the beauty of his language and delivery and the organization of his lectures and their fitness to the students before him, filled me with a desire to teach as much like that as I could. Here was a definite service I could seek to perform.

As time went on and I studied with other fine teachers as a graduate student in the Philosophy Department, my ambition went a step further. I began to hope that I might even do something as a creative philosopher. So, I would not only be carrying on the service to men by teaching as my grandfather had, but perhaps also by creation as my father was doing.

So there was that original persistent craving for knowledge to which was added a pervasive urge to be of service to man, to which was later added an ambition to elevate that service to some degree of creative achievement. To become a philosopher by profession rendered all these possible. To what degree these aims could be actualized, only events could tell.

So much for my initial motivations at the time I launched into professional life with a Ph.D. in philosophy in the year 1916. My real teaching, however, did not begin until after the end of World War I in 1919. That year I went to the University of California, Berkeley, where, except for numerous sabbaticals and visiting professorships, I have remained ever since. Those original motivations never left me. I am still pursuing knowledge for all I am worth. I have sought with earnestness and without let-up to be as good a teacher as I could for all sorts and sizes of classes, and for many sorts of students. And I am still seeking to be a creative philosopher towards increasing our comprehension of things. And now these motivations aside, what results over the intervening forty or fifty years do I seem to come up with? What are my final convictions today? I will take them up under three heads—knowledge, society, and education.

Regarding my convictions about knowledge, I was, when I left Harvard, close to what would now be called a physicalist, or materialist. I was deeply impressed with the methods and results of the natural sciences, accepted the reducibility of the more complex levels of nature to the simplest, and took the ultimate physical properties as the basic cosmic facts. I was not willing, however, to deny like J. B. Watson, the existence of introspective qualities. I merely held that they were of no scientific importance and tried to pay no more attention to them.

This materialist dogmatism of mine was shaken in the mid-twenties, partly by contact with some pragmatists in Berkeley and particularly by Mead, whom I met one summer while I was a visiting professor in Chicago, and partly by the Gestalt school in psychology to which I was introduced while on sabbatical with Edward Tolman in Europe. The characteristic atomism of the mechanist was severely challenged by both groups with the evidence for intrinsic connections within events. The result upon me was not a conversion from one view to the other, but a conviction that both views were giving alternative interpretations of the "same facts." The difference lay in their basic presuppositions or categories of explanation and description. But this was more than a verbal difference. It penetrated into our very cognition of the structural and qualitative nature of the universe. I came to regard the two views as alternative world hypotheses based upon different incompatible sets of categories.

Kant's theory of categories now meant something to me it had never meant before. Any person immersed in a set of categories would inevitably perceive and interpret all things as they appeared through those categories. Kant's release from his dogmatic slumber in which he had thought he was seeing things just as they were in themselves, freeing him to realize he was seeing them through the categories of his mind, merely lifted him out of one stage of dogmatism and lodged him in another. For if, as Kant believed, there was only one set of categories which determined the structure of all he saw, then how could he distinguish the appearance of things seen through his categories from what these things were supposed to be in themselves? As C. I. Lewis once pointed out, how could you know you were seeing things through a set of categories unless there were at least two sets of categories which brought out incompatible differences of appearance through their interpretations?

This was the new insight that came to me. And having found two world hypotheses with very persuasive sets of categories, I looked about for others. Roughly I found that what divided the so-called schools of philosophy in the history of the subject were generally sets of categories yielding incompatible interpretations. Some of these world hypotheses were much better grounded than others. The more adequate ones were those that had wider scope and greater precision in their interpretations. In the end I decided there were only four of these. And I published a book, *World Hypotheses,* describing them. In a way there was nothing new about them. They were the same old school theories we had read about in every extended history of philosophy. The only difference was that they were set up separately and displayed side by side on exhibit, so to speak, as hypotheses.

This procedure, I thought, did have some salutary consequences. It brought out prominently the pivotal sets of categories and their divergencies. It showed clearly how the diversity of interpretations arose from the divergencies of the guiding concepts as categories of being. More important still, it undermined the legitimacy of all the traditional appeals to certainty. It showed that the illusion of certainty came from absorption in a set of categories. For to anyone immersed in a set of categories their particular interpretations of data seem absolutely indubitable and the presuppositions which produce them seem like self-evident principles. Once one is aware of diverse sets of categories one is alerted against such parochial dogmatisms. At the same time one is made aware of a limited number of relatively adequate interpretations of evidence, from which one can make a reasonable judgment in deciding upon certain types of difficult issues.

So the outcome of my urgent pursuit of knowledge has been a partial scepticism. Such restrained scepticism does not block the accumulation of knowledge. Quite the reverse. It is dogmatism that blocks the pursuit of knowledge. Man has come to know a great deal. The accumulation of various degrees of predictable knowledge among the special sciences over the last two or three centuries has been spectacular. Just how to interpret these results on a world-wide scale is still a big question. But I also think it is a step of progress to become aware of the interpretive effect of categorial sets where wide comprehension is needed. And I hold that there is a limited number of relatively adequate categorial sets, and that through them we can get approximations to a true conception of the nature of things. I believe, moreover, that we may come upon still more adequate world hypotheses than those we now have. I have even ventured to suggest what may be a new one.

While working on world hypotheses, I came upon an idea of how they originated. There are evidences that they start from analogies derived from human experience or from common sense or other sources. I called them root metaphors. The root metaphor for my own world hypothesis came out of my studies in value theory which revealed the key concept of selective system which for values is a special sort of feedback system. This concept seems to be capable of unlimited extension and promises to be a fertile root metaphor for a world hypothesis.

When a root metaphor emerges in the history of philosophy it is generally rather vague. As it develops it becomes clarified. Its structural features are extracted and become a set of categories. With these categories the facts of the world are confronted and interpreted in their terms. If they are fertile, a consistent system of carefully described facts develops with increasing scope and precision of interpretation. And then we have a world hypothesis. If it is taken up by a number of philosophers, it creates a school which may become very influential and shape the thought of a whole society, seeping down even into the common sense of the period.

This root metaphor theory is merely a theory about the origin and development of world hypotheses, and need not be accepted by persons interested in world hypotheses themselves. But so far as it is found acceptable, it greatly simplifies an understanding of the history of philosophy and of cognition generally, for the special sciences have not been immune to the categorial presuppositions of world theories. The root metaphor concept also has an evaluative function in cognition. It reveals the fallacy of eclecticism; that is, the incoherence and confusion that occurs when incompatible categorial sets are mixed up together. It can also reveal the futility of empty abstractionism when categories get separated from their root metaphors and their factual rootage in concrete human experience and are treated as self-evident truths immune to criticism.

Let me now turn to my convictions about social matters. Here we enter the domain of ethics and value theory. In this area I have reached the conclusion that the key concept is that of the "selective system." From the beginning of my study of values, as early as the writing of my Ph.D. thesis on the subject, I have held that values are facts open to descriptive procedures. A theory of value is a descriptive hypothesis subject to confirmation by the field of human acts it refers to. The recent diversion of the study into the anomalous emotive judgment concept and the linguistic concentration on imperative, optative, prescriptive and other forms of non-descriptive sentences, strikes me as essentially irrelevant and most unfortunate at this strained period of history when we need the best confirmed cognitive studies available for our intelligent guidance.

I have done my best on this subject, utilizing the accumulated wisdom of the great empiricists from Aristotle down through Hobbes, Spinoza, the utilitarians, the idealists, and the pragmatists, to John Dewey and R. B. Perry and others still more recent. In *The Sources of Value,* which presents my final systematic conclusions on the subject, I began with a detailed descriptive study of purposive behavior, borrowing heavily from E. C. Tolman's psychological experimental work. Here I found that a detailed description of a complete purposive act from the initial dynamic impulse to the terminal goal fulfilling the conditions of satisfaction inherent in the drive, contained not only the value factors of desire and satisfaction typical of the hedonic theories but also a sanctioning imperative factor typical of rationalistic theories.

For a purposive act is a dynamic systematic structure with an initial drive and a terminal goal and a succession of intermediate acts leading from the drive to the goal. The imperative factor is imbedded in the system in the dispositional requirements of the drive for a specific pattern in the goal to reduce the drive and yield satisfaction. Any intermediate acts that fail to lead towards the goal are dismissed as errors as soon as the mistake becomes evident. They are acts which the system rejects as acts that *ought not* to have been chosen. And all intermediate acts that serve to lead towards the goal are retained in the system. The latter are the acts dynamically sanctioned by the system as those that *ought* to be performed. Such a system which dynamically within its own structure selects acts that ought to be chosen as against those that ought not for the furtherance of its inherent dispositional aim, I call a "selective system." And here is the concrete unit of value behavior in human experience.

Now I find many levels of such selective systems extending from the single purposive act, to a personal situation including a number of such purposive acts and requiring the obligation of prudence, to social situations where several persons are involved requiring obligations of mutual consideration, to social institutions with institutional sanctions demanding conformity, to cultural demands for harmonious institutional integration, until finally there are the demands for individual and social adaptation through the action of biological natural selection.

Furthermore, I find that at the two poles of this series of selective systems there are two distinct dynamic agencies. At the pole of the single individual purpose, the dynamic agency is the particular drive of that purpose that has its seat in the individual person experiencing that drive. But at the pole of biological natural selection at the other end, the dynamic agency is that of the genes and the chromosomes controlling the inheritance and adaptation of the species to its biological environment. In man as a social animal the impact of natural selection comes not primarily (except rarely) upon individual organisms but upon the social organization. And in man as an intelligent organism who can make different forms of social organization or human cultures, the impact of natural selection is upon the culture pattern adopted. This is in contrast to the social insects, whose social structures are imbedded in their instinctive behavior and cannot be changed. Man can change his culture and is consequently much more adaptable than the bees and ants and termites. But man is by no means immune to the impact of natural selection. The impact is upon his cultural system. So, ideally, it would seem important for men to develop adaptable cultural systems. This is my belief and my recommendation. The ideal human society I have called the adjustable society.

Unfortunately, however, man is extremely rigid and inertial in regard to changes in his culture. Anthropologists have noticed this particularly in primitive cultures. But civilized man is perhaps not much better. Among civilized societies two opposite types of society have been lauded as ideal. Each centers on the opposite dynamic pole of the series of selective systems. One centers on the dynamics of individual desires and satisfactions. It sets up the political structure of the open individualistic society with the ideal of maximizing individual satisfactions, decentralizing authority with checks and balances to give the individual as much freedom of choice as possible. The other sets up the so-called closed, or centrally integrated society with the aim of maximizing efficiency of organization for security and continuity of survival, developing a centralized authority and ideally an organic distribution of functions in which every person can find his place for the fullest realization of his capacities in the harmonious service of the whole. The classic exposition of the open individualistic society is found in Locke's and J. S. Mill's political writings. The classic exposition of the closed functional society is to be found in Plato's *Republic*. The British and American democracies of the last two centuries may perhaps be taken as fair exemplifications of the open society in actual practice. The feudal-ecclesiastical societies of Europe in the middle ages are perhaps corresponding exemplifications of the closed functional society, as also, presumably, are the communistic societies of today.

In my judgment both of these social structures in their ideal forms are justifiable depending on the attendant circumstances. The principal determining circumstance is the degree of social pressure internal or external bearing on the social group. The greater the pressure the greater the need of centralized authority for the preservation of the group. This condition leads at once (as soon as one thinks about it) to the conception of an adjustable society as the overarching ideal to be aimed at. There are, of course, many degrees and combinations of centralized and decentralized social structures. Rarely would the extremes be appropriate throughout. And there are debased variations of each, towards irresponsible tyranny on the one side and irresponsible anarchy on the other.

Actually I believe our American society has exhibited in practice many of the traits of an adjustable society, and that this form of organization is latent in the American constitution through the fortunate chance that it was drawn up as a compromise between the individualists following Jefferson and the exponents of a strong central government following Hamilton. For three times under great stress within our brief history have we centralized our powers to meet an emergency and then decentralized (probably too quickly) when the emergency was over—for the Civil War, and World Wars I and II. But we are so imbued with the ideal of individualism to the point of dogma that we fail to see the greatly superior ideal of social adjustability under which we actually (though sullenly and with jerks and growls) conduct our affairs. We are socialized today much more than our ordinary citizen realizes and cares to contemplate. And with the pressures of population, and integration, and the pollution of our environment we shall need to socialize—that is, to adjust with effective centralizing authority—more and more.

And there is more than this in the offing. The general assumption in the foregoing paragraph is that men live in relatively autonomous groups and that some such groupings are what must be preserved on the average for the survival of the human species as a social animal. So it was with primitive man preserving his tribal security. So also for the early civilized nations. In the biological competition of tribes and nations the better adapted would survive and so insure the survival of the species. But the scientific industrial progress of men in the recent past has transfigured the whole situation. There is no question in my mind that the very concept of nationality or any other strongly autonomous social form today is a cultural lag. The world is too small with us. Moreover, man's ingenuity and intelligence has created the means of his total annihilation. The pressure on mankind for his survival as a species is mounting with terrifying speed. The uncontrolled autonomy of nations is the supreme threat of this era. A powerful United Nations is the only safe solution I can see. And I should wish it to move as smoothly and fast as possible into a United Mankind with a strong, intelligently flexible, adjustable society.

And now because I am a college professor, let me lower my sights considerably and examine the present crisis in the colleges. Looking back I am surprised to discover that the span of my life nearly covers the whole course of the development of the American University. For it was Eliot at Harvard who was most responsible for changing what was little more than an academy into a university. Though Eliot had just retired when I entered Harvard in 1909, my class was the last to experience the free elective system which was part of Eliot's program. A student's only requirement for the A.B. degree was sixteen year courses with a C average. The idea was to give a boy a chance to range over the whole field of knowledge under the ablest scholars available and find out for himself his chief interests and capacities. For many students, including myself, it was an ideal program. Through it I discovered philosophy in my junior year. Yet following the spirit of the plan I did not specialize in the field till I became a graduate student, but continued to spread out over other subjects, feeling it would be my last chance to extend my knowledge freely. The trouble with the plan was that too many less conscientious students found it too easy to select sixteen of the easiest courses available, acquiring the so-called "gentleman's C." To block off this escape route, Lowell who was Eliot's successor, set up the plan of a group of breadth requirements together with an intensive major in a special field, a plan that soon became practically universal in the American college.

Meantime, after Eliot's initial impetus, the American University spread across the continent and became probably the most productive research institution in the world. And it proved a good teaching institution too, in spite of a few more or less justifiable criticisms it received. Yet now after about a century of extraordinary development it is being shaken with disruption. The crisis is the more amazing in that the research productivity of the American University has reached today the highest level ever and gives every indication of being able to maintain this level indefinitely—unless it is knocked down.

What is the trouble? It is easy to oversimplify the trouble. But I will risk suggesting that it centers in the aspersion of "irrelevancy." Irrelevancy, however, to what? Certainly not to the search for knowledge, nor to the training of experts to apply the knowledge from our efficient schools of engineering, medicine, agriculture and the like. It seems to be irrelevancy to the acute social discontent and needs of the society outside the

University. But why pick on the University rather than the government? This may be partly due to the accident at this time of the draft for an unpopular war that happens to hit precisely the students of university age. But it must also be admitted that the increasing emphasis on published research in the universities has led to some neglect in regard to undergraduate teaching.

An overemphasis on "relevancy," however, can also do real damage to the universities. For one of the central principles of the effective pursuit of knowledge is that it be pursued for its own sake without thought of how or where it might be relevant to some human use. One of the principal achievements of the American University during its develop-ment has been to attain this condition of freedom from political or other special influence. It looks as if that happy condition is drawing to an end, especially in the State universities. We must probably also look forward to more centralized authority even in the university government itself. On the basis of the ethical generalizations made earlier, the pressures within and outside the university will almost surely lead to more central govern-ment surveillance, and some loss of academic freedom. Much will depend on the trends of American social organization in the years to come. If the trend can be toward a greater awareness of the ideal of an adjustable society, or at least more flexibility of social action in that direction so that freedom as well as security will not be forgotten, there would be no reason to fear for the vigorous continuance of the great American Univer-sity. More concern with its "relevance" to political issues and social needs integrated into its teaching and research projects might actually increase its excellence. A genuinely adjustable society could hardly fail to discover the social importance of essentially untrammeled research for whatever is true and particularly for what is truly good for mankind.

Forty Years After:
A Clarification of Outlook

Roy Wood Sellars

Forty years ago, American philosophers were moved to publish two volumes on the contemporary, American scene in philosophy. The essays included were to contain information about influences working on the writers and were to bring out specific features of their own thought. This project paralleled similar efforts in Germany and England. Evidently, philosophy was seeking to move into an era of analysis, comparison and self-comprehension. It was assumed that the days of complete dominance by the thinkers of the past, such as Hume and Kant, were over, though they might still give leads. New approaches were needed. I answered the call by stressing realism, naturalism and humanism.

Forty years is quite a lapse of time in an adult's life. Only two of the contributors are, I believe, still alive. What I shall try to do is to indicate a kind of maturation in my outlook. I am still a critical realist but stress more the mechanism underlying natural realism. This, as I see it, is a from-and-to affair in which sensory information is referentially used to give *facts about* the stimulating object. The new realists oversimplified this rather complex activity and read it in terms of presentationalism. That is, they held that the external object was itself given to the percipient. Such presentationalism is usually called naive realism. It was in contrast to it that I spoke of critical realism. I thought of perceptual cognition as a rather mediated achievement informed by sensory informa-tion. I still think that the new realists had such a set against any idea of representation that they did not see any possibility of an intermediate position. Nature, as I see it, was too clever for them. Too clever for the logical positivists also.

Now I don't think nature planned this development but that one thing led to another. As I see it, the sense-organs were evolved as instruments of adjustment of the organism to its environment. Smelling, touch, and hearing all gave guidance. So I think that guidance was the first function and not cognition. Cognition emerged later in man from this first stage. It involved a growing concern, with a social background, with the things around him. Language and concept formation aided. The interrogation, What's that? symbolizes this shift. Factors used in guidance by birds and animals began to stand out as informative. I suppose sight as a distance-receptor had much to do with this. It permitted delayed response. Man's big brain was operating.

Cognizing was, accordingly, an emergent. And it involved the use of sensory information to give facts about objects. As I see it, then, the category of *facts about* emerges with cognizing. I don't think that Wittgenstein realized this connection. His *Tatsache* are rather mysterious. Sensory information, cognizing, and facts go together. In perceptual cognition we are concerned with the things around us. It is tied up with looking at and handling. This activity is the basis of reference. It is a directed affair.

Nor do I think that traditional representational theories did justice to this mediated directedness. Locke made ideas the primary objects of thought and then wondered how he could have knowledge of physical things. This involved his famous two steps in knowing. And Kant opposed phenomena to things-in-themselves. I can quite understand why the new realists thought this was a dead-end. Hence they moved to presenta-tionalism. It seemed to them the only alternative to idealism. Even Russell stressed a primary knowledge of acquaintance. This made sensa-tions, or sense-data, terminal. There is little doubt in my mind that the subjectivism which went with Cartesian dualism played a part. Man, as it were, painted himself in. Philosophy moved to idealism of a grandiose type while science concerned itself with the vast inorganic world and with mensurational methods and experimentation. It is only in our day that the possibility of a basic integration is dawning. I shall have something to say about that possibility later when I try to fit perceptual knowing into the scientific scheme of things. I shall then show that the mechanisism of perceiving is explicable in terms of physics and biology and that it gives a frame within which scientific knowing with its stress on bodies and observation can develop.

One other point I want to make. Cognizing emerged without any theory as to its nature being given. Aristotle, following in the footsteps of Plato, appealed to forms somehow transmitted. But modern science rejected his forms as barren virgins. And it is true that Aristotle's physics was quite inadequate. Descartes fell back on an intuitive reason but British empiricism put forward sensations and ideas. Modern epistemology was thus inaugurated. But ideas became terminal. As I have indicated, the new realism rebelled against subjectivism and idealism and resorted to presentationalism. I acknowledge this temptation in natural realism just because sensations stand out *as functioning* and are not labelled as sensations. I have already noted that representationalism had secured a bad name because it stood for a two-step operation which fizzled out. The job was to achieve a better idea of the function of sensations as informing directed perceiving. As I see it, critical realism consists in an exploration of the conditions of such an operation. It moves between presentationalism and representationalism. In essentials, it is concerned with the path to cognition taken by man.

Since I am inevitably covering a large territory, I am obliged to make remarks on kindred movements. A word, then, upon the use of behaviorism. It was the weakness of introspective psychology that it put percepts in place of external perceiving. The cause of this is obvious. It had no realistic epistemology at hand. It was continuous with the subjectivistic, empiricistic tradition. This, we saw, terminated in ideas. Behaviorism was a natural development connected with biology and animal experimentation. I was in the know in this development since I talked with John Shepard, Maier and Schneirla. Maier was, in point of fact, one of my students. I had later talks with the neurologist, Herrick. I had no objection to animal experiments and admired their ingenuity. But I wanted to keep continuity with an objective human bio-psychology with a stress on external perceiving. On the whole, I found this in the *Gestalt* movement. Man is a symbol-using animal and I fear that formal behaviorism cannot do justice to this evolutionary level. That is why I am somewhat skeptical of the vogue of the term, behaviorism, in the social sciences. Of course, there is objective behavior to be studied. But there is motivation and thinking lying back of it.

Since I am concerned with driving home a philosophical approach, I shall permit myself returns to much the same topic from different angles. I pointed out that nature did not include an explanation of the nature and conditions of the human knowing it achieved. And, as I see it, philosophy when it arose, made a rather bad job of it. This should not be surprising since it was a rather subtle operation. Only in our own days can the various threads be put together. We can, I think, see the limitations under which Hume and Kant suffered. Perhaps I was fortunate in being put in a situation dominated by a scientific outlook. But I still think that was not enough. I kept a sense of basic problems. From the start, I was intrigued by perceiving, the mind-brain problem, evolution and the nature of valuing. I grasped the opportunity by organizing a class in the philosophy of science, perhaps one of the first in this country. I did not pretend to be a scientist. I was frankly a philosopher interested in science. But I soon found that scientists interested in philosophy seldom took the trouble to get inside philosophy. I have in mind Pearson's *Grammar of Science,* Mach's *Analysis of Sensations,* etc. I found the same attitude in Carnap and the logical positivists, even in Wittgenstein. Expertness in logic was not enough, important as that was. My first book (1916) *Critical Realism* was clearly exploratory. I started from natural realism, as I do now, and sought to show its ambiguities. I still think this is a better approach than the Hume-Russell one. It at least puts the onus on subjectivism.

I interject here my disputes with my colleague, Parker, and with Dewey and Hook. Parker could not see how I could get to matter. Ultimately, he stressed intuition or acquaintance, as did Berkely, Hume, and Russell. Actually, I did not reduce knowing to acquaintance. I thought of it as a referential achievement mediated by sensory information. Basically it arrived at facts about. I held that we gain, in perceiving, facts about material things. Electrons, neutrons, positrons, etc., seemed to be ultra-microscopic constituents of material, molar bodies about which, by scientific methods, we gain facts about. I rejected the ideal of the intuition of matter. As I saw it, Dewey and Hook made experience ultimate. But they could not find science's *matter* in experience and so sought to make it a construct. To me, this is one test of the adequacy of instrumentalism and pragmatism. I shall mention this again when I come to ontology. One reason I moved to evolutionary materialism from naturalism is that naturalism was vague in its ontology, often reducing naturalism to methodology.

Since this is a semi-autobiographical account, I may mention the fact that F. H. Bradley, the dean of British philosophers, after reading my *Critical Realism,* wrote me that he could see advantages in realism but could not imagine how one could get beyond appearances. In my terms, appearances were, for him, terminal. The reader, I hope, can see that my analysis of perceiving brought out the referential use of sensory information to inform the externally directed act of perceiving. Animal life passes from sensory guidance to knowledge claims in man.

I do not overestimate the amount and the penetrative character of perceptual knowledge. But it sufficies for everyday adjustments. And the natural realism which results can absorb a good deal of scientific knowledge. But, as I shall show, science began with a new technique of measurement and experimentation on what it called *bodies having mass*. It stressed theories, laws and verifying observation. Perceptual description was left as a kind of background. This continued to bother philosophers. If one looks at the history of modern philosophy, it is easy to see why.

The framework with which it started was a combination of mind-matter dualism and perceptual subjectivism. Since there was no theory of evolution as yet, mind stood out as philosophy's business. Science was, at best, natural philosophy while moral philosophy was set over against it. There developed patterns of thought, such as British empiricism, Kantianism, Hegelianism, idealism, subjective and objective. I entered the field just as Anglo-American idealism was breaking down. The pragmatic revolt of Peirce, James, and Dewey was making itself felt. This still kept an experiential context and did not emphasize epistemology. It is not surprising that some of the younger men became suspicious of this neglect. The obvious thing to do was to examine sense-perception. And so arose, almost simultaneously, the new realism and critical realism.

The new realists, as I have already indicated, embraced presentationalism. They could see no dividends in anything savoring of representationalism. The critical realists were a mixed bunch. I had given the name to it but found the essence-wing dominant. I shall later examine Durant Drake—who was in touch with Strong and Santayana—and try to bring out my divergence. Their essences seemed to me to have a Platonic flavor and to have no clear empirical base. I, on the other hand, stressed the from-and-to mechanism of perceiving and the informational role of sensations, arguing that concepts were responsible to them and that the object gave the information used in testing statements. But I fear that I was not much listened to. Montague gave a rather biassed story of American realism and Dewey did not like epistemology. After the Great Depression, American philosophers turned to European models and movements, seemingly satisfied with the *cliché* that the new realists could not explain error and the critical realists could not account for truth. I have been criticized for speaking of American Neo-colonialism. But I think there was some justification for it. Time will give its verdict. This, I think, has already begun.

I have indicated that, while making no pretence to being a scientist, I kept closely in touch with science. I worked out a broad base, keeping in mind the mechanism of perceiving, the mind-brain situation, the nature of evolution and the difference between cognizing and valuation. I sought to fit these strands together. Despite Schilpp I may be a living philosopher, whatever that may mean. At this point, I just shrug my shoulders. I wish Americans were better historians. I note that my *Evolutionary Naturalism* is not even mentioned in the bibliography on emergence in Edward's *Encyclopedia* though Lloyd Morgan wrote an essay on it in his book *Emergent Evolution;* and the discussion on *materialism* makes no reference to the book, edited by Farber, McGill and myself, called *Philosophy for the Future: The Quest of Modern Materialism* (MacMillan, 1949). I do not think Farber and McGill should be thus ignored. Young American Philosophers when they write on materialism go to Australia, to Smart and Armstrong. They are good men but I suggest consideration of the title, *Look Homeward, Angel.*

To continue, I became increasingly interested in what was called a cognitive relation. Was this postulated relation internal or external? The idealists held that it was internal. Following Berkeley's lead, that to be is to be perceived, they advanced to Hegel's rejection of things-in-themselves and settled on thought as ultimate. The real is the rational and the rational is the real. Here we had a kind of logical immanence. When Royce was confronted by a realistic revolt he argued that realism involved the denial of any meaningful cognitive relation and implied the absurd postulation of a reality lying beyond cognition. What, indeed, was the external cognitive relation some realists talked about? I note that Blanshard falls back on the duplicity of an internal meaning and an external meaning, modelled on Royce.

I was convinced that there was a certain blindness to possibilities in this controversy. Was not the idea of a cognitive relation misleading? As I looked at the mechanism of perceiving, I noted the interplay of responsive reference and the use of incoming sensations as informational about their external source. As I saw it, cognition is an achievement founded on this interplay. The first stage is guidance and the second stage is referential claims. What is called transcendence and which, on its face, seems mysterious is an expression of this from-and-to operation. If we could not referentially respond to the things stimulating us and if the messages coming from them did not contain information which could be directionally used, then there could be no human knowing. But merely to label it transcendence left it unexplained. But, once we can denote objects and think of them in terms of the information they send us, the road is clear both for natural realism and scientific realism. We humans gain facts about external things. Microscopes and telescopes can come into use. These increase the information received. And the cosmos grows.

A few words now on the dispute between epistemological monists and epistemological dualists, since there has been some misunderstanding on this topic.

The idealists were epistemological monists with their idea of an internal cognitive relation. The new realists shifted to what they called an external cognitive relation, that of presentational realism. Objects are just given to awareness. This is a form of naive realism. R. B. Perry was quite frank about this. Over against this they put the mistakes of representative realism with Locke and Kant as prime exhibits. This was called epistemological dualism. Montague, of course, put the critical realists in this category. Lovejoy, I think, came nearest to this classification. But the essence-wing of critical realism and my own analysis of knowing sought a reformulation between presentationalism and traditional representationalism. I shall examine Drake later on this point. He thought the essence before the mind was identical with the essence in the object known. I, as you will expect, put sensations and concepts within the cognitive act, as having a cognitive function, and regarded the denoted external thing as the terminal object. It is thus a non-presentational, epistemological monism. That is, it is a one-step view which recognizes mediation.

This is important, since I hold that we never *intuit* external realities, such as matter and energy, but only gain facts about them. This fits in with my rejection of a cognitive relation.

I shall now pass briefly over traditional puzzles about perceiving, the look of the face in the mirror, the stick bent in water, the changing appearances of things as we walk away from them. I recently argued with C. I. Lewis about the situation.[1] Torn between the difficulties confronting both presentationalism and representationalism and not understanding my intermediate position he could only conclude that presentations are *"ingredients* in objects, the bent stick in water is an ingredient in the really straight stick". This, as I point out, shows the influence of Whitehead. Whitehead, as I shall indicate, turned back from Hume to a reformed and panpsychistic subjectivism. I, on the other hand, pressed forward to a realistic analysis of perceiving in which sense-impressions are

1. *The Philosophy of C. I. Lewis,* edited by P. Schilpp.

used in the act as informational. This is, in my opinion, far better than to regard presentations as ingredients in objects.

The point is crucial. One escapes from the old dilemma of a choice between presentational realism and a two-step representationalism. And one can do justice to the from-and-to mechanism of perceiving. One should perceive the stick as bent in water. Given the *from* conditions, one should see one's face in the mirror as reversed. Things should look smaller as we walk away from them. The pictures on the screen result from projections and reflections of light patterns. I think all this confirms my analysis.

The next task is to integrate science and philosophy, to show how they can be fitted together.

Science clashed with medieval philosophy in its beginning by attacking, first, Aristotle's physics and, second, the Ptolemaic astronomy. By developing the ideas of mass and inertia, it put *bodies having mass* in place of qualitative things. This led to the experimental discovery of the law of falling bodies. After this came the law of gravity and celestial mechanics. But there was, as yet, no new epistemology. Descartes made his effort. But philosophy had to grapple with perceiving and the role of mind. As we have seen, this was not easy. And so science went ahead from physics to chemistry and thence to biology, developing method and techniques. In my own day, I saw that the theory of evolution might undercut Cartesian dualism. The idea of levels in nature and emergent qualities and abilities focussed on life and the brain-mind situation. But, first, one must escape from idealism and subjectivism. I sought to do this in my revision of natural realism which brought out the mechanism of perceiving and rejected mere presentationalism. I called this critical realism. Since I was always seeking to integrate science and philosophy I had a rather broad context for my thinking.

How, then, do I see the situation? First, I think science and philosophy can agree on a realistic epistemology. That will be a big step forward. The molecular theory of life is, also, an advance in my lifetime. Now comes the mind-brain situation. I outlined a double-knowledge approach which could harmonize behaviorism and neurology with introspectionism. This is an *identity* outlook. But now we come to ontology, to the theory of being, of what is. Philosophy long speculated on this topic. On the whole, modern philosophy frowned on materialism. This was partly because science tended to take a rather narrow, external view of matter and energy. I suppose this outlook reflected the dominance of the inorganic sciences. Philosophy, as we have seen, was, itself, dominated by the thought of mind.

And so we come to ontology and metaphysics. I have given this much space to epistemology since I regard it as the gateway to the consideration of ontology.

A matter now of terminology. I had used the term, naturalism, in my book, *Evolutionary Naturalism* and in my contribution to *Contemporary American Philosophy*. It was a good contrast term to supernaturalism, but I had expressed misgivings already in my first book, *Critical Realism*, as to its ontological adequacy. I quote: "If the critic desires to follow the present liking for the word *New*, he is at liberty to call my position, Neo-materialism or the New Materialism." My colleagues in editing the book, *Philosophy for the Future*, pointed to the tendency among Columbian pragmatists to identity naturalism with the use of scientific method. I was willing to recognize that connection but, as a physical realist, that did not seem to me enough.

And so we turn to a reconstruction of ontology in terms of bodies having mass, bodies moving through space in clocked time, subject to the laws of motion, particles combining chemically in fixed proportions. All this is now conceptual and yet linked with mensurational observations. It is felt to be more penetrative and to give more adequate knowledge of the world. And common sense absorbs it, adds it to natural realism. But the question will not down. In what sense have we still to do with the *sensible world?* We want to *see,* if possible, these atoms and molecules, welcome the electron microscope and atom-smashers.

This, I think, is a healthy instinct. But it must be supplemented by a keener awareness of the nature and reach of everyday perceiving. I have argued that we cannot intuit external things but that we have in perceiving a blend of sensory content and the facts about objects which they convey. The new realism was misled and emphasized the sensory presentation arguing that the only alternative was two-step representation, a bankrupt alternative. I, on the other hand, have tried to show that sensory content is used as giving information about the denoted object. It is quite inevitable that the two factors are blended in natural realism. A sophisticated epistemology can distinguish them. Hence even the electron microscope reproduces this situation. We see an atom or a molecule much as we see a marble. But if we could not do this we would be puzzled and slightly skeptical of their reality.

I am arguing, therefore, against Eddington's two tables, the table we perceive and the table in terms of scientific, mensurational facts about. I am also arguing against idealism and the pragmatic notion that scientific objects are constructs. The alternatives here are basic for ontology.

What we start with ontologically at the level of natural realism is the *existential reality* of persons and things in their intercourse. Persons throb in their awareness of doing and feeling. Things are acted on, must be adjusted to, resist, behave. And we develop criteria of existence. Fairies, ghosts and phlogiston do not exist. But existence is not a stuff we intuit. It is, rather, a basic category of thought. When we say material things exist we mean they are part of our world and must be reckoned with. The same holds for persons, a peculiar part of the material world. And here we must examine arguments for dualism and theism. Have we good reasons for granting existence to immaterial things? Ontology must study such questions.

My friend, Parker, used to question my employment, now and then, of the term "stuff". To me, it was a category reflecting the idea of something to be handled and used. To the Latins, wood stood out as a stuff. It was typical of matter, material. In contrast to Plato, Aristotle had introduced an unknowable something as a foundation for forms. But the atomists had been more forthright. Atoms were bits of material. As I see it, modern science is particulate, even as regards energy. There are quanta of action. Thus stuff is a kind of preliminary category which must fit into space, time, and causality. I take categories very seriously as concerned with knowledge about the constitution of the cosmos. Evolutions stands for the emergence of new categories such as life, mentation, knowledge, valuation. All these categories are, to me, instances of knowledge about the world and not *a priori* endowments, as they were for Kant.

I am now going to compare my outlook with that of Durant Drake and Whitehead. The first represented the essence-wing of critical realism with a panpsychistic ontology. The second is a panpsychist with touches of essence views in his epistemology. I confess I like these grapplings with ontology which I miss in pragmatism. It was because Dewey never quite faced up to the problem of perceiving and fell back on a vague experientialism that his outlook seemed to me unsatisfactory. But this does not mean that the brain-mind situation is not puzzling. It must be approached with circumspection. Drake and Whitehead offer an approach which emphasizes the psychical. I, on the other hand, argue that the psychical emerges within the physical, *properly understood*. This was a thesis in my first book.

But let me turn to Drake. I shall use his contribution to *Contemporary*

American Philosophy, Vol. I, as a base. There are two steps in his outlook, first, his theory of essences and, second, his rejection of emergence. He regards the latter as involving ontological discontinuity. This is a serious charge which must be met. Whitehead, also, rejects the idea of emergence. I take the path of the importance of organization and *Gestalten* and of levels of causality. I argue that the content of being reflects varying structure and function. That is, I do not begin with a fixed image of material systems as reducible to isolated components but stress patterns and processes. My view of perceiving emphasizes an interplay.

What is an essence? On page 285, Drake defines it as that which confronts us in perception, blue skies and red sunsets. These are the *data* of perception. They are this or that "physical object out there." This would seem to me an expression of what I call natural realism, which I regard as a growth founded on the referential use of sensory information. What Drake wants to avoid is mentalism and representationism. He speaks of projection as giving us supposititious physical things. Since these are products of projection they are not the essences which make up our mental life. And then he goes on to examine the complexities of introspection.

It is obvious that I do not accept his rather mysterious projections for I stress the interplay of reference and sensory information. With his projection theory Drake is nearer to the new realists than I am. In veridical perceiving his essences are, supposedly, one with the external thing. I take the sensory information as giving facts about the external thing. All of us try to escape two-step representationalism.

I turn now to the question of emergence. Drake seems to have identified it with dualistic vitalism. I, on the other hand, stressed levels of causality. Molecular biology illustrates what I had in mind. In DNA and RNA we have *codal causality* at work, the gene pools controlling growth.

But the neuro-muscular system has its own causal job to do, that of responsible adjustment to a complex and changing environment. It must use the information coming to it through the sense-organs. This requires alertness to signals. As organisms pass from the instinctual level to the greater flexibility of guidance by the use of experience, responsive *awareness of alternatives increases.* Decisions must be made. This involves a still higher level of causality. The brain, as a whole, must function. Now this involves functional compresence. As this develops we reach, as in morality, what I have called agential causality. The self with its dispositions must function as a control. But I cannot here go into that. I must step back in history to the two-substance theory of Descartes which, in my opinion, embodied a both pre-evolutionary outlook and a bad episte-mology.

When the physical is opposed to the psychical, I find operating the assumption that we have a sort of intuition of the stuff of the material world. That was, certainly, true in the early stages of Newtonianism. But I do not think this assumption is valid. Even in 1916 I argued that consciousness was, in its way, spatial since it functioned within neural operations. As I see it, scientists tend to be puzzled by the rise of consciousness since they are dominated by impersonal, quantitative facts. I, myself, can see no *a priori* reason why sensory qualia and raw feels should not arise in neural patterns and processes. I note that Lord Brain argued that sound tones are connected with paths in the auditory area. Smell, taste and vision are similarly connected with specialized sense-organs and cerebral areas. I have no doubt that science will study such sense-organs and cerebral areas in great detail. But, from my point of view, it must accept sensory experiences as data. The rising identity outlook rejects any assumed prior intuition of the content of being, such as Descartes's. In its way, idealism reenforced this tradition in a converse fashion by making ideas terminal. Berkeley's to be is to be perceived illustrates this outlook. Dewey and Hook could not see how we could know matter and made it a construct. I, on the other hand, point out that we begin with facts about molar things and move to the microscopic. But it is always facts about, never intuition.

Merely a few words about Whitehead. As I see it, he was near to Drake. But his attitude to Hume is strategic. Many take his defense of causality as against Hume as focal. I am, also, a defender of causality as a category. But I see Whitehead's reformed subjectivism as based upon Hume's acceptance of sensations as terminal. I do not. I regard them as used as informational in referential perceiving. Whitehead then proceeds to change them into essences, eternal objects. Platonism and logic then take over in ingenious ways. I regard him as a belated Victorian. But I have great respect for his intellectual stature. I tried to dig to a new founda-tion. Whitehead moved from above downward and was opposed to evolutionary emergence. I moved from down upward stressing new levels of causal operations. And so I arrived at man and his precarious condition and at humanism. I spoke of the next step in religion and studied the *dramatics of historical religion* with critical sympathy. Religion will *come of age as* it reorientates itself to man's actual situation.[2]

2. See my book, *Religion Coming of Age*. New York: MacMillan, 1928.

But I have about exhausted the space permitted me. I want, in conclusion, to say something about values and valuation.

It will be recalled that I contrasted the role of cognition with that of valuation. I argued that man was a doer as well as a knower. Valuation is closely connected with action as in morality. As I see it, feeling must interplay with knowledge to arrive at a justified attitude and appraisal of objects and projects. These concern the role of the objective in the personal and the social economy.

As we would expect, language reflects this activity and we have terms uniquely expressive of appraisals and criteria and good reasons given for their adoption. When we say that this picture is beautiful we not only mean that we like it but that we can point to features of the picture which back our aesthetic judgment. There has been an interplay between feeling and features in our attitude. Moral judgment, likewise, reflects a similar interplay between moral feeling and awareness of social consequences.

The point I would make is that value assignments are not like cognitional descriptions but are, nevertheless, of objective import in their context. That is, their objectivity is not factual and transcendent but immanent and functional. They are tied in with the human scene. This is one reason why I did not like G.E. Moore's approach with its view that 'good' referred to a non-natural property. It is simply not a factually descriptive assignment. One must have a keener sense for the leads given by language. And this reflects the fact that man is both a knower and an agent. He must size up possibilities of action in their bearing on his life.

I want, finally, to make some remarks on the old dilemma of determinism versus free-will. We are now, I take it, at the level of what I called agential causality. The agent is aware of alternatives in action. These, if he is reflective, he will try to evaluate in accordance with moral opinion. But the self is a growth affected by education and disposition. The best he can do is to deliberate and make up his own mind on the question. We call him free when he is in that situation. That is, he is not dictated to by others. This is, of course, a matter of degree. There are various pressures at work.

As I see it, the term "free-will" is rather ambiguous. It may stand for moral autonomy or, sometimes, for a kind of erratic spontaneity of a faculty called "will". I do not believe in such a faculty though I fully recognize the purposive side of man's nature. What I object to is the assumption that man is a puppet enmeshed in the working of a fixed mechanism. I object as much to theological determinism of the foreordained type. My point is that making up one's mind is not a predetermined operation.

It is because of this personal situation that doubt and hesitation may arise. And, after an act, regret and self-condemnation may manifest themselves. The human self is not a fixed, static reality. It is, in some measure open to revision, sometimes drastically so. A new value perspective may manifest itself. In all this man differs from the massive, inorganic world. Here my idea of levels of causality comes to the front. I am in no sense reductive but stress man's uniqueness. But I want to see it in natural setting. And there is, alas, too much human bondage, as Spinoza saw.

This approach is in line with the recognition of self-determination. I, myself, speak of agential causality. But the human self is a growth. Growth tends to be too passive a term. There is, in human affairs, much struggle and tense decision-making. The historian and the sociologists both warn me that most people are creatures of habit and of situational setting. This is, in part, a matter of social pressure and lack of a vital education. One must not expect too much. Varying attitudes to war illustrate this. I, myself, hate war as immoral and dangerous to civilization. But I find that many people are insensitive to its inhumanity and danger.

While, then, I am a naturalistic humanist, I am not unaware of man's uniqueness and the dramatic implications of the human condition. I do not thrust aside the old religions with disdain but look upon them as no longer quite adequate. Religious thinkers must raise their sights and deepen their moral and intellectual integrity.[3] Man's outlook on himself and the cosmos in which he finds himself is changing. I, myself, am prepared for an ecumenical dialogue on such matters. And I do not think it can long be escaped. Religion, ethics, and social and political philosophy are now intertwined. All this will require grounding. I make no snide remarks on America's great, or notorious, men but do not think all is well. I could think out a number of slogans but they all come to the need of sympathy for our fellow man and the enduring importance of enlightenment. Such is the foundation of social wisdom.

3. I cannot close this essay without paying my respects to Professor Brightman of Boston University, a contemporary of mine. He belonged to the Bowne tradition but was more of a realist, stressing epistemological dualism. He was much concerned with the problem of evil and introduced a surd in the theistic scheme. He was modernistically inclined and I found him very suggestive. I have often wondered what his reaction to Tillich and German existentialism would have been.

Roy Wood Sellars
University of Michigan

Ethics for Fellows
in the Fate of Existence*

Herbert Spiegelberg

"A sense of justice is grounded in the mental operation by which a person puts himself in someone else's shoes." *The New Yorker,* January 6, 1973, Notes and Comments.

1. *Basic Concerns.*

What follows is not a personal creed. I doubt that in my case such a self-important profession, even if I could offer it in good faith, would make sense to my fellow beings. I doubt even more that this is the job of the philosopher in the Socratic tradition. What I want to try instead is a first formulation of certain ideas which have become increasingly important to me. They were sparked by experiences of my childhood during the First World War in my native Alsace, then on the German side of the battlelines. They have grown in me since my adolescence in response to the circumstances into which I found myself born and which I have encountered in my later life, including the expulsion as a German from Alsace, now French again, the rejection by Nazi Germany because of racial "impurity," and the admission as an immigrant to the United States in 1938 on the French quota because of my birthplace in what was retroactively considered France. For these ideas I have found no real support in past and present philosophy and too little in recent existential thought. I believe that they contain the most relevant insights I can offer

*Carl Wellman, my colleague and friend at Washington University, helped me greatly by his constructive challenges.

to my fellow humans at this time. Hence I no longer feel the right to withhold them, while still hoping for a chance to develop them more adequately, and particularly to put the proper phenomenological foundations under them. Much as I believe in the possibility and necessity of such foundations, this paper should not yet be considered as a valid sample of phenomenological philosophizing. At the present all I can do for additional support is to refer to a series of papers listed in the footnote[1] which were published since the Second World War.

My title should speak for itself. But I would like to make it plain that by "ethics" I do not understand a mere theory of moral conduct, let alone a meta-theory of ethical language, but an attempt to offer some guidelines for approaching the mounting problems of our day. I will try not to dogmatize. But I shall have to appeal to the empathetic efforts of my readers, hoping that my attempt to present my findings will evoke in them similar experiences, or help them to think through those they have had thus far.

What will need most explaining is what I mean by the phrase "fellows in the fate of existence." Even before doing so, I would like to account for the cumbersomeness of the expression "fate of existence." Why do I not speak simply of "fellows in existence" or simply of "fellow-beings"? Firstly, I want to make it plain that I consider the fate of "existence" a special and ultimate basis for fellowship. Moreover, in talking about "existence" I want to bring out the affinity of my thinking to existential philosophy. However, in so doing I do not want to subscribe to any specific form of "existentialism." In particular I have found no support

1. (1) "A Defense of Human Equality," *The Philosophical Review* 53 (1944), 101-24.

(2) "Equality in Existentialism," *Nomos* IX (1967), 193-213.

(3) " 'Accident of Birth': A Non-utilitarian Motif in Mill's Philosophy," *Journal of the History of Ideas* 22 (1961), 475-592.

(4) "Human Dignity: A Challenge to Contemporary Philosophy," in Gotesky, R. and Laszlo, E., ed., *Human Dignity*. New York: Gordon & Breach, 1970, 39-64.

(5) "On the 'I-am-me' Experience in Childhood and Adolescence," *Psychologia* (Kyoto) 4 (1961), 135-146; republished in *Review of Existential Psychology and Psychiatry* 4 (1964), 3-21.

(6) "A Phenomenological Approach to the Ego," *The Monist* (1965), 1-17.

(7) "Phenomenology through Vicarious Experience," in *Phenomenology: Pure and Applied*, ed. by Erwin Straus, Pittsburgh: Duquesne Univ. Press, 1964, 105-126.

(8) "Toward a Phenomenology of Imaginative Understanding of Others," *Proceedings of the XIth International Congress of Philosophy* 7 (Brussels, 1953), 235-239.

(9) "On Some Human Uses of Phenomenology," in F. J. Smith, ed., *Perspectives in Phenomenology*, The Hague: Martinus Nijhoff, 1970, 16-31.

for my position in Sartre's version of it. I consider his failure after thirty years to supply the explicit promised ethics one of existentialism's sadly lost opportunities. This is true especially of Sartre's failure to spell out the ethical implications of his emphasis on the essential contingency of human existence. What to me remains the main significance of existential theory is that, thanks to Kierkegaard, the wonder and terror of man's way of existence has been highlighted in a new and sensitizing manner, something which the mere term "being" or "fellow being" cannot convey.

But why call "existence" a fate? For at least two reasons:

(1) Without implying fatalism, for which I hold no brief, the word "fate" stresses the inexorableness of existence as the prime and ultimate fact about our being, which cannot and must not be glossed over.

(2) Without identifying fate with "blind fate" the word expresses the fact that the victims of this fate are totally ignorant of any possible meaning in it or purpose behind it. In this sense the mere fact of our existence is something that has befallen us, has happened to us as an "accident" in a sense which does not imply a denial of cause. This is one of the meanings of the phrase "accident of birth," which is basic for my present approach to ethics. However, what I would like to keep out, especially at this stage, is the connotation of a sinister power which has "thrown," "thrust," or "flung" us into existence. These melodramatic terms, injected into the discussion without real clarification of their implications especially by Martin Heidegger, introduce a kind of anthropomorphism and Promethean revolt for which we have as little ground as for a more theistic interpretation implying a mission entrusted to us. Instead we had better face our situation and in fact our predicament soberly without such futile emotions as cosmic rage or exultation.

I shall begin with an attempt to clarify what I mean by the idea of fellowship and particularly by "fellowship in the fate of existence." I shall then simply state some of the general ethical premises which will form the basis for my subsequent ethical reflections, without trying to justify them. The balance of the paper will consist in an attempt to spell out some of the implications of my approach for the most burning moral issues in the present crisis of humanity, which can no longer afford its past provincialism. For mankind can survive only if it develops a sense of planetary fellowship without which the ideas of world citizenship and world government must remain powerless dreams.

2. Types of Fellowship

"Fellowship" is an idea which thus far seems to have had surprisingly little consideration in ethical literature. Only the phrase "fellow feeling" figures conspicuously in Adam Smith's ethics as an equivalent of "sympathy."[2] Even more noteworthy is the fact that in this context Smith stressed the need of putting ourselves imaginatively into the places of our fellow beings. But he supplies no clear and cogent connection between the fact of fellow feeling and the ethical duty of imaginative self-transposal.

One might think that the idea of fellowship is nothing but that of human brotherhood or "fraternity." But quite apart from the "male chauvinism" expressed in this metaphor, its implications are different and more problematic. Already the expansion of the original meaning from the relation of brothers within the nuclear family unit to larger groups and finally to mankind as one family is far from obvious. Moreover, it makes sense only if mankind is a family with two common parents, one father of all mankind clearly not being enough, as commonly asserted, whether these be human fathers and mothers or superhuman ones. From this point of view the idea of fellowship is certainly less loaded than that of brotherhood, and certainly theologically neutral.

But what does the appeal to fellowship imply? The history of the English word with its etymological connotation of partnership in a business venture (from *feoh*, cattle, money, i.e., one who lays down money) hardly throws much light on the present ethical implications of this term. Even though there must be some historical connection between these meanings, at present it hardly carries any live meaning. Here the main division is that between two types of fellowship. The one is based on choice, be it by co-optation, as in the case of academic fellows, or by free joining, e.g., through a financial contribution to an association, or the mutual "good fellowship" of an informal group of more or less "jolly fellows." The other fellowship is none of our own choosing and doing but of finding ourselves "in the same boat," of being caught in the same unchosen predicament. Coming from the earlier idea of fellowship as a voluntary association[3] one might well wonder why such an involuntary

---

2. *The Theory of Sentiments* (1759) Part I Section I ("Of Sympathy").
3. The seeming priority of voluntary fellowship or association may well be characteristic of the English language. Thus Greek *hetairos*, a word whose etymological roots seem to be far from clear, refers to all kinds of being joined, voluntary and involuntary; Latin *socius*, related to *sequi* (to follow) also does not presuppose an act of association; French *camarade* refers to sharing the same chamber or room; German *Genosse* is based on the relation of enjoying *(Genuss)* something jointly, such as a house *(Hausgenosse)*; similarly the common western word "companion" expresses the sharing of the same bread *(panis)*.

condition can make any claims on us, let alone more valid claims than those based on voluntary association. But this is precisely what I maintain. To show this requires some more basic considerations not based on the mere study of words and their history. What is it then in the natural human condition that establishes a real bond among persons who have not chosen such a binding relation?

Fellowship in the basic sense is always fellowship in a certain respect. It does not make sense to speak of Tom, Dick and Harry as being fellows, except in the colloquial sense of being "nice fellows," without saying *in what* they are fellows or what they share. Now this sharing can refer to practically everything under the sun (and in a sense even the sun and the universe beyond). It need not mean sharing identically the same object; even having different but equal or similar conditions in common may be the basis for such sharing. It can begin with such relatively trivial circumstances as sharing the same house or address or public conveyance, and extend to sharing the same country ("fellow countrymen"), the same planet, or the same time in history ("fellow contemporaries"). Fellows who in this manner share identically the same fate may be called *same-fated* or *fate-joined* fellows.

But there is also a very different kind of "sharing." Having the same height or skin-color, sex or class and ultimately human kind or simply being does not mean that we are connected by real contact with the same thing or situation. Here our sharing consists in having parallel, i.e., equal or similar, characteristics without being linked by them. Fellowship based on such sharing may be called *like-fated* or *parallel-fated* fellowship. It hardly needs pointing out that fellowship in the fate of existence is of this latter kind.

It seems noteworthy that not all fellowship is essentially conscious. While choice-based fellowships are essentially conscious, this is by no means true of fellowships in fate. It may be relatively frequent in same-fated fellowships based on actual living together in relation to the shared object or situation. But this is not the case with parallel-fated fellowships such as the class-fellowship of the proletariat. To make us conscious of them takes comparing, pointing out and even awakening. No wonder that we are so little aware of our fellowship in existence.

3. *Fellowships in Parallel Fate*

Let us now consider some more momentous instances of such parallel-fated fellowships.

There is the fellowship of those struck by the same disease like polio or cancer or by physical suffering in general—according to Albert

Schweitzer the basis for a "brotherhood of those marked by pain." This should not rule out the possibility of a fellowship among those who "struck it rich", i.e., those "fortunate" few or many who have been spared disaster and suffering and enjoy the bliss of a great aesthetic or religious experience, as in a concert or on separate pilgrimages.

But while such instances of shared departures from normal experiences may stand out and give rise to a special kind of bond and fellowship, they are by no means the most important ones, since they are based on common accidents or coincidences. The basic instances are those grounded in our essential conditions. In ascending order of relevance I nominate here:

(1) our common fate of belonging to one rather than to another group of beings, such as:

    (a) being female or male (fellows in sex)

    (b) being young or old (generation-fellows)

    (c) being black, yellow, brown, or white (race-fellows)

    (d) being in one particular place or time (neighbors)

    (e) being Chinese or American, Arab or Jew (fellow nationals).

(2) But there are even more common and non-discriminatory parallel fates, predisposing to potential fellowships:

    the fate of being born human, rather than animal (fellow humans), or

        being alive (fellow living beings)

    and finally of "being,"

        both in the form of "mere being" (fellow beings)

        and of existing (fellow existers).

It is on this condition of sharing the fate of being human and of existing, with all its assets and liabilities, that I would like to base my approach to ethics.

4. *Accidents of Birth as Parallel Fates*

Why should such parallel fates have any ethical significance, establishing ethical relationships among us? After all, isn't it understood that in this case there is no direct social bond between us, as in the case of partnership and companionship?

It is probably true that in our usual lives we are not very ready to pay attention to our ethical bonds with parallel-fated fellows, something which we are almost forced to do in the cases of fate-joined fellows sharing the same real "boat" with us. However, it takes not much sensitizing or reminding to see that the new situation is at least analogous—and infinitely more momentous. But we have to be awakened to it. What we have to appeal to for such an ethical awakening is what we at times casually, if not thoughtlessly, call "the accident of birth" which assigns to each one of us a specific lot and no other. To take this phrase seriously is, I firmly believe, the lever which can move the dead weight of our social lethargy.

What specifically does it mean to take the accident of birth seriously? At first glance one may think that this phrase is nothing but a manner of speech which makes little if any real sense. After all, what sense is there to speaking about "birth" as an accident? Even if we do not share the deterministic or fatalistic view that there are no accidents but only ignorance of definite causes, is it not obvious that scientifically there is nothing accidental about birth or, for that matter, conception, and in fact about all the accidents which threaten our lives, and against which we take insurance policies?

But it does not take much reflection to realize that something quite different is at stake when we begin to fully realize the accidental character of our station. How else could it be that a determinist such as J. S. Mill was greatly influenced by this motif throughout his social and political thinking?[4] Here I shall not attempt to show the real meaning of our talk about the accident of birth. I shall simply submit that what is involved is not a mere denial of natural causation, but a fundamentally novel conception. Its thrust is to bring out the absence of any moral title to whatever accidental, non-essential position we find ourselves and others to be in, be it economic plight, sex or skin color, which were Mill's prime concerns.

And now for the positive aspect of the "accident": In denying any moral claim to our congenital position I am pleading for a novel concept of existential justice (and injustice). I mean by this that existence as such involves for the existers certain basic claims, regardless of whether they are fulfilled or even fulfillable, in fact and even in principle. Specifically,

(1) The fact that "I am me" is something not of my choosing or doing for which I can claim any credit or can be legitimately blamed. At best I can have some responsibility for my further becoming, for the "nature" I shape by my choices and efforts out of my initial me-ness. My being-me is therefore an "accident of birth," a fate into which I am "cast" without my consent. Now I submit that whatever is done to a person without his consent is in principle an existential wrong, regardless of whether it is an objective benefit, a harm or something neutral: even benefits forced upon

4. See "Accident of Birth: A Non-utilitarian Motif in Mill's Philosophy," see note (1).

a beneficiary, in order to be valid gifts implying obligation, have to be freely accepted. And one cannot take it for granted that such benefits will be accepted, if only because such acceptance diminishes one's moral freedom, as even the proverb knows (*beneficia accipere est libertatem vendere*). Hence the fate of one's own very self-being involves essentially an "existential" wrong in the sense of a "slight" to one's basic freedom. There is something morally incongruous about the lack of consent, and even the impossibility of being asked for one's consent, to one's own basic being. There is perhaps even an essential indignity in this predicament. To this extent the repudiation of his existence by the suicide is not only a defensible protest but an act of reaffirmation of his dignity.

(2) The fact that I am or exist is likewise a condition on which I have had no say—and actually could not possibly have had any say. But this impossibility does not preclude the fact that to be exposed to being is a "condemnation" without a prior hearing. Regardless of whether the infliction of a temporary existence with the attached price of having to die is a clear objective benefit; there is something morally outrageous about this situation and the implied imputation that I have to acquiesce to it. To be, to exist is in this sense an affront to one's freedom. In this sense it means: being an innocent victim, a pawn, at least at the start of one's career.

(3) The fact that whatever one is at the start by way of one's congenital endowment, from one's genetic heritage to one's intellectual and emotional constitution, is something one never asked for or could have asked for, despite Plato's telling myth of Er in the *Republic,* telling because it concedes that on moral grounds we really should have had a say about our "lot" and even our character. This applies particularly to

(a) being a human. The very idea of the migration of souls (metempsychosis) emerging independently in several cultures (e.g., Greece and India), is an indication that being oneself is by no means identical, and experienced as identical, with being human. Totemism, animal worship and even plant (tree) and mountain worship is another confirmation. There is simply no essential, let alone morally necessary relation, between being a self and being cast in human shape. *A fortiori* this is true of

(b) being male or female,

(c) being of one race or another,

(d) being of one constitution or temperament or another, including various kinds of physical "beauty" or "ugliness,"

(e) being born normal (healthy) or with various "handicaps."

(4) The fact that our initial station, i.e., our belonging to any particu-

lar (historical) time, (national) culture and (social) situation is none of our choosing. There is therefore an essential moral unbalance in being born into any such station, whether it turns out that this station is one of overprivilege, as in being born into the aristocracy or into the most powerful nation, or into the proletariat, or an underprivileged (under-developed) nation.

Whatever pride (or shame) we may feel, and may be exhorted to feel and display on such occasions by our current education, is therefore morally and existentially indefensible, apart from being socially disruptive. There is no excuse for pride and shame over congenital conditions, which are all accidents of birth.

5. *Some Premises for Ethical Implications of the Fellowship in the Fate of Existence*

In outlining some of the implications of fellowship I am clearly making some general and specific assumptions about ethics which I shall not spell out in detail, let alone justify explicitly. They include the following beliefs:

(a) There are "objective" qualities and conditions which, regardless of our whims and wishes, demand our respect (usually called "values," "worths," dignities"), such as harmony, fairness, freedom.

(b) Our freedom and power to "realize" them in the sense of both noticing them and actualizing them involves for us a responsibility, however limited, for their place and survival in the world.

(c) The accident of birth involves for its beneficiaries and victims at least the duty of imaginative self-transposal and empathy.

6. *Ethical Implications of Fellowship in the Fate of Existence*

a. *Why fellowship in fate commits us*

It is relatively easy to see that fellowship in the sense of a companionship freely entered by mutual promises or consent involves mutual obligations and responsibilities. These are the obligations based on promises or similar free commitments. But the situation is quite different where we find ourselves as fellows who never asked to be matched together, caught willy-nilly in the same predicament. And here there is an additional important difference between the situation where we share identically the same plight and that where we find ourselves merely in a parallel but separate plight. In the former case we are tied together by the bonds of neighborship among individuals depending on one another, receiving aid from or giving it to one another, since we have a joint stake in the preservation of what we share. But such a comradeship or mateship of people thrown together by circumstance is very different from the fellowship of those who "share" merely a similar situation in different corners of this planet. "Why on earth" should they be at all ethically related to one another?

Perhaps the best way to show that they are indeed so related is to imagine a case where, among people of roughly similar condition, one were struck by a tornado, while most or all others remained safe and perhaps even profited from the misfortune of the one less "fortunate." It is certainly no accident that witnessing such scenes and even hearing or reading about them, we cannot suppress the thought: How come that the twister struck him rather than me? Can we then simply shrug off such ideas and rejoice in our better luck or fortunes? True, Lucretius wrote:

> " 'Tis sweet, when, down the mighty main, the winds
> Roll up its waste of waters, from the land
> To watch another's labouring anguish far."[5]

The very revulsion we may feel against such seeming smugness is an indication that there is a tie between us and those in conditions parallel to our own, such as equal physical and economic distress, the basic human condition, and even being itself.

Why? I submit that there is something like a moral unbalance if people sharing similar situations are subject to a "discrimination" which favors those more "fortunate" by the mere "happenstance" of "good luck," and disfavors the "unfortunate" victims of "bad luck." There is clearly a special sense of injustice behind our words when we say that it was "unfair" that a person struggling under a physical handicap should also be struck by the loss of his supporting friends. Something, we feel, is basically wrong about such a fate and, what is more, something ought to be done about it.

In a different context I have asserted by way of a tentative premise that unearned advantages call for redress, and apparently this "axiom" has appealed even to such original thinkers on justice as John Rawls to the extent that he seems to take it for granted.[6] I consider this as additional support for the belief that fellow beings are tied to each other

5. *On the Nature of Things,* translated by W. E. Leonard, Book II.

But even he added:

> "Not that we joyously delight that man
> Should thus be smitten, but because 'tis sweet
> To mark what evils we ourselves are spared."

6. "A Defense of Human Equality," *Philosophical Review* 53 (1944), 113, as quoted in John Rawls, *A Theory of Justice,* Cambridge: Harvard University Press, 1971, 100.

by the similar fates of their very being to the demands of a compensatory existential justice.

Lately, there has been a poignant confirmation of this belief in the case of the so-called Hibakusha, the survivors of the man-made cataclysm of Hiroshima. Robert J. Lifton in his study of the after-effects of the bomb concludes his chapter on "Survivor Priority Guilt" with these italicized sentences:

> "The survivor can never, inwardly, simply conclude that it was logical and right for him, and not others, to survive. Rather he is bound by an unconscious perception of organic social balance which makes him feel that his survival was made possible by others' deaths: If they had not died, he would have had to; if he had not survived, someone else would have."

And he ends (without italics):

> "Such guilt, as it relates to survivor priority, may well be that most fundamental to human existence."[7]

Moreover, I maintain that such compensatory existential justice requires our putting ourselves vicariously into the places of our fellow beings whether privileged or handicapped. Without such imaginative self-transposal we could not adequately realize what it means for the fortunate or unfortunate to experience their fates and make appropriate amends. Such an operation is actually nothing new in philosophical ethics, and even less so in everyday ethical thinking. Consider how often in our discussions or in our appeals to others we introduce such fictions as:

"Suppose you were black (or yellow or white). . . ."

"Suppose you were poor (or rich). . . ."

"Suppose you were young (or old). . . ."

In fact, such invitations to "supposals" and especially to imaginary self-transposal occur not infrequently in the thought experiments of moral philosophy. Even the golden rule makes full sense only if interpreted as: "Do unto others what you would want them to do unto you *if you were in their place*" (otherwise you might inflict your taste on them). Similarly, thinking through the greatest happiness principle commits us to determining the quantity and quality of other people's pleasure, which ultimately requires our imagining how we would feel in their places. Thus, self-transposal is a basic part of our moral thinking. How far has moral philosophy paid real attention to it?

7. *Death in Life*, 54.

However, one might object: Does it make sense to attempt such self-transposal? After all, it is based on assumptions not only contrary to fact but impossible to perform in reality. For "I am I and you are you; and nothing can be done about it. And I can't ever be anything else but me, and you can't ever be anything else but you."[8] Moreover, the request for such a supposal sounds at first like a noncommittal invitation to our imagination to participate in an intellectual or aesthetic adventure. Is this really all there is to it? Suppose we refuse this invitation? Isn't there something much more serious behind it: a duty to accept the invitation, to put ourselves into the place of the other? If so, how can we account for it and justify it? I submit it is again the accident of birth and the existential unbalance implied which commits us to compensation, beginning with an effort of imagining ourselves in the place of the other, realizing that we might have occupied it, were it not for the accident of our actual birth.

b. *To what fellowship in fate commits us*

But now for a more specific consideration of the ethical implications of the accident of birth as characterized above.

(1) The fact that "I am me"—and of course on equal terms also that "you are you," (only that I have no comparable access to and insight into you and your world except by way of your letting me in on it)—points to a dimension of personal existence whose full depth and richness can here merely be asserted. The fact and experience of this rarely realized and fathomed "wonder" seems to give each self a unique "dignity" in a sense which certainly calls for much more clarification. It calls for a respect approaching awe. This is one of the reasons why we feel or ought to feel the "unconditional regard" (postulated by Carl Rogers but never justified), for everyone who shows signs of such consciousness of selfhood. In the light of this realization all treatment of human beings as numbers, as "material" or as bodies (to be counted as measures of military success) stands condemned as a crime against human dignity. So does all "rubricizing" of human beings, i.e., treating them primarily as specimens, as "one of those. . . ." or rather as representatives of a type rather than themselves.[9]

8. Carson McCullers, *Member of the Wedding.* Boston: Houghton Mifflin Co. 1946, 138.
9. W. James, *Varieties of Religious Experience,* N. Y.: Mod. Lib., 1902, 10: "Probably a crab would be filled with a sense of personal outrage if it could hear us class it without ado or apology as a crustacean, and thus dispose of it: 'I am no such thing,' it would say; 'I am *myself, myself* alone'." See also Abraham Maslow, *Toward a Psychology of Being.* Princeton: Van Nostrand, 1962, 126-130.

(2) The fact that I *am*—(and on equal terms that you *are*)—while rarely fully experienced in its stark irrevocableness, establishes at the same time a right to continued existence, regardless of whether I had a right to come into existence at the start.[10] Once I have been put into existence and am now a personal self capable of realizing and taking charge of my being, no one else has a prima facie claim on this my existence. Such being, which is more than mere life, has claim to unconditional respect—(unless waived or forfeited)—perhaps to the degree of reverence (for life), although the latter term and feeling may be excessive for a being as imperfect as man.

One may well hold that being in itself, no matter what it is that has this being, has value *("omne ens qua ens est bonum")* and a claim on our respect, and that destruction, even of "worthless" things, is a kind of cosmic "misdemeanor." All the more is any interference with personal existence an attack on basic values.

(3) The fact of the "accident" of our congenital *"nature"* calls for a primal tolerance for and patience with one another's natures. It is very easy to get impatient, critical and contemptuous of the characteristics of people other than ourselves (at times even with our own), as if they were to blame for them. But at least congenital characteristics are by definition those for which no one is to be blamed except those parents who could have known the high probability that these characteristics were hereditary. Otherwise we are all the victims or beneficiaries of accidents over which we have had no control. None of us has earned or deserved his endowment or lack of it.

Race may be at the moment the major occasion for this reminder. Once all of us realized that being born black is as much of an accident of birth as being born white, we might be more ready to transpose ourselves into the places of our alternates in racial fate. But it does not hold any less for such characteristics as being born into either sex or into another physique.

Realizing the origin of these congenital differences may seem primarily a reason for deepened patience with the other's differing characteristics, though not necessarily for resignation over them. It might be one reason for compassion, only that there is something much too pharisaical about

10. Recent discussions of the wrong we may inflict on future generations by exposing them to the prospects of nuclear disaster, overcrowding and pollution may well imply that they as non-beings have a moral right to non-being—violated by bringing them into this world—a right which can perhaps be construed in less paradoxical, e.g., hypothetical terms.

this attitude if it is practiced by the self-righteous haves toward the have-nots.

What must also be realized, harder though it be for handicapped victims of existential unbalance, is that the targets of their understandable envy and resentment did not ask for the silver spoons they discovered in their own mouths. To this extent even the fortunate ones are victims of fortune, and it is usually not even in their power to divest themselves of their congenital advantages without committing suicide. All they can do is to try to make up for their better luck. This is why we might hope that even the handicapped, or those who rightly or wrongly believed or believe themselves to be handicapped, will eventually come to realize that their opposite numbers are no villains, that they could not help being privileged and that even each born "aristocrat" deserves to be looked upon as a new human being.

(4) The most urgent need may be to become aware of the ethical implications of the accidents of our congenital *status*. For it is these accidents that keep us apart on the social, national and particularly on the international level. To begin with the last: realizing the accident of our national birth as Americans or Asians, as Arabs or Jews, as French or Germans, should remove all occasion for one of the most fateful obstacles to international union, the pride of national birth, now considered almost the most basic feature in one's social nature to the extent that "I am an American" not only takes precedence in consciousness over "I am a world citizen," but colors one's view of human nature; to put it in the form of a pun, man seems to be a national rather than a rational being. Pride of being born as a member of one nation rather than another is just as misplaced (if not silly) as the pride of aristocracy for "having taken the trouble of being born" (Beaumarchais, *Marriage of Figaro*). The same is true of being ashamed of being born in a nation humiliated by defeat or disgraced by collective guilt.

Such an approach should also allow us to break the stalemate in our hereditary national blood feuds and hatreds. Once we are fully aware that each new generation is born without any doing of its own, and is, as a matter of historical accident, either a Montague or a Capulet, a Greek or a Barbarian, a prince or a pauper, it becomes morally indefensible to hold one another responsible for such differences. By the same token each new generation could and should make a fresh start by challenging these accidents. In fact, the best hope for reconciliation—or rather conciliation, since the new generations have never been in conflict—is the replacement of one generation by another ready to dissociate itself from its predecessors and to realize that both sides are the innocent victims of a history they did not make. This is the place where the generation gap is one of the greatest opportunities for mankind. It could imply a call to the new generations of the world to unite; for they have nothing to lose but the heritage of a fratricidal history bequeathed them by their elders.

Realizing that the generation gap is a matter of the accident of birth could also be a means for bridging it. The older generation, deploring the decline of authority and damning the younger one as immature and irreverent, might do well to realize that its "riper" age and greater experience (not always such a blessing anyhow) are matters of an accident of earlier birth entitling it to nothing. But also the younger generation might consider that the older generation is older not of its own choosing but can't help belonging to another age and is powerless to cross the gap. Both are captives of the accidents of chronology. But they can liberate each other to some extent by mutual imaginative self-transposal.

Such a new approach to the generation problem may also offer hope for a novel solution of such tragic historical conflicts as the one between Arabs and Israelis. There was little use to contest the legal international right of an Arab majority to their territory and even to keeping out immigration that would make it a minority. Compared with this right the millennia-old claim of the Jews to their ancestral home may have weighed little. What did weigh was their claim to *some* place on this globe where they could escape oppression by those who tried to deprive them of their chance of survival and their very right to existence, particularly when the rest of the world refused to give them further asylum. Their best hope was and still seems to be a return to their ancestors' underdeveloped land which they have a special chance to develop. On what basis can this moral issue be adjudicated? What I submit is that once the new Arab and the new Israeli generations come to realize that it was merely the accident of birth which made them Arabs or Jews respectively, they should be able to make a fresh start: realizing that they are fellow victims of one of history's most tragic conflicts, who ought to forgive each other for sins they themselves never committed. Besides, they, as well as every other group and individual, must come to realize that no new generation has a birthright to the soil on which it is born, that we all, not only our ancestors, are new settlers, if not squatters, in new land, and that we have no moral right to exclude those who have as little claim as we have to any part of the earth where we happen to be born. Even inheritance is no unconditional and unlimited right of the heir, but at best a right of the testator if he does not harm others by his dispositions.

The mutual realization of the accidents of birth may also build new bridges across the generation gap in its primary area, the modern family. It is obvious that no child chose his parents and his entire family. This fact should make it clear that his mere birth does not put him under any obligations to his family until he has accepted them freely. It is less obvious that even parents have a choice only as far as the *existence* of the new generation is concerned. But even if they knew all about genetics, they could not "make" and "create" their children in "procreating" them. What these children are is to that extent an "accident." Such a coexistential understanding of the contingencies of the basic existential constitution of the family may well be the basis for authentic tolerance combined with the effort to a mutual respect and cooperation.

Realization of the accident of birth also throws a new light on membership in one religious denomination rather than another. Actually it is not so much the ignorance of the truth or untruth of religious beliefs and dogmas, but the ostensible accident of being born Moslem or Hindu, Catholic or Protestant, which is the deepest reason for genuine tolerance. Re-consider John Bradford's exclamation on watching a "heretic" being led off to execution: "There, but for the grace of God, go I."

At least equally serious is still the matter of social and economic class, now that this parallel fate has become a matter of "class consciousness." Granting, what should not be granted as a dogma, but only after much more critical examination, the fact and the necessity of the class struggle as the basic social reality of our society with the rigid division between the exploited proletariate and the bourgeois exploiters: how much for the class strugglers is this division a matter of accident or of choice? Under a rigid historical materialism there clearly is no real choice anyway. Being born a bourgeois is an unalterable fact and there is no chance for him to ever change sides. All the revolution can do is to liquidate the exploiters, never convert them. (Apparently Marx and Engels, the born bourgeois turned fathers of the revolution, are in a special class.) But even so, being born in either class was an accident of birth. One is a proletarian, but also a bourgeois, as a matter of a blind fate. In that case, is there no reason for "mercy" with those bourgeois who make an honest effort to repudiate their capitalist past and their inherited capital by joining the "disinherited"? Or is this as impossible as a change of sex or color?

The basic truth of the matter is that there is no such thing as a moral birthright to nationality, creed or class, even though to a limited extent some of these can become a matter of choice by change of allegiance, granted grudgingly and disapproved by the native groups as a case of "disloyalty." Unless we believe in original sin in the sense that the children inherit the guilt and possibly the merits or grace of their forefathers, we must reject the idea that we have any right to any "native headstart."

7. Final Pleas

This leads me to some final pleas. As an attempt to sum up some key principles of the ethics of fellowship in the fate of existence I shall put them in the form of simplifying imperatives not meant as commands, but as appeals to spontaneous "realization," both in the sense of insight and of actualization in practice.

(1) Approach every human person as a being who has been cast into his lot without his own doing. In particular think of him as a person who has not chosen (a) to exist, (b) to be he himself, (c) to be whatever he is as far as his congenital characteristics such as race are concerned, (d) to occupy his station in life as far as national, religious or class differences are concerned.

(2) Whether handicapped or privileged, consider all human beings as fellow victims of a morally unaccountable fate.

(3) Considering his basic condition, treat every human person as a new being in his own right, never merely as a continuing extension of his biological ancestors and never as a specimen only.

Such don'ts imply do's like:

(1) Respect each new being in his own dignity.

(2) Transpose yourself in imagination into his plight which is *his* merely by the accident of birth, but could have been *ours* as well.

(3) Be patient with, and tolerant for, his congenital differences, however alien to us.

(4) Be compassionate with those who do not know what they have done to us and others.

(5) Have mercy with others and yourselves threatened by our self-righteousness and callousness in pursuing a collision course in the name of national honor, which can lead only to the victimization of innocent new generations.

(6) Redistribute burdens and privileges rather than take revenge on and exterminate those equally victimized by the accident of birth.

Accident of birth is not the last word of the new ethics for fellow beings in fate. But it is the first word. The second word is the free choice by which we can respond to and redeem this accident. The way from chance to choice is the path of human reclamation of a "universe we never made." Hence we ought to consider human beings not only as fellow victims of the accidents of birth but also as fellow agents capable of accepting and rejecting this fate by converting their congenital endowment into a new order based on choice.

What, then, is the significance of this new approach to ethics? It tries to make us face the fact of our existence in all its inexorableness, cosmically and morally. Against this background we can best plot our course individually and jointly as coexisting fellows, each one for himself, but not alone, and develop the kind of ethics that makes sense where before there was no sense or only potential sense. Such an ethics may provide a way out of the impasse in which we victims of history find ourselves caught at this juncture. It may also help us to develop the sense of planetary solidarity instead of the nationalist provincialism which seems to doom us to reciprocal suicide.

What fractured mankind needs desperately now is a fresh start. The new generation must really begin as a new set of human beings, not identified with their inherited past, free to reject and accept the lot into which they were cast. As fellows in the fate of such coexistence they have something in common that allows them to throw off the shackles which their predecessors have bequeathed them. We all are victims of this past, but we are not enslaved by it. On the contrary: the fact that we are new existences gives us the chance and the obligation to confront it as an alien accident and to redeem this old world of chance by innovating choices.

Confessions of Faith

Robert Ulich

Since I have been asked for a confession of my faith, I may just as well give a bold preliminary answer and say that I am inclined toward a form of cosmic pantheism though without any of the typical sentimentalities about the kindness of nature which sometimes go with pantheistic philosophies. Nature nourishes us and can be kind to us, but it cares for us only to the degree to which we care for it, in body and mind. Otherwise it can be extremely cruel. I also confess, that my pantheism has a mystical overtone. I am not at all ashamed of it, for I believe that all radical thought leads finally into mystical regions. Concerning that belief, I am in good company.

Furthermore, there is no philosophical endeavor that could answer all the questions which man may ask in his confrontation with the enigma of life.

I also know that my faith is not merely the result of logical reasoning. No faith is; otherwise it would not be a faith. Even our great and towering philosophical systems have their origin not merely in the brains of their authors, but also in the subconscious levels of their personality, from the pre-Socratic philosophers Heraclitus, the progressive, who conceived of the world as continual flux, and Parmenides, the conservative, who admired the Abiding in all its changes, to Hegel, the idealist for whom the world was an enterprise of the Mind, or Spirit, struggling for its self-realization. If a thinker tried to solve the existential problems of humanity merely by use of his intellect, his answers would certainly be false (which, of course, is no excuse for undisciplined emotionalism).

Evidently, every person with pantheistic leanings considers himself not merely as an isolated individual, but as a being embedded in a great Whole, or in an encompassing All, which he feels in breathing and walking and eating, which nourishes him in the womb of his mother, and accompanies him until it recedes from him in his hour of death.

THE ENCOMPASSING

No language has an unambiguous word for that ultimate power of being, or reality, which we feel is the source of all living. The vocabulary is endless—Maya,[1] with its thousands of attributes for the Indians, the Hen Kai Pan, (The One and All) for the Greeks, The Order for Confucius, and God for the Christians. But there always remains in us a feeling of inscrutable depth. Some of the profoundest thinkers, in Asia as well as in the West, have called it the coincidence, or the identity of opposites, for they felt that the world abounds with contradictions, such as good and evil, love and hatred, growth and death. We stand in awe before it when asking such ultimate questions as "Why is there something rather than nothing?" "What emerges out, or immerges into, the ever flowing waves of time?" Of, in more colloquial terms, "What is it all about?"

However, in our confrontation with the universe we can distinguish four different basic attitudes, if we exclude those which express merely a negative position such as "scepticism", "atheism", or "nihilism."

1. The first attitude I may call the *scientific* attitude (science to be understood in the widest sense of the term). It is characteristic of modern man, who in his attempt to understand the world around him applies mainly the category of *inherent causality*. The world consists for him of myriads of smaller worlds, all interconnected by bonds of cause and effect within ever widening combinations. One of these worlds is the human person.

As long as we are healthy, we take it for granted that the various parts of the body interact smoothly. Only when we are sick, in other words, when one part refuses to interact with the total body, or when we convalesce and feel the delight of gradual re-integration, only then do we pay attention to the miracle of a smoothly functioning organism.

The apparent causality we observe in the world around us has led earlier generations to make an analogy with the mental life of humans

1. See Heinrich Zimmer, *Myths and Symbols in Indian Art and Civilization.* New York: Harper and Row, 1962.

and to suppose that nature is directed by inherent motives. Our scientists, from Newton onwards, have replaced the older animistic-spiritualistic by a mechanistic aspect of the universe. Of its consequences for the relation of man to the world in which he lives we will speak in the next section on ethics.

2. Besides the scientific attitude, there is a second one, which I may call the *cosmic*.

Whereas the causal-scientific attitude treats the world as an object to be investigated and to be handled according to methodical principles, the cosmic attitude is emotionally laden. It appears in our feeling of empathy when we see a magnificent tree cut down by a sawing machine, or when helpless animals are tortured for scientific purposes. Actually, cosmic metaphors appear constantly in our daily conversations. Unconsciously, like ancient men, we attribute to nature our own personal feelings and motives which she probably does not have, such as serenity, sorrow, or fatigue. The finest expression of man's feeling of unity with the whole universe we sense in the language of the poet, the painter, or the composer. As an eternal religious testimony of our brotherhood with nature we still admire the sun-hymns of the Egyptian King Ikhnaton and of Saint Francis of Assisi. Even the ascetic and dualistic church-father, Tertullian, compares Pentecost with Spring. Later the Church was wise enough to let the dates of Christian festivals coincide with solstices, or other changes in nature, celebrated by the pagans.

3. The deepest form of the cosmic conception of life is a form of *mysticism* which endeavors to unite the human individual with the inner unity of the world. Through deep and absorbing contemplation a person can detect in the subconscious level of his personality his "self." Whereas the "ego" is constantly exposed to fighting, irritating and "egotistic" tendencies, the self connects the individual with the trans- or sub-personal realms of existence. In intense forms of ecstasy (being beyond oneself) the individual consciousness can dissolve itself in the divine whole. Genuine cosmic mysticism should be carefully distinguished from the morbid "mysticism," better called "obscurantism," which we find in the religiosity of Christian saints, of pietists and some modern sects. They do not seek unity with the cosmos, but are engaged in a form of dualistic, often ascetic, spirituality, sometimes going together with a morbid craving for self-identification with the suffering of Christ and other miraculous events. This kind of religious trance (see the life of St. Theresa of Avila as only one out of hundreds of instances) *contradicts* reason, whereas true mysticism *transcends* it. The former denies man's unity with

the world; in the second he becomes conscious of his mooring in the grounds of existence. But there will always be hours when we suddenly feel that the order we believe to exist in the universe is interrupted by some force which defies all attempts toward rational explanation, which is senseless, destructive, and indescribably cruel. What do we feel when a healthy and beautiful mother of young children is killed by incurable cancer, or when the brain of a great scholar, such as Pierre Curie, is smashed by a team of horses before a heavy truck? We may learn the cause of cancer just as we learn the causes of accidents or of avalanches. There is causality in the foreground, but what is behind it? What did Sophocles want to tell us with his story of Oedipus, the brave man who by mistake killed his father, saved the city of Thebes, became the husband of his mother, and then blinded himself under the unbearable weight of guilt? However much science may explain to us the causal order of the universe, it can suddenly, as by unexpected lightning, be disrupted by an event of utter nonsense.

Let us have no illusion. There may be those who resort to miracles or who comfort themselves by referring everything, even the greatest cruelty and injustice, to the inscrutable will of an Almighty God. But what kind of God, a thinking man will ask? At the last frontiers of destiny, all our thinking and searching breaks down. We stand before a gigantic whole in which the most radical contrasts unite: spending and nourishing on the one side, fury and destruction on the other. No philosophical or religious system can explain this mystery. All we can hope is that it show us its kindly and not its frightful sides. If not, we will have to bear it in stoic resignation. But we will understand why, for the Hindus, Maya, the primal substance of the world, is at the same time creation *and* destruction, evolution *and* dissolution, the dream-idyll of the inward vision of the god *and* the desolate nought, the terror of the void, the dread infinite.[2] We will also understand why, for the Greeks, even the Olympians had to submit to the inscrutable *Moira,* and why, in a similar mood, Germanic mythology speaks of the power of the *Wurt.* Every culture, so it seems, has an awesome vision of a force that turns even the will and might of the gods into their contrary. Therefore, the claim to possess a definite answer to the riddle of destiny is either a sign of mental laziness—one just stops thinking—or of intellectual arrogance. In his admission of the limits of reason concerning ultimate questions, Kant, probably the sharpest analytical intellect in Western philosophy, is closer

2. Zimmer, *op. cit.,* p. 46.

to the mystics than the creators of presumably comprehensive world views which only deceive us about the human situation in a world of uncertainty.

It is evident that the various attitudes toward the universe influence our moral behavior, provided we assume, as I do, that morality is not merely the result of calculations about how "to get along" with one's neighbor and one's smaller and larger community, but that our conscience, though very much the product of interhuman relations, points towards deeper and more universal layers of existence than mere social utility. In our better hours, most of us believe that through productive thinking and acting we help not only ourselves and our friends, but also the creation in which we live in its continual attempt at harmonization and integration, whereas spite and aggressiveness destroy the whole precarious texture of living.

This leads us over to our next section.

THE MORAL PROBLEM

It was inevitable that, while indicating the four attitudes towards Being, I already touched on their ethical implications. But I may now become more explicit.

1. The interpretation of reality as an unfeeling causal nexus has changed the old community of faithful believers, praying to a divine Governor of the world, into an aggressive society endowed with a dangerous master-complex. Man the inventor believed he could handle the earth as an object without realizing that he is its guest, not its owner. The effect of this attitude has been twofold. On the one hand, man has wrung benefits from nature undreamed of in earlier times. On the other hand, nature suddenly tells us that it is unwilling to give us more of its treasures than it can afford.

Small and insignificant as man appears before the universe, he is nevertheless the being that can choose between supporting the creation and acting like an alien, or even like a destructive element within its surroundings—not knowing that his alienation from nature involves his alienation from himself.

Hence our great problem: first, how to restore health within sick, because maltreated, nature itself; second, how to regain health in our own souls, split between the desire for a life in contact with nature and the requirements of our modern industrial society. This is not merely a matter of skillful planning. All our attempts at cleaning the polluted air of our cities and the dirty waters of our lakes and rivers, to save our woods and to control the rise of the human population, all these attempts will not succeed without the cooperation of men with a new conscience. No longer must conscience reign merely between persons and persons, but between humanity and life as a whole. Whether the universe is merely an unconsciously self-perpetuating causal order, or whether it emanates from and is directed by a superior mind, as long as each of us lives, he does not live of himself, by himself. Rather is he part of an immense reality.

But while discussing the moral consequences of the causal-scientific world-aspect I must not neglect its positive quality. This is the attitude of the true scientist himself. Of course, there are men in the field of science as in every field who consider their work as a relatively interesting routine which provides a living. Everything else is of minor importance. But creative scientists are generally men of deep and selfless devotion, of methodical discipline, of infinite patience and of readiness to correct themselves, or, in contrast to many theologians and philosophers, to be corrected. Nowhere, it seems to me, is the will to international coopera-tion greater than among scientists. They do not believe that nature has a soul, nor do they know whether it rewards their endeavors, but they put their own souls into their work. Take these virtues together and you have, from my point of view, the basis for an ethics of *intellectual devotion* which, when becoming part of man's conscience and followed in other fields of life, could lead us not only back to nature, but also forward to a new world-awareness.

2. Nevertheless, the fact remains that science has succeeded in treating nature only as an object, either of intellectual or technical manipulation or both. Despite all passion put in the work as such, a certain impassionate coolness must reign between the man of research and nature, if the work is going to succeed. Therefore, "Science is not enough" has now almost become a slogan. Its truth has been felt particu-larly by our greatest scientists. Whereas as investigators they stand *before* the universe, as men endowed with a sense of reverence they try to enter *into* it; they ask questions concerning the meaning of their work and their own existence, and they hope that the universe will respond to their questions. And so do we all. In one way or another, we ask for permission to participate in the gigantic enterprise of Being, or whatever names our language may offer. From existential isolation we enter into a fellowship between men and nature; we become co-responsible partners. Wherever the attitude of scientific causality engenders the ethics of disciplined

devotion, the cosmic attitude produces the ethics of *respectful sympathy*.

3. What, now, are the experiences of a person with the third kind of our world-attitudes, the *mystical*? At present the Western world has learned about cosmic mysticism through Eastern meditative practices such as Yoga and Zen, which are generally combined with specific bodily postures supposed to facilitate the immersion of the ego in the self and of the self in the All. But of profound cosmic unity we have a supreme example in the great medieval theologian, Master Eckhart (1260-1327) who in his *Anweisung zum Schauenden Leben* tells us: "Now do away with all things visible and unite with the undivided and formless essence of being." (*So streift nun alles Bildhafte ab und einigt euch dem bild—und formlosen Wesen.*) He also says: "Without seeking yourself, you should penetrate into the truth: the pure unity which itself is the Godhead. Thus you will experience unexpected surprises." *(Und danach soll man vordringen in die Wahrheit: Zu der blossen Einheit, die die Gottheit selber ist—ohne dabei das Seine zu suchen; so kommt man in sonderliche Wunder.)* Characteristically, Master Eckhart likes to avoid the term "God" because of its anthropomorphic connotation. "Godhead" means not a personal God, but the *essence* of the Divine Principle.

A person with this experience has no need of ecclesiastical intermediaries between man and the Divine. Therefore Master Eckhart can dare the sentence: "You must overcome the Son and even the Father."

Inevitably, the Inquisition accused him of heresy, and rightly, from its point of view. But at the same time it interrupted a tradition which, if pursued, would have changed the development of Western religion. The sporadic emergence of cosmic mysticism in religious sects at the time of the Reformation, or in contemplative minds such as Jakob Boehme's, was always looked at with suspicion by the hierarchy, both Catholic and Protestant. This suspicion caused not only profound dilemmas in the minds of pious Christians, but it also caused the tragical conflict between the Christian dogma and modern science, a conflict which we have not yet completely overcome.

Essentially, mystical experience is the opening of the self to the All, or, as the devotees also may say, the invasion of the All into the self. The All, as it were, breaks the walls of individuality. It is characteristic of our individualistic era with its separation from the totality of being that the older and fuller word "person" has been replaced by the term "individual," or the ego isolated from other egos.

The result of the mystical confrontation of the self with the center of all existence is a sense of liberation from the noises and pressures of the outside world, a feeling of silence, and, together with it, a feeling of inner strength and rejuvenation.

Essentially, the experience can only be had, but not analyzed. Indeed, mystical cultures, especially the Indian, employ an innumerable number of opposite terms for describing the indescribable, e.g., "fullness of being" versus "the void;" "the overwhelming" versus the "hidden;" or "the light" versus "the dark."

All this sounds strange to the rationalist. But he should ask himself whether he was not shaken by similar contrasting experiences in the face of traumatic events, such as sudden death or natural catastrophies. And although it is not the same, these experiences nevertheless point to similar psychic phenomena that creative poets and artists also seem to undergo when a transcendental power seems to dictate to them what to do. However, it should be remembered that mental phenomena of this kind do not occur without a long mental preparation that assembles in the subconscious a potential energy which, at a given moment of high intensity, breaks through the foreground. Mystic experiences are not like sunrays which suddenly shine through a closed window. It is a dangerous mixture of ignorance and frivolity to believe one can produce them by means of drugs. Mysticism is the very contrary of hallucination. Its moral is not individualistic self-delusion or phantastic illusion, but *transcendental unity,* just as the *mythical* attitude, of which I am now going to speak, does not belong to the realm of fairy tales or arbitrary plays of fancy.

4. The *mythical* attitude represents the primal, or most original, relation of the human race to the universe. Myth originates when the inner life of man projects itself symbolically into images he finds in nature—still undiluted by verbal concepts and therefore so significant for our own self-recognition, for primitive man is still in us. Primitive man conceived of the world not as one governed by the laws of causality; but he felt embedded in it with all its demoniac and unpredictable forces. Just as old folk songs, myth emerges out of the collective subconsciousness of the race. Animals were much nearer to ancient man than to us, either as friends or as enemies. Some became images of light and greatness, others of darkness and destruction, and many, just like human beings, harbored in themselves both good and evil. As in nature itself, animals were not yet separated from each other.

Animals had souls. Therefore, they served as interpreters between man, on the one hand, and the world of gods and demons, on the other. The eagle, as other birdlike creatures, symbolized the heavenly spheres, or strength, as it still does in modern heraldry. In Greek mythology, just as does the thunderbolt, it belongs to Zeus, in German mythology to Wodan. It can be found on a sacrificial goblet of King Gudea of Lagash of the Sumerian period (ca. 2600 B.C.).[3]

In distinction from birds, the earthbound bull represents the terrestrial element. So did the lion. When Heracles, alone and without weapons, strangles the Nemean lion in its dark cavern, or wrestles with the Cretan bull, he "wrestles with the negative elements of the procreative power of the bull in its lower material aspects"[4] and thus overcomes the dark forces in himself. Yet, it was the same Heracles who served as a maid and lost his self-respect as a sexual prisoner of the voluptuous Omphale.

In Indian legends the serpent Ananta, the ancestor of earthly serpents, symbolizes the cosmic waters on which Vishnu, often identified with Maya, rests when he is immersed in his world-dream. Sloughing itself, the serpent reminds the Indian of the wonder of rejuvenation and Buddha's doctrine of rebirth. On the other hand, creeping on the earth, it reminds him of low sexuality and bondage. There is almost nothing in the multitude of metaphysical opposites in Indian myth with which the serpent is not connected. But the same opposites are brooding in man himself; therefore his feeling of identity as much as his feeling of horror in relation the serpent-world.

One of the most profound and at the same time charming tales of Zen-Buddhism pictures a shepherd who, in order to find his self, has first to find, and then to tame and ride, an ox—the tale being nothing but the symbol of discovering one's own struggling ego. Christian myth, also, projects the conscious and mostly unconscious contrasting qualities of man into a number of symbolic images. The angels, representing the celestial sphere, have wings. God has to fight the goat-footed devil from the beginning of the creation, as man has to fight him from birth to death. The serpent persuades Eve to disobey the Lord. Dragons have to be killed by saints such as St. George. The whale, like the dragon, the symbol of the mysterious abysmal forces of water, swallows the prophet Jonas in its dark body, but is forced to disgorge him under the rays of light. And Daniel, in the lions' cave, is confronted with beasts which in all their ferocity submit to the power of faith. Similar stories can be found in many cultures. The evangelists and saints have animals attributed to them. The lamb, often adorned with the cross, symbolizes the

3. See Dorothy Norman, *The Heroic Encounter*. New York: American Federation of Arts, 1958-1959.
4. *Op. cit.*, p. 11.

kingdom of peace, and one has only to study old illuminated manuscripts or to go through medieval churches in order to comprehend the close connection between early Christian men and the animal kingdom—despite the dualism of the doctrine.

Superstitions!—so the rationalist will say. Indeed, when changed from symbol to concrete fact—and how easily is man tempted to do so—the myth of Satan, to mention only one of many examples, has tortured many sensible souls. More than that, with its demoniac accouterments of witches and tempting spirits, it raised to the level of conscious action the most devilish fear and persecution complexes in man.

Thus, what I wish to suggest here is by no means a relapse into myth as such but to discover in it the oldest intuitions of man about his complicated and polar inner self. Or, to use a famous concept of Carl Jung, myth helps us to reconstruct in ourselves the "archetypal" experiences of the human race in all their depth and contradictions.

Myth is inexorable, often cruel, realism. It contains no illusions, neither about the dark forces within man, nor the dark powers behind him. It confirms the irreconcilability between the world as it is, and the world as we would like it to be. Tragedy and destruction may befall the best, and the wisest may become the victims of stupid rulers. Even the gods and their sacred animals harbor in themselves the germs of their contradictions, and the best moral intentions may in the course of time develop their own contrasts. Love may turn into hatred, and joy into suffering, but the reverse may also be true. Even bad things may become our helpers. There is nothing entirely bad and nothing entirely good. I am often reminded of the serpent symbol when thinking of the history of our great religions. The founders wanted peace, love, and rejuvenation, but they also created the spirit of aggressiveness, hostility, and dogmatism. Jesus himself, like the Bible, is full of opposites. He preached love, but he also said "Think not that I am come to send peace on earth: I came not to send peace but a sword" (Matthew 10:34). Indeed, I know of no simple answer to the moral problem when I turn from the surface of traditional human relations to its depth.

Yet, the fact that in the last analysis life remains a mystery of whirling opposites is no excuse for discouragement to mythical man. He is neither a relativist nor a nihilist. Although he does not know for certain whether the better will always be the better, he is nevertheless willing to fight for it, for he knows that life decays without courage and the risking of values. Every heroic deed is an inspiration. It lifts the hero above the reign of the ordinary and serves as example for others. For the Indians it makes manifest Dharma, the moral order of the cosmos. Although Dharma has been in virtual existence before the beginning of the world, it likes to express itself in particular occurrences, such as in deeds of selflessness, in purity and in contemplation of the Absolute.

But what can we do in order to master the ambiguities within us and even force them to accompany us on the difficult path towards wholeness and maturity?

First, although it seems rather theoretical to the practical mind we have to learn the art of self-examination. "The unexamined life," says Socrates, "is not worth living." Indeed, the person who refuses to probe into himself, his motives and his intentions, is swayed to and fro by the winds of chance. He does not hold himself together, but is held together by the framework in which he happens to live. If the framework of habits and conventions, his security and his conventional beliefs, are shattered, he too is shattered. Therefore, all developed cultures have rituals of self-scrutiny, by dint of which man confronts himself with a divine censor. In the Catholic tradition it is the confession, with the priest acting as the intermediary between man and God. In all religions prayer is demanded to lead man into and above himself. In secular cultures such as ours the danger emerges that man tries to probe his worth primarily in terms of success. The vertical line dissolves in the horizontal, until he is finally overcome by inner emptiness. The priest then, or prayer, or contemplation, is replaced by restless activity, the hunt for pleasure, and finally the psychoanalyst. However, in one way or another, every healthy person stands as a judge before himself. It depends on the criteria he uses; whether they are superficial and thus end in the frequent interaction between arrogance and self-pity, or between superiority and inferiority complexes, or whether they reach into the deeper layer of human conscience.

But self-examination, however important, will not suffice. In connection with religious contemplation, as it is exercised in certain parts of the East, it may lift a person above, or away from, his ego. Nirvana may be the goal. But in our activist and possessive Western culture we do not like to drown in self-oblivion. We are even inclined to sense a degree of morbid self-centeredness in persons too much occupied with their precious self.

But whither to go in order to maintain our moral integrity and self-respect in spite of the confusion of contradictory opinions and inclinations?

A German of my generation may be pardoned if, once more, he quotes

Goethe. As an old man, Goethe he said: "If in the multitude of tasks you cannot decide what to do, fulfill the duty of the day." I think the advice is good. But it is incomplete. Activity alone, even the most useful one, offers no final solace to the human soul. Goethe would have been the first to agree, otherwise he would not have been the creator of Faust, the symbol of the restless seeker. And, in spite of his indifference about conventional religion, he was convinced that the decisive battle of history would not be the one between warring nations, but between faith and faithlessness. In other words, in what *spirit* should we act? Identical acts, if pursued in a different attitude of mind, in love, in moods of obstinacy or of indifference, will have an entirely different effect. They may enchant, or they may disappoint.

The final answer to all these problems Goethe gives in his doctrine of the fourfold reverence. First, man should act and live in a spirit of reverence *(Ehrfurcht)* for that which is above him. Second, he should be imbued with reverence for that which is like him. "While trying to understand his relation to his equals and thus to mankind as a whole, as well as his relation to his environment, be it necessary or accidental, he lives in the cosmos and thus in the spirit of truth."

The third, reverence, is the reverence for that which is below us, "even loneliness and poverty, scorn and disdain, insult and misery, suffering and death."

Only when a person has absorbed these three reverences, can he arrive at the highest one, the reverence for himself. He may then respect himself as the "highest product of God and nature, without being pulled down into a state of profaneness by self-conceit and selfishness."[5]

Here, in the words of a great poet and thinker, we have, so it seems to me, the sum-total of the ethical problem. The horizontal line, on which we all move most of the day, is not forgotten—do what the day commands you to do. Goethe's fear that the mechanization of modern civilization may destroy the deeper moorings that prevent it from dissipating itself in uninspiring activities is expressed in the polarity between faith and non-faith. But what kind of faith? Goethe gives no answer which would satisfy the dogmatic mind. Faith for him is not a certainty, but an attitude that expresses itself in the form of reverential awe toward the totality of the creation, in its productive as well as in its destructive aspects. Thus Goethe, who in his later years became increasingly attracted to the wisdom of Asia, comes close to the symbolism of ancient myth.

5. Quoted from Carlyle's translation of *Wilhelm Meister*, Second Book, Chapter I.

The abstractions of Kant and the speculations of Hegel never interested him.

We modern city-dwellers can no longer have this intimacy with nature as ancient man had it before he was overwhelmed by organizations and institutions. The old Goethe already foresaw man's alienation from nature and the cosmos as a result of the coming age of the machine. We have driven the great Pan into far away forests, rivers, and mountains where he desperately defends himself against the encroachment of fighting humanity. Therefore, we have to reconstruct the lost homestead in the embrace of nature through an inner operation, namely, going into that depth of our existence where we feel the currents of the cosmos flowing through our souls. Even then we may not always know whether our thinking and acting are right or wrong. We will hesitate to judge others because we know of the dark forces in our selves. We will always be seekers. But we will do so in the right spirit even though we may err.

EDUCATION

If we pursue the thoughts discussed in the preceding sections, the question emerges, how can we educate a man who lives in some accord with these ideals. Indeed, this is more or less the question about the future of humanity. And it is characteristic of our time of confusion that never in human history has education loomed so large as today.

From the elementary school to the university, the teacher has to familiarize the younger generation with an extent of knowledge unknown a century ago, with the accent increasingly shifting from the humanities to the sciences. Most fathers are no longer capable of helping their children with their home assignments in mathematics, which today succeeds the tyranny of the ancient languages and is just as useless for most adults. Inevitably, with more and more children of the less educated classes, and also with an increasing number of less talented youth participating in relatively advanced courses, the institutions multiply which attempt to understand better than was possible so far the processes of learning and teaching—which is all the more difficult since we do not know what fundamentally happens when an individual learns. Still less do we know whether there exists such a phenomenon as collective learning. When observing that whole groups and nations repeat the same deadly errors again and again, one may well conclude that there is no such thing.

But looking at all these new institutions devoted to intellectual advancement, I ask myself what aim they conceive of within and behind that whole "development," just as, when reading the many "Reports" on our schools, I question whether their authors have even asked themselves what kind of desirable man they want to provide for humankind.

Unless our schools, if possible in continued connection with the family, penetrate the learning with an attitude of respect for the thousandfold wonders of life, we may bring up learned barbarians who constantly destroy what they produce. It makes no difference whether we express this attitude as Hindus, Buddhists, Mohammedans, Catholics, Protestants, Humanists, agnostics, or atheists. A premature attachment to any particular faith may even close the minds instead of opening them. The faith we need in the future is neither a possession nor an anarchical meandering through the whole span of human beliefs. Rather is it a direction in the pursuit of which man learns to clarify and structure his self in a reverential dialogue with the powers of life.

Three characteristics, so it seems to me, would a concerned person derive from such a dialogue. He would avoid dangers of delusions as well as illusions, but just as much would he avoid a life of disenchantment. Although he would enjoy the great achievements of our modern technical civilization, he would not allow himself to be engulfed in its often aimless turbulence and its *delusions* of grandeur which have destroyed modern man's cosmic conscience and alienated him from the deeper resources of his own existence. But how can he develop such a cosmic conscience when the traditional religious systems no longer comply with his request for inner certainty and when new answers with similar potency cannot, and probably never will, be found?

Surely, science has freed us from the bonds of magic—at least to a degree. But the mind of man transcends the world of matter and causality which is the subject of science. He knows of delight and love, of admiration and wonder, but also of the invasion of the demoniac and the tragical. Despite all his knowledge, he often stands perplexed and helpless before inscrutable powers. Thus, as he must learn to live without *delusions* about his relation to nature, so he must also learn to live without *illusions* about his rational powers and about his dependence on destiny.

Yet, despite the loss of delusions and illusions, caused not only by his existential situation, but also by world wars, revolutions and the ambiguity of modern technology, man has no right to *disenchantment*. Whereas in earlier times he was inclined to be dogmatic in religion, arrogantly proud about his knowledge, overconfident in his managerial talent, and then despondent or cynical when the world did not respond to his approaches, he must now learn to be modest without losing initiative, to remain the eternal seeker without expecting ultimate answers, and to believe in the worth of his moral intentions—knowing that they too, like all life, may harbor the germs of their own distortion.

Now I contend that our present school system, in spite of all its cognitive achievements, is utterly unconducive to the development of the new piety I am here demanding. Our schools train the intellect at the expense of the emotions with the result that they underfeed even the intellect, for without feeding on a rich emotional base, the intellect becomes sterile. With the emphasis on science, the situation will even deteriorate. Every great intuition, invention, and discovery, not to speak of works of art or related to art, results from a combination of thinking and feeling, including the will. Fundamentally, the three are inseparable. Every creative act is a product of the total personality, in its consciousness as well as in its subconscious life, and this totality is exactly what we neglect in most of our schools. How, otherwise, would it come about that after the age of twelve the artistic creations of children often decline in spontaneity?

Fortunately, an increasing though still small number of schools enter a new path. They enliven not only the children, but free the teachers from the deadly routine that hangs like a dark shadow over their work. Their delight is to observe the development of the young who wonder while they learn, who learn discipline without being disciplined, whose minds are not stuffed but open up to the degree to which they conquer new territories of knowledge and experience. In such a school the beginning of biology, or observation of life, plants and animals, is not just a process of *looking* at something, but of *looking at something with a soul.* Mathematics is not a mere skill but a second language, the one by means of which man induces measure and order into his observations of otherwise bewildering data. And history is not a mere series of events, but the history of successes and failures on the way of man from primitive isolation toward mankind consciousness.

I am far from contending that this kind of schooling alone can arm a growing person against all the vicissitudes of human existence. But it can prevent him from travelling through life, seeing and experiencing more and more, and at the same time straying farther and farther away from his inner self.

Eventually, all attempts of man to develop his physical as well as his still not fully used mental potentialities in a world of polarities—all these attempts should be motivated by one guiding principle, expressed by the Bible in these beautiful words (Matthew 16:20):

> For what is a man profited, if he shall gain
> the whole world, and lose his soul? Or what
> shall a man give in exchange for his soul?

The World I Live In

W. H. Werkmeister

I am sufficiently old-fashioned to believe that philosophy is worth its salt only when philosophers are concerned with problems that transcend mere technicalities and pertain to what it means to exist as a human being. That problems of this type encompass the whole of human existence—its cognitive, evaluative, and activistic aspects, individually and in their manifold interrelations—is obvious. In the end, only an integrative view of the whole can satisfy our drive to know, to understand, and to find meaning (or the lack of it) in our existence. As far as I can remember, this concern with the whole of human experience has always been the driving force in my own philosophical efforts.

To be sure, in *The Basis and Structure of Knowledge* (1948), I dealt exclusively with problems of cognition and with the foundations of our most exact sciences. But I did acknowledge even then that "unless our philosophy is sufficiently broad in conception to include all aspects of human experience, it is inadequate as an ultimate point of view" (p. x). *Man and His Values* (1967) was conceived and written as a supplement to the earlier book. Even so, however, the argument remained incomplete. What was needed was a statement and a clarification of the metaphysical presuppositions and implications of the ideas set forth in those two books. What was needed, in other words, was the development of a broad perspective that would make it possible to accept human valuations and human aspirations as part and parcel of cosmic reality. In a forthcoming book, *Man in Perspective,* I have attempted such a projection. What I wish to do here is to give a thumbnail sketch of the point of view developed in those three books and to relate it to our present-day human scene.

I

My task is facilitated by the fact that my approach to the problems of ultimate concern, first formulated in *The Basis and Structure of Knowledge,* has remained the same throughout all these years. I speak of it as methodological solipsism—with the emphasis on *methodological,* for I am not a solipsist in any other sense. In fact, I believe (with all realists) in the reality of an external world—a world that existed long before I was born and that will continue to exist long after I am gone. But the warranty for my belief in that world I can and do find only in my own first-person experience. I have no evidence of any other kind; for even what I read or what others tell me can support or invalidate my beliefs only because the reading and the being told are themselves part of my first-person experience. Even the existence of other persons I can assert only because of the evidence I encounter in my experience.

In this perspective, epistemological problems take on a special significance; for the question now is, On what grounds can I assert that there exists a real external world with real people in it? A naively realistic appeal to "perceptual" evidence will not do; for if the "things" constituting the world are identical with my "perceptions," then they are not truly part of an *external* world. They can, in that case, in no way transcend the perceptions themselves, coming into being when I perceive them, and ceasing to be when I no longer observe them. And to argue that the "things" are the causes of my perceptions will not do either because such an argument presupposes the point at issue—the existence of "things." But if I know of the "things" that constitute the world around me because I so interpret certain "givens" in my first-person experience, then I must find within that experience itself a criterion in terms of which I can and do justify such an interpretation. Is there such a criterion?

Before I answer this question, let us take a brief look at first-person experience itself. What is involved here?

The experience is obviously relational: A "something" is "aware of" a "something else." There is a "subject-pole" and an "object-pole" in this relation; and both require interpretation. In my own first-person experience it is, of course, "I" who is the "subject-pole." For the moment, however, I shall concentrate on the "object-pole" of "my" experience. This "pole" is highly complex and variable, consisting of all sorts of "objects"—colors and sounds and shapes and feelings and desires, memories, and thoughts and hopes and aspirations. And among them are the "objects" which are also things in an external world. How to distinguish them from the rest is, of course, our problem.

The whole of "my" experience has its temporal aspects: "Objects" occur simultaneously or follow one another. And some of them appear side by side and as themselves spatial. But even the "objects" of an apparently spatio-temporal character cannot all be identified with things in an external world; "objects" of hallucinatory experiences prove that. However, "my" belief in the reality of an external world and of the things in that world would be warranted if "I" could relate at least some of the "objects" into a pattern of interactions by subsuming them under a general Principle of Causality. "I" could then say that "objects" of experience are also things in a real world when they are causally efficacious. This assumes, however, that the Principle of Causality itself is warranted by the facts of first-person experience.

The Principle cannot be justified as an empirical generalization, for any attempt to do so is a *circulus in probando*. I submit, however, that the Principle is firmly grounded in the basic uniformity (or, if you prefer, the homogeneity) of time which, in its emptiness, does not explain why any particular "object" occurs in my experience at this particular time and not at some other. Such occurrences become intelligible only when the "object" in question can be taken to be the result of antecedent conditions. I submit, in other words, that the Principle of Causality in its broad sense is the *conditio sine qua non* of the intelligibility of "my" experience and also of the world around "me."

To be sure, as naive realists we have always acted on the assumption that causal relations prevail in the world of things. There is, however, much firmer support for the Principle of Causality. It is this: The uniformity of time just referred to is more specifically defined in the various conservation laws of the physical sciences. Newton's First Law of Motion may serve as an illustration of my argument. The Law states: Any body at rest or in rectilinear uniform motion will continue at rest or in rectilinear uniform motion unless acted upon by some external force. It follows at once that any understanding of some deviation of the "object" from rest or rectilinear uniform motion depends upon the Principle of Causality. That Principle, therefore, is basic to our knowledge of the world around us, for it is constitutive of that world. Even Heisenberg's much-discussed and misunderstood "Principle of Uncertainty" is rooted in causally induced conditions.

Viewing the world around "me" as a nexus or context of causal interactions, "I" can now discover the more specific laws governing those interactions—such as Newton's law of gravitation and Maxwell's equations. But as new evidence becomes available to "me" in "my" first-person experience, any particular conception of the world around "me" may have to be modified. At no time, therefore, can "I" say with finality that *this* view which "I" *now* hold is the truth. "I" can speak only of warranted belief—finding the warranty in first-person experience itself as "I" interpret the "objects" of that experience in terms of causal interactions. The shifts from a geocentric to a heliocentric conception of the universe and, ultimately, to that of an "exploding" universe illustrate my point. And they illustrate also the fact that, starting with the "givens" of first-person experience, "I" encounter ultimate problems for which, in principle, there is no solution because they are but versions of the question, Why is there a universe at all, and why is it as it is? Is it finite or infinite? And what happens to the galaxies when their radial velocity outward reaches the velocity of light? They will then have passed beyond the reach of our observations. But do they still exist? Is there an ever renewed creation of matter at the center of the universe from which the galaxies derive? What is the origin of the hydrogen gas so widely distributed throughout the universe and whose condensation under gravitational pressures generated that tremendous heat necessary for the formation of all the other "elements" we find in the world?

When we turn to the atoms themselves and their internal structure, our experiments (depending upon causal interference with "given" states, conditions, or processes) reveal an almost unbelievable complexity and a great variety of particles and anti-particles which only the quantum mechanical equations of Schroedinger-Dirac and, more recently, of Gell-Man render intelligible. Is "matter" ultimately of the nature of particles or of waves? Apparently only the conception of superposed "fields" accounts for all the facts from the transmission of light to the structure of atoms. But the facts of observation, interpreted in terms of causality, reveal even more; for if an elementary particle collides with its corresponding anti-particle, they both disappear in a burst of energy; and, conversely, when sufficient energy is available, new pairs of particles and anti-particles can be created. Are we then to say that, ultimately, reality is energy? Any answer to this question must remain purely hypothetical—unless, that is, we can view the facts within a broader framework.

But whatever the answer may be, this much at least is warranted by our causal interpretation of the world of things: Nature, as we know it, is essentially process—causally determined process. Moreover, it is character-istic of any particular causal nexus that it is an "open" process; that it does not have a predetermined goal but can be deflected in a variety of ways as diverse causes interact with it.

II

Now, in the world around "me" there exist not only atoms and rocks and planets and galaxies, but also plants and animals and human beings. That they, too, are part of the real world follows from the fact that, as bodied entities, they are integral to the causal nexus that is constitutive of the realm of nature. Their existence, their life, is also process. Metabo-lism alone suffices as proof. But the question is, Is the process which is the life of an organism the same kind of process that we encounter in non-living nature? And to this question the answer must be that it is not. The essential difference is that the causal nexus *per se*—the causal nexus that is constitutive of the external world (including the organisms)—is "open" in the sense indicated above, whereas the process identifiable as "living" is centrally determined in a very specific sense: It is self-regula-tory, self-reproductive, and morphogenetic.

Since I have discussed most of the relevant facts at some length in *A Philosophy of Science,* Chapter X, I shall be very brief here. But the case must be argued.

An example of central determination is, of course, the behavioral response of various organisms (including man) to the world they live in—be that response reflexive, instinctive, or volitional-intelligent. The facts in the case are obvious and I shall not dwell upon them. I am here concerned only with the physico-chemical aspects of organismic exis-tence.

In the case of higher animals, central determination is certainly in evidence in what Claude Bernard called "the fixity of the *milieu intér-ieur.*" That is to say, it is in evidence in the processes of "equilibration" which tend to preserve the inner stability of the organism—the stability of body temperature and of the sugar-content in the blood, for example. Although inexplicable in terms of causal relations pure and simple, such "equilibrations" are at least understandable as "feedback" interactions which exemplify the wholistic character of organismic processes and their central determination.

More important for my argument are the interrelated processes known as metabolism. Here we deal with physico-chemical interactions of organism and environment in the course of which the molecules of the "nutrients" absorbed by the organism are broken down into their constituent elements which are then re-synthesized into molecules that are necessary for the maintenance, the growth, and the proper functioning of the organism—be that organism plant or animal, unicellular or multicellular. That is to say, in metabolism the organism is not absorbed by the environment but selectively utilizes it; and only some form of central determination can account for this.

But there are facts which point up even more forcefully the unique form of organismic determination. I refer to the facts of ontogeny, of the development from ovum (or seed) to full-bodied maturity of a multicellular organism—a process that is directional (its result being a structurally and functionally well-integrated whole) and morphogenetic. Although DNA (deoxyribo-nucleic acid) is the species-specific determinant in this process, it alone is not sufficient to account for the epigenetic character of the development. This is so because all cells of a multicellular organism are equipotential. They all contain the same DNA molecule which is capable, initially, of generating the whole organism. However, at any given stage in the development of an individual only that part of DNA in each cell which corresponds to the specific "needs" at that stage will become effective; all other parts remain dormant. And at each stage the conditions necessary for the emergence of the next stage are being produced. In a very specific sense this morphogenetic development is, thus, epigenetic.

The process as a whole cannot be understood simply as the unfolding of the structure of DNA, for the DNA molecule is in no sense the structurally and functionally articulated organism itself; it only determines the specific direction of the development. What this means is that, in morphogenesis, the place of a cell within the developing whole is an additional factor in determining the outcome. One might be tempted to speak here also of a feedback mechanism; but (a) all feedback mechanisms necessary for organismic existence are themselves being produced in and through the process of ontogenetic development, and (b) experimental displacements of cells in the early stages of ontogeny—displacements that would destroy any preformed feedback mechanism—do not materially affect the outcome. The developing organism readily overcomes such displacements. We are here obviously face to face with a "wholistic" type of determination for which the conception of a DNA-determined "gradient field" might be the only adequate one.

In reduplicating itself and preserving its identity in cell-divisions and genetic transmissions, DNA is centrally determinative not only of the ontogenetic development of some particular organism but of generations of essentially the same kind of organisms. That is to say, every specific form of DNA is determinative of some particular species of plant or animal life, and through DNA the species lives in the individuals. Slight variations in DNA must therefore entail slight variations in the species. Large modifications, however, must result in a new species. It is thus at the level of DNA that we encounter not only the problem of the origin of life but the problem of biological evolution as well.

How the first viable DNA molecules were formed in the course of cosmic evolution is by no means clear. We can only surmise that, somehow, under "favorable" conditions and in the course of many millions of years, the first nucleic acid chains came into existence; that some of them were capable of synthesizing protein molecules that could transform sugar, phosphate and ammonia into nucleotides, thus establishing something akin to a metabolic process. But all of this remains conjectural—an interpolation *post factum*. So far at least no interpretation of the data of our first-person experience can carry us beyond this.

But the origin of life on earth is no more of a problem than is the process of the emergence of new species in biological evolution. Actually, the idea of evolution is one of the broad Principles enabling us to bring together in orderly interrelation an immense variety of observational data. There are countless forms of unicellular organisms; there are the grasses, the flowering plants, and the trees; and there are the fish, the reptiles, the birds, the insects, and the mammals; and in the perspective of Evolution they all came into existence as the result of specific modifications of the original DNA. Reference to the "survival of the fittest" is in itself no explanation of that fact. After all, unicellular organisms have survived to this day, as have survived countless other species of plant and animal life. And, obviously, indispensable for the survival of a new species is the emergence of viable new forms in preadaptation. Moreover, it is not sufficient that only one individual of a new kind appear at a time. For the survival of a new species many individuals are necessary; and when bi-sexual reproduction is involved, the two sexes must emerge together. To be sure, "natural selection" does take place; but basic to the process of evolution is that "upward thrust," that surpassing of levels of existence already attained that characterizes the multi-directional progress of evolutionary development. And, in the end, the development is not simply biological; for it gives rise also to instinct-determined forms of behavior, to consciousness, and to animal and human intelligence. The process is clearly epigenetic, and we ourselves are a product of it. That is to say, Reality manifests itself in us as it does in everything else in the world, and in our cognitive endeavors it is beginning to understand itself.

III

But let us return to our first-person experience, for it is not limited to cognition alone. There are also our affective-conative responses to the "givens"—to the "objects" and "events"—of that experience; and in them are rooted our valuations and evaluations. I have dealt with them at some length in *Man and His Values* and shall, therefore, again be very brief here.

Even the most basic value experience is complex. It always involves in inseparable fusion a "feeling tone" and an attitude, the "feeling tone" being the warranty for the attitude. If the "feeling tone" is hedonic, we take a pro-attitude toward it and toward any object, situation or event that elicits our affective response—i.e., we approve. If the "feeling tone" is algedonic, we take a corresponding anti-attitude—we disapprove.

The "feeling tones" themselves are experienced at various levels and in manifold interrelations. On the positive side there are the purely sensory pleasures, the gratifications of appetites, the feeling of well-being, the satisfactions of communal living, a deeply felt peace of mind, the joys of enterprise and creation, and the sense of fulfillment, of happiness. And there are corresponding levels in our algedonic experiences.

The qualitative differences in experience at the various levels are indicative of an order of rank of values; and this finds confirmation in the fact that at the various levels we ourselves are at stake in different degrees. At the purely sensory level we are only tangentially involved. At the level of self-fulfillment, however, we are totally involved as human beings; we are wholly at stake as persons. And the drive for self-fulfillment is intrinsic to human nature. It is but a manifestation of that same thrust upward that is the creative aspect of evolution no less than of ontogenetic development—the drive toward the realization of all potentialities.

Since the attitude warranted by the "feeling tone" of our experience generally encompasses whatever elicits that "feeling tone" in us, all our valuations and evaluations of objects, events and situations are rooted in that experience; but crucial for the ascription of values to the things and events of the world we live in is our understanding of the nature and causal interrelations of those things and events. Cognitive judgments must therefore augment the affective-conative aspects of our value experience.

In fact, in a very specific sense they are basic to all truly warranted value ascriptions.

It is obvious, I believe, that the whole of human culture is ultimately rooted in our valuations and value ascriptions. The exchange of goods in the market place, for example, depends on differential valuations on the part of the buyer and the seller; and our agricultural-industrial complex is geared to that exchange. The social institutions of any society—educational, judicial, and political—but reflect prevailing valuations within that society. Art in all its forms is quite clearly an expression of human valuations—as are our moral codes. And at the very heart of religion we find a concern with ultimate value standards.

Each society is thus a conglomerate of diverse valuations—of valuations that are embedded and therefore "objectified" in the customs and laws, the institutions and practices that prevail. Children are molded by the valuational patterns of the society into which they are born; but, feeling their own potentialities unfulfilled by the possibilities of development open to them under existing conditions, they may also rebel. The value patterns themselves are always subject to revision and will be re-evaluated as men see new possibilities of human living and of a fuller realization of human potentialities. Seeing such possibilities and striving to realize them is in itself perhaps the highest mode of self-fulfillment; for man is not truly a person unless he is a lawgiver unto himself, restraining and directing his impulses and desires in the light of a projected self-image that could be normative for all mankind. In his commitment to such an ideal the individual grows beyond the merely biological and psychological levels of existence and truly exemplifies that upward thrust characteristic of cosmic evolution.

If it now be argued that evil also "lurks in the hearts of men"; that history reveals again and again what barbaric deeds men are capable of; that the Attilas and the Hitlers have sought self-fulfillment in atrocities beyond description; and that, therefore, my thesis is utterly utopian; I can but appeal to the fact of historical non-survival, on the one hand, and to the slow but progressive emergence of societal forms of existence more conducive to the realization of human potentialities, on the other. Admittedly, human history is in many respects not a pretty picture of man, but it is not all black either. There is enough constructive achievement in it as far as I am concerned to warrant my belief in the future. And while man is not a thoroughly rational being, he is sufficiently reasonable on the whole, I believe, not to destroy himself and his highest aspirations.

IV

But to see man in proper perspective we must consider his long, long journey from the days of *Pithecanthropus erectus* and *Sinanthropus pekinensis* (the early and middle Pleistocene) through *Homo heidelbergensis* (the first truly human being on earth) and *Homo neanderthalensis* (who inhabited the whole of Europe from the Third Interglacial until well past the climax of the Fourth Glacial Period) to *Homo sapiens* (the Cro-Magnon or modern race) who suddenly appeared in Europe some time between 25,000 and 10,000 years ago and replaced the Neanderthalers. The evidence we have in the form of fossil remains, though fragmentary, is proof of a progressive ability of man to use and to manipulate the raw materials and forces available in nature, and to create new ways of dealing with the conditions of his existence. The over-all picture is one of Man pressing on in manifold ways from one level of achievement to another; for to press on was inherent in the very nature of Man—as it is inherent in all forms of life.

Man's creative genius is exemplified in all of his inventions—in the chipped flints, the stone knife, the spear point, the stone axe; in bow and arrow, the throwing board, the boomerang. It is exemplified also in weaving and pottery, in the complicated methods of preserving food, and in the techniques of starting a fire. This inventiveness in practical matters is augmented by man's early interests along aesthetic lines. Even Neanderthal Man made use of mineral colors. Beads and pendants of stone and bone, bracelets and rings, and even a triple-strand necklace date back to early Aurignacian times—as do carved figurines, painted stones, and monochromatic cavewall paintings of the wooly mammoth, the cave-bear, the Celtic horse and wild cattle. Sculptures in stone and bone of human and animal subjects date back to the Salutrean culture, as do the magnificent polychromatic paintings of the bison on the ceiling and walls of the cave at Altamira. And even Neanderthal Man must have wondered about the meaning of human existence and about life after death. His ceremonial burials prove it.

What all this amounts to is that, because of his creative abilities, Man could and did leave mere animal existence behind him; that he could and did "cross over" into a new, a socio-cultural environment of which he himself was pre-eminently the creator. After four billion years of cosmic evolution, a creature had emerged that could and did contemplate himself and his fate; that could and did evaluate in his own terms the world he lived in, making use of what he found in that world for his own purposes.

No environmental determinism can account for these facts; for it was Man himself who creatively exploited the opportunities available to him in nature.

And this Man, so we have seen, is himself a manifestation of Reality. His creativity and his achievements—but also his failures and frustrations—are part ,and parcel of a cosmic process in the course of which initial potencies are gradually transformed into actualities. The only adequate conception of Reality, therefore, must find its warrant in the human situation taken in its entirety—cognitive, evaluative, activistic. Anything short of this is metaphysically inadequate.

But if this is so, then neither "Being" nor "Becoming" truly describes the ultimately Real. There is not only process—a process that is epigenetic; but there are cognitions and valuations as well, and these are neither mere Being nor mere Becoming. And one other fact is of special significance here. In "crossing over" from animal to human existence, Man left the sureness and security of instinctive determinations behind and became increasingly dependent upon his own choices and decisions, all of which, in turn, depend upon his insights and valuations. But Man's understanding of the possibilities inherent in an existential situation is limited and often quite faulty. His valuations, therefore, are frequently distorted and his actions misdirected. The result is conflict—in the life of the species no less than in that of the individuals; and human history attests to this fact. Misjudgment, wrong decisions, devastating conflicts—these are the price Man has to pay for the freedom he has in molding himself and his culture. It is from this perspective that I wish to take a quick look at our contemporary scene.

V

All human beings are born into and grow up in socio-cultural environments in which specific patterns of conduct and diverse institutions (hospitals, places of learning, governmental agencies, etc.), reflect historically developed valuations and value commitments. To such environments individuals respond in complexly varied ways. They may readily accept some aspects of the established pattern because they find them to be congenial to their own potentialities and aspirations, and they may react critically to other aspects, adjusting to them the best they can or rejecting them outright, opposing to them their own valuations, their own vision of what human existence should be. And such responses provide the dynamics of all socio-cultural development.

To be sure, every concrete socio-cultural situation admits of two extreme and opposed attitudes toward its inherent valuations. There exists, on the one hand, the possibility of a complete and unquestioning acceptance of the established order; and there exists, on the other hand, the possibility of a total and unselective repudiation of the prevailing order in its entirety. The first attitude means cultural stagnation; the second entails socio-cultural anarchy. But in times of transition, such as ours, the problem of a total and unquestioning acceptance of the prevailing patterns of valuations and of their embodiment in social institutions need not concern us here. It is not a pressing issue; for our whole culture—and on a world-wide scale—is presently affected by the flux of shifting valuations. The other extreme, however—"revolution for the hell of it" (Abbie Hoffman)—is clearly in evidence; and it is both a denial of historical accomplishments as foundational to future achievements, and a disavowal of reason (as manifest in the drug-sickened mind of Jerry Rubin). There is nothing redemptive in the irrationalism of a drug-indulging and drug-dependent culture. That way leads to the end of the road for mankind.

The civil rights movement is, of course, an entirely different matter. It derives direction and force from the shocking discrepancy between the projected ideal basic to our society (that "all men are created free and equal") and the actualities of existence of large minority groups. Conflicts of this type are inherent in the dynamics of progress; for it is always the projection of an ideal closer in harmony with human potentialities that points the way and inspires the actions for historical development.

This fact is exemplified also in the activities of students who, facing life from here on out in the shadow of the H-bomb, see war as a symbol of moral crisis in a nation that aspires to leadership in the world. The projected ideal of "perpetual peace" points the way in a world that has only recently witnessed the carnage of two world wars and is currently witnessing the devastating effects of war upon innocent people in Southeast Asia. The defunct League of Nations and the enfeebled United Nations are but tentative beginnings of a trend in history that alone can lead to conditions under law conducive to the fullest realization of mankind's true potentialities. But pursuit of this course of action (perhaps the most difficult of all, considering the wide-spread appeal to "national interests") requires restraint and reason—even on the part of its most fervent advocates. Violence as a protest against current failures to achieve the goal is itself more of an obstacle than a solution of the problem.

I have dwelt upon these problems not in order to solve them but in order to illustrate through them my conception of history as itself a manifestation of Reality. My point is that the projection and the pursuit of goals is the essentially human mode of action—individually and cooperatively as "subjects of history." Deterministic interpretations of history fail to account for the epigenetic or creative aspects of human achievements. To be sure, at any given time the historically developed basis of action contains the conditions reaction to which gives rise to the problems that require solution. But it is our human understanding of those problems and our projection of possible solutions that determine our actions. To be sure, our understanding may be faulty, our valuations may be in error; and, because of this possibility, our projections and actions may be misdirected. But they are subject to revision—and at times to radical revision in the light of consequences that were not or could not have been foreseen. However, in the perspective of Man's long, long journey from the times of Neanderthal Man to our own days there has been undeniable and manifold progress in history. There has been an increasingly cultural embodiment of Reality through the agency of Man.

For the rest—I quote "Miss Madrigal" in Enid Bagnold's play *The Chalk Garden:* "I shall continue to explore—the astonishment of living."

The Philosophic Quest*

Paul Weiss

QUESTIONER: What is your conception of philosophy?

WEISS: I conceive of philosophy to be a creative endeavor at understanding being and knowing. Philosophy is a sympathetic and critical examination of these and the universe in which they are. Philosophy's task is the clarification and extension of a vision of man and his universe. I do not wish to disparage the indispensable development of technical skills, but without vision, technical skills are only sharp tools with no function.

I realize this view is not popular. Today, most philosophers are content to pursue limited, specialized questions, usually as defined by some school or leading man. They are "academics". This situation does not unduly disturb me, for throughout history only a relatively few men have taken the categorial understanding of reality to be their primary concern. At the close of the Middle Ages, while hundreds of now forgotten scholastics worked on highly specialized problems in logic and rhetoric, only a few, like Thomas Aquinas and Dun Scotus, gave themselves to philosophy in the broad sense. And it is these who are the true philosophers, philosophers who have contributed significantly to the history of thought.

QUESTIONER: Why do the others concentrate on the more limited questions?

*This essay is a revision, by Paul Trainor, of a recently taped interview between Professor Weiss, Rosemary Desjardins, and Stanley Hoerr. (Ed.)

WEISS: It is dangerous to ask the big questions. You risk going counter to what everyone has been thinking about. You raise difficulties for yourself and others, and you have no well-understood place where you are to go. Your method is not clear and your categories not complete. You are adventuring and may fail. It is safer to do a highly competent job that does not have promise of great revolutionary success. Most men would not venture if there is danger of abysmal failure.

QUESTIONER: Isn't this interest in specialized questions also the result of the sometimes acrimonious and fruitless disputes which arose in the history of philosophy? Has not the apparent sterility of philosophical debates on fundamental issues led philosophers to concentrate on the more manageable specialized questions?

WEISS: Yes. But the attitude rests upon an erroneous interpretation of history, which in turn supposes that intellectual clashes are sterile or that they invalidate the arguments of all the participants. But this simply isn't so. The same misconstruction is to be found in accounts of science, when it is supposed that this presents us with a straightforward, persistent united front inevitably arriving at final truth. Ptolemaic astronomers conflict with Copernican astronomers; post-Darwinians clash with Darwinians; Lamarckeans quarrel with the orthodox Darwinians; and so on. And the victory of one over the other is never complete or permanent. There is no going back to the past, but there is also no complete forgetting of it either. The next stage often accomodates something having its roots in what had been set aside.

QUESTIONER: Isn't the real difficulty the fact that this history of philosophy is a catalogue of failures, a list of unsuccessful solutions. Doesn't this lead one to suspect that the great metaphysical questions are, after all, insoluble?

WEISS: Are they insoluble? We know that they have not yet been solved. But that isn't sufficient to show they are insoluble. We cannot say in advance that such and such a question cannot be solved. I am devoting my life to the task of solving metaphysical questions. Others devote theirs to trying to find out the origin of life or the nature of cancer. They have not found the answers. Yet, we cannot conclude that there are no answers, or that they cannot be found. Questions persist as legitimate challenges for us.

QUESTIONER: Nonetheless, we can discern a distinctive development in science. Modern science has superseded its predecessors. We no longer return to Ptolemy for our astronomy. Philosophers, by contrast, do go back to the ancients. Why is there not a comparable development in philosophy?

WEISS: It is true that philosophers can read Plato with the kind of benefit that the astronomer could not gain by reading Ptolemy. This is in part because philosophy is not science. In part it is due to the fact that the insights of previous philosophers are still significant. This should make us look upon the history of philosophy with more sympathy rather than less. Later periods bring new perspectives. Insights of previous philosophers must then be integrated into the new perspective. In this qualified sense, we may speak of philosophical development.

QUESTIONER: In light of what you have just said, what do you think might be the advantages and the disadvantages of the recent linguistic turn in philosophy?

WEISS: The linguistic turn, as I see it now, is a variant on the Hegelian scheme. It abides by a doctrine of coherence, and translates the Hegelian problems about concept into linguistic ones—but without making an advance in clarity or solution. The vocabulary is rooted essentially in the logical movement that flowed out of *Principia Mathematica* and Wittgenstein's work. But the attitude toward reality is Hegelian; what is real or known is syntactical, universal, formal, self-enclosed.

QUESTIONER: Would you be rash enough to predict where it might lead us?

WEISS: I think it will soon pass away—as other revisionistic forms of Hegelianism did. It will most likely be replaced by a richer Hegelianism—perhaps a kind of neo-Deweyanism. Dewey had scientific and humanistic as well as linguistic concerns. He was interested in art, politics, and psychology. But he also had a rather thin grasp of religion and art, and had little tolerance for speculative and systematic philosophy. His kind of view will in the end merely provide an entrance to a more solidly based, wider-ranging, more imaginatively envisaged account of all there is, here and beyond.

QUESTIONER: Since philosophy is not merely the pursuit of academic skills, what is its relevance to life?

WEISS: I think philosophy should not try to influence life. It has its own problems. Of course, it contributes to civilization, and, in some indirect way, has repercussions upon the values and, ultimately, the lives of men. It has relevance to life to the degree that it ignores life in order to attend to an intellectual understanding of the nature of reality and of knowledge. Its relevance to life should be incidental—just as it is incidental to a poet, and to one who is devoting himself to a life of religion. If philosophers forget this they will tend to turn philosophy into a vocational discipline. But it is good in itself. The repercussions philosophy has on life will take the best possible form when philosophy is pursued for its own sake and on its own terms.

QUESTIONER: I find your view of philosophy—philosophy as the pursuit of wisdom—largely absent among professional philosophers. I think we may conveniently divide most professional philosophers into either job-holders or intellectual toolsmiths. On the one hand, the job-holders tend to view philosophy as just another business; at times, even a racket. I wonder what might be the attraction or advantage of philosophy relative to any other business for these people. The toolsmiths, on the other hand, see philosophy as a mere sharpening of the mind, as a tool in argument. Few, if any, give a satisfactory answer to the question, What is the tool for?

WEISS: These people have settled upon one aspect of the philosophical enterprise. They forget that philosophy must nurture and articulate a vision of reality, not merely subject someone else's vision to intense and severe criticism. Wisdom requires this vision, but wisdom takes years to accumulate. The very sharp tools of criticism may be developed in relatively short order. Philosophy tends to attract young people who are quite bright, who have nothing much to say. Because they are sharp-witted, they can be easily lured into producing clever distinctions and rejections. It takes wisdom to use this critical apparatus in the service of an articulate and muscular wisdom.

QUESTIONER: What do you suppose these people are looking for who are attracted to philosophy in so far as they don't yet know what it is?

WEISS: Many young people are attracted to philosophy because they know how to argue. They nourish a suspicion of positions presented by other disciplines and even by previous philosophers. Theirs is a kind of inquiring mind. The great hope is that they will not be fixated on that process, but will eventually see the kind of truth that lies beneath the surface, and will try to grow out—to expand the vision—without losing their critical powers.

QUESTIONER: I should like to turn to the relationship of philosophy and education. Do you think that philosophy should seek to provide an integrated "overview," or should it conceive of itself as an academic discipline along with all the others?

WEISS: The former, I think. Philosophy offers a measure for, and a challenge to, everything accepted without adequate examination of its presuppositions. It should examine, sympathetically but critically, the dominant outlooks everywhere. If made to fit an academic pattern, it may lose the detachment it needs to carry on its radical adventure. It might become conventionalized and timid.

QUESTIONER: To what extent do you see education in philosophy, especially graduate education, as training, as opposed to education in a wider sense?

WEISS: 'Training' has a number of meanings. It may refer to the mastery of skills, of knowing how to read and dissect a text. It may have to do with mastering the position of some dominant thinker. Or, "training" may pertain to learning what it is to think as a true philosopher. These meanings are not altogether incompatible, but it is perfectly possible to concentrate on the first two and ignore the third. When this happens, we arrive at an academic way of looking at philosophy. A graduate school should provide an opportunity for young philosophers to listen to and acquire something of the insight into the meaning of philosophy as understood by those who have devoted their lives to its pursuit in a large-spirited but yet disciplined manner.

QUESTIONER: On your view, then, it isn't simply a question of listening to a man, or reading what he says, but rather actually engaging him in philosophical dialogue that matters in the education of the student?

WEISS: There need be no discussion. In fact, it is often impossible to have a dialogue, because the interlocutors are not equal. This was true in my own case.

I had the good fortune of listening to Alfred North Whitehead when I was a graduate student. I realized that the kind of dialectical, critical life I had been leading as an undergraduate, even in confrontation with a teacher of the stature of Morris Cohen, was rather thin. I wasn't on Whitehead's level; I cannot say I had a dialogue with him. I would have difficulties, and I would raise problems. More often than not, I would find him answering questions which I hadn't asked. He was formulating answers directed to questions much larger than any I had even envisaged.

QUESTIONER: Was he answering your questions?

WEISS: No. It was not important that he should. My questions were formulated the way young people formulate the questions. I had hard questions of a precise sort. He was thinking about what the thing looked like in a larger context. When I saw him do this, I was disappointed at first. But then I began to benefit from his outlook, much broader, much richer, much more significant than anything I had ever thought was possible.

QUESTIONER: Is it fair to conclude that, by and large, you think neither students nor teachers should look for, or at least should not expect, the give-and-take of a two-way exchange?

WEISS: In some ways it is. But let's not be dogmatic. I think philosophers should be masters who open up a whole new way of thinking and examining matters that the young man with his quick mind and sharp formulations might be able to utilize, to some degree, then and there. But always the young man should be made aware of an adumbrated background which he could never hope to master except by giving himself honestly and wholeheartedly to the philosophic life.

QUESTIONER: Listening to you, I find myself wondering why the philosopher wouldn't prefer to concentrate on his own research and thinking. Why would he bother to teach?

WEISS: No one should teach except so far as he is able to learn. The true philosopher learns by finding that the young have difficulties formulated in a way he himself had not envisaged, or perhaps raise difficulties that are not yet articulated in his over-all scheme. My joy in teaching derives from the challenges of the students whose impact they do not see immediately, perhaps because I offer satisfactory answers at the moment. But the answers I provide very often do not satisfy me. They dislocate me, and make me reflect upon what I have done.

QUESTIONER: Philosophy, on your view, requires technical discipline and vision. Discipline can be taught. Is there any way to teach vision?

WEISS: Only by modeling yourself on those who have it, as the way one builds character, the way one builds a general outlook or tries to capture the spirit of a saint. Let me try to say that in another way.

We teach in this country by having someone transmit what he knows to someone who is uninformed. But in the East, there is another method—that of the Guru which is closer to what I have in mind. Here pupils try to achieve the wise outlook of their masters. They risk constricting their vision to a traditional pattern. But they do enable the student to become part of a civilized world, with a rich past and a promising future.

Index

A

Abel, E., 121
Apollonius, 165
Aquinas, T., 240
Aristophanes, 55
Aristotle, 31, 50, 51, 86, 138, 181, 185, 188
Armstrong, D. M., 184
Arnold, M., 97
Artmann, P., 123
Aurelius, M., 88
Ayer, A. J., 29, 130

B

Bagnold, E., 239
Bailey, M. J., 85
Beer, A., 121, 124
Beethoven, L., 124
Benne, K., 69
Bergman, G., 127
Bergson, H., 55, 85, 86, 143, 144, 148
Berkeley, G., 107, 141, 171, 182, 184, 190
Berkson, I. B., 76
Bernard, C., 231
Bidney, D., 70
Blumberg, A., 127, 129, 130
Boehme, J., 217
Bohr, N., 137

Boltzman, L., 121, 125, 129
Born, M., 125, 137
Bosanquet, B., 23, 34, 41, 44
Bowne, B. P., 192
Bradford, J., 208
Bradley, F. H., 20, 41, 44, 141, 146, 182
Bridgman, P. W., 129
Brightman, E. S., 85, 197
Broad, C. D., 125
Brooks, P., 37
Browning, R., 43
Bruckner, A., 124
Bryan, W. J., 36
Buddha, 150
Bühler, K., 127
Burtt, E. A., 66, 68

C

Caird, J., 37
Campbell, R. J., 37
Carlyle, T., 222
Carnap, R., 126, 127, 129, 132, 133, 182
Carritt, E. F., 30
Chambliss, J. J., 63
Childs, J., 69
Clarke, S., 133
Cohen, M., 244
Coleridge S., 140
Copernicus, 241
Counts, G., 69

Courbet, G., 50
Crusius, 144
Curie, P., 214
Curti, M., 69

D

Darrow, C., 66
Darwin, C., 63, 241
De Broglie, L., 144
Descartes, R., 28, 41, 48, 61, 85, 109, 111, 144, 165, 180, 181, 185, 189, 190
Desjardins, R., 240
Dewey, J., 20, 31, 37, 45, 52, 53, 60, 64, 68, 69, 76, 89, 90, 104, 144, 182, 183, 188, 190, 242
Drake, D., 183, 185, 188, 189, 190
Duns Scotus, J., 240

E

Eastman, M., 68
Eddington, A. S., 186
Einstein, A., 121, 125, 128, 129, 137
Eliot, C. W., 177
Emerson, R. W., 45
Engels, F., 63, 67, 208

F

Farber, M., 184
Fechner, G. T., 142, 148
Feuerbach, L., 63
Fichte, J. G., 58
Fox, G., 39
Frank, P., 126, 127
Freud, S., 28, 45
Frost, R., 147
Fuller, B., 118

G

Gell-Man, M., 230
Giles, H. H., 69
Gödel, K., 127
Goethe, J. W., 124, 222, 223
Gomperz, H., 127, 129
Gotesky, R., 194
Goulet, D., 147

Green, T. H., 37
Gunsaulus, F. W., 36

H

Hahn, O. H., 126, 127
Hamilton, A., 176
Hare, R. M., 29, 32
Hegel, G. W. F., 23, 37, 63, 82, 86, 107, 142, 146, 183, 184, 211, 223, 242
Heidegger, M., 86
Heisenberg, W., 125, 127, 137, 142, 143, 145
Hempel, C. G., 127, 129
Heraclitus, 221
Herder, J. G., 167
Heyting, A., 127
Hobart, 137
Hocking, W. E., 41, 86, 142
Hoerr, S., 240
Hook, S., 182, 190
Hopkins, M., 37
Housman, A. E., 23
Hughes, E. A., 36
Hume, D., 126, 13, 134, 137, 141, 142, 144, 179, 182, 185

I

Inge, W. R., 37

J

James, W., 37, 40, 42, 85, 86, 133, 140, 142, 183, 204
Jefferson, C. E., 37
Jefferson, T., 176
Joachim, H., 20, 38
Jordan, P., 125
Joseph, H. W. B., 30
Jung, C., 220

K

Kaila, E., 127
Kant, I., 44, 47, 58, 63, 107, 120, 121, 144, 145, 171, 179, 180, 182, 183, 185, 214, 223
Keynes, J. M., 125
Kierkegaard, S., 85, 86
Kilpatrick, W., 69

Kluckhohn, C., 70
Kraft, V., 126, 129
Kroeber, A., 70, 71, 82
Kuhn, T., 95
Külpe, O., 129

Lamarck, J. B., 241
Langer, S., 130
Laski, H., 68
Lasswitz, K., 122
Laszlo, E., 194
Lee, O., 86
Leibniz, F. W., 41, 133, 141
Lenin, V. I., 67
Leonard, W. E., 202
Lessing, G. E., 167
Lewis, C. I., 20, 86, 130, 171, 185
Lifton, R. J., 203
Locke, J., 47, 48, 144, 180, 185, 175
Lovejoy, A., 185
Lowell, A. L., 177
Lucretius, 202

M

Mach, E., 120, 122, 125
Mahler, G., 124
Maier, N. R. F., 181
Malthus, T. R., 153
Mannheim, K., 16
Martineau, J., 37
Marx, K., 63, 67, 68, 146, 152, 208
Maslow, A., 118
Maxwell, C., 143, 230
McCullers, C., 204
McGill, V. J., 184
McLuhan, M., 118
McTaggart, J. M. E., 41
Mead, G. H., 66, 82, 171
Mead, M., 70
Menger, K., 127
Mill, J. S., 28, 31, 137, 175, 199
Miller, D. S., 127, 129
Milton, J., 167
Montagu, A., 70
Montague, W. P., 20, 37, 183, 185
Moore, G. E., 20, 30, 191
Morgan, C., 37
Morgan, L., 184

Moulton, J., 38
Mumford, L., 76, 79, 118

N

Natkin, M., 127
Neurath, O., 126, 129
Newlon, J., 69
Newman, J., 37
Newton, F., 37
Newton, I., 137, 145, 190, 213, 230
Niebuhr, R., 147
Nietzsche, F., 58, 121
Norman, D., 219
Northrop, F. S. C., 142
Nowell-Smith, F., 29

O

Ortega y Gassett, J., 152
Ostwald, W., 120
Otto, M., 66

P

Palmer, G. H., 169
Parker, De W. H., 182, 188
Parmenides, 211
Pascal, B., 40
Pauli, W., 129
Pearson, K., 182
Peirce, C. S., 133, 140, 141, 142, 143, 144, 183
Perry, R. B., 20, 31, 86, 130, 141, 143, 185
Pfleiderer, O., 142
Planck, M., 121, 125, 129
Plato, 23, 25, 51, 63, 85, 155, 175, 181, 183, 188, 190, 242
Poincaré, J. H., 52
Popper, K., 128, 129, 133, 134
Prall, D. W., 86
Prichard, H. A., 20, 30
Ptolemy, 241, 242

Q

Quine, W. V. O., 130, 131

R

Rashdall, H., 30
Raup, B., 69
Rawls, J., 202
Reichenbach, H., 126, 127, 129, 133
Reid, T., 47
Reidemeister, K., 126
Reininger, R., 127
Riehl, A., 122, 129
Rodin, A., 23
Rogers, C., 204
Rolland, P., 67
Ross, W. D., 20, 30
Royce, J., 41, 42, 44, 52, 140, 142, 146
Royden, M., 37
Rousseau, J., 63
Rugg, H., 69
Russell, B., 34, 45, 120, 122, 128, 134, 136, 137, 139, 141, 180, 182
Russell, E., 36
Ryle, G., 109

S

St. Augustine, 37, 50, 150
St. Francis, 45, 213
St. Theresa, 213
Sankara, 23
Santayana, G., 13, 134, 183
Sartre, J. P., 156, 158, 159
Schelling, F. W. J., 107
Schilpp, P., 20, 184, 185
Schlick, M., 121, 122, 125, 126, 127, 128, 129, 137
Schneirla, T. C., 181
Schopenhauer, A., 58, 121, 144
Schroedinger, E., 125, 230
Sellars, W., 146
Shoemaker, S., 142
Sheffer, H., 130
Shepard, J. F., 181
Sidgwick, H., 30, 137
Smart, J., 184
Smith, A., 196
Smith, F. J., 194
Smith, N. K., 108
Smith, T. V., 66, 68
Snow, C. P., 97
Socrates, 30, 55, 96, 155, 159, 223
Spengler, O., 158

Spinoza, B., 23, 41, 85, 111, 124, 143, 144, 192
Stephen, L., 40
Stevenson, C., 29
Straus, E., 194
Strawson, P. F., 142
Strindberg, A., 138
Strong, C. A., 127, 129, 183
Sumner, W., 93

T

Tagore, R., 128
Tarski, A., 127
Teilhard de Chardin, 118
Tertullian, 123
Thirring, H., 127
Thouless, R. S., 28
Tillich, P., 147
Tolman, E., 171
Toulmin, S., 29
Toynbee, A., 118
Trainor, P., 240
Troland, L. T., 141
Trotter, W., 28
Tufts, J., 66
Tylor, E., 63

U

Urmson, J. O., 29

V

Vaughan, W. F., 85
Verne, J., 122
von Hügel, F., 37
von Mises, R., 126, 127
von Neumann, J., 127, 137

W

Waismann, F., 126, 127, 128, 129
Ward, B., 118
Watson, J. B., 171
Webb, C. C. J., 39
Weiss, P., 130
Wellman, C., 193
Wells, H. G., 141
Whewell, W., 129
White, L., 74

Whitehead, A. N., 23, 25, 86, 87, 130, pp. 140-150, 185, pp. 188-190, 244
Wigner, E. P., 145
Wild, J., 86
Wittgenstein, L., 25, 30, 109, 110, 124, 127, 128, 129, 139, 180, 182, 242
Wolfson, H. A., 85
Woodbridge, F. J. E., 20

Woods, J. H., 85
Woolman, J., 45
Wright, O., 163

Z

Zilsel, E., 125, 129
Zimmer, H., 212, 214